'99

Gemisphere
LUMINARY

COMPILED AND EDITED BY MICHAEL KATZ

Gemisphere

P.O. BOX 10026

PORTLAND, OREGON 97296-0026

503.241.3642

ISBN: 0-924700-08-4

Library of Congress Catalog # 97-071982

Gemisphere Luminary

FIRST EDITION

Parts of this book were originally published as *Gifts of the Gemstone Guardians*

Copyright © 1989, 1994 by Michael Katz

Co-editor: Katherine Hall

Designer: Principia Graphica

Typographer: Blue Sky Research

Printer: Dynagraphics

THIS BOOK IS A COLLECTION OF INTERVIEWS GIVEN BY THE GEMSTONE GUARDIANS. THE INFORMATION CONTAINED HEREIN SHOULD NOT BE CONSIDERED AS A SUBSTITUTE FOR CONSULTATION WITH A LICENSED HEALTH-CARE PROFESSIONAL OR AS A REPLACEMENT FOR ANY MEDICAL TREATMENT.

THE GEMSTONES REFERRED TO IN THIS BOOK ARE OF THERAPEUTIC QUALITY, WHICH MEANS THEY MEET SPECIFIC STANDARDS OF COLOR, CLARITY, AND CONSISTENCY. THESE STANDARDS ARE SET BY THE GEMSTONE GUARDIANS AND ARE DIFFERENT FOR EACH GEMSTONE. THERAPEUTIC-QUALITY GEMSTONES ARE OF THE FINEST QUALITY AND SHOULD NOT BE CONFUSED WITH MORE COMMONLY AVAILABLE COMMERCIAL-GRADE GEMSTONES.

Printed in U.S.A. on recycled paper

MY DEEPEST GRATITUDE

To my co-editor Katherine Hall, who held the torch of love, wholeness, and integrity throughout the writing of this book; her support for me and the Gemstone Guardians radiates from the core of her being. To Dr. Pauline Alison for her insights and brilliant efforts to make the information in this book more accessible to the Guardians' readers; her clinical perspective has helped bring the Guardians' teachings more fully into this world. To my children Emily, Eleena, and Eranel, the greatest blessings in my life. To the staff at Golden Age Institute, whose support has cleared the way for me to focus on this book. To the dear one, who, without her ability to relay this information from the inner planes, this book and this work would not have been born. And, especially, my most loving thanks to the Gemstone Guardians, their Overseer, and the inner council to which she belongs.

CONTENTS

The
EARTHSTONE
Guardians

The
OCEANSTONE
Guardians

The book you are about to read contains interviews with thirty remarkable individuals. These individuals are Gemstone Guardians, the inner-world beings responsible for fulfilling the purpose and maintaining the effects of gemstones everywhere. ◊ The interviews with the Guardians were conducted in nonphysical realms through a spiritual practice which involves moving one's consciousness into these inner realms or dimensions. Once present in and aware of these inner dimensions, one may meet and speak with other beings there, much as we do in the physical world. ◊ Conducting these interviews was a team effort involving myself and a female partner who wishes to remain anonymous. It was her extraordinary task to convey the words of the Guardians to the physical world. It was my role to interview the Guardians, edit their discourses, and oversee publication of this book. ◊ My partner was fully aware of the events transpiring in the inner worlds and describes her experiences there prior to and following each interview. These descriptions, as well as my questions, are set in italics to distinguish them from the words of the Guardians. ◊ The words, ideas, and love of life communicated in these pages come from the Gemstone Guardians. They invite us to open our awareness to ever greater possibilities and experience their insights with our hearts and intuitions as well as with our minds.

In Spirit,

Michael Katz

1

THE ASSIGNMENT IS GIVEN

Late one evening I sat on my living room sofa, closed my eyes, and turned my attention inward. I began to hear what I thought was the sound of the wind. Then I remembered the air outside was calm and realized that the sound was coming from somewhere deep within me. ◌ Suddenly the sound grew louder and a scene appeared in my inner vision: About thirty individuals sat in a circle around an enormous crystal. A column of light poured into the crystal from above and flowed out of its base, spreading evenly to everyone seated around it. ◌ The individuals before me were as real as any I had ever met. Some resembled nothing more than a vortex of energy in human form. The others were distinctly human-looking, and each of these wore a different style and color of clothing. I could see by their gestures that the members of this group were engaged in a lively conversation. ◌ I stood outside the circle. Moments later Michael appeared at my left side. On my right was a spiritual master with whom I'd had previous encounters; his knee-length maroon robe, weathered skin, and short dark hair and beard were familiar features. ◌ "They are discussing a book," the master said, "a book which will soon be written about them." His deep brown eyes looked sharply into mine. ◌ A man in the circle stood and took a few steps toward the crystal. Then he turned and faced us. He had a long white beard, was dressed in purple robes, and held a staff of white wood. He motioned for us to join the group. The conversation in the circle stopped at once, and all heads turned to us. ◌ With a growing sense of wonder and curiosity, Michael and I entered the circle. As we moved toward the man in purple robes, I had the sudden feeling that something even more extraordinary was about to happen. ◌ "It is time that the people of Earth learn some truths about gemstones," the man said, "specifically about the missions and healing effects of gemstone spheres. ◌ "The individuals you see here are Gemstone Guardians. They are the caretakers of the gemstones. It is the time-honored duty of each

Guardian to help fulfill the purpose of a particular gemstone and to maintain its effects. Recently all the Guardians have been given yet another responsibility: to start working directly with human beings to teach them the correct ways to use gemstones. ○ "The Gemstone Guardians gathered in this circle have been discussing a series of discourses they will be giving in the form of interviews. These interviews will be an important step in the fulfillment of their new responsibility: they will allow the Guardians to share the knowledge of the gemstones for which they are responsible. When these discourses are completed, they will be edited and compiled into a book." ○ My curiosity was growing more intense by the moment. Michael and I glanced at each other. We had been working with gemstones for many years in Michael's business and had become deeply interested in their healing properties. We had reviewed many books and articles on the subject and, to our surprise and disappointment, had found their information vague, incomplete, or too general. ○ Often each of our references had something different to say about the properties of a given gemstone; sometimes it seemed as though they must be describing different gemstones altogether! We had become frustrated but determined not to give up our search for a true authority on the effects of these powerful tools. Now questions began to form in my mind: Had these "Guardians" known of our search? Would they help us find the information we were looking for? ○ As I listened and wondered what was to come next, I studied the rich purple eyes of the man who spoke to us. They reminded me of the finest quality Amethyst. Then he answered my unspoken questions. ○ "Through the teachings of your spiritual path, the two of you have learned the art and science of following the light and sound of Spirit and of traveling in consciousness to nonphysical places such as this. The tests and trials you have undergone in the past several years have been arranged to teach you discipline, trust in your inner guidance, and how to maintain the focus of your attention." ◌ Indeed, the daily practice of certain spiritual exercises was an important aspect of both Michael's life and mine. The sound I had heard when I closed my eyes was part of this daily experience. Nevertheless, I considered it a great blessing when, on occasion, I was able to shift the focus of my awareness away from my physical surroundings and consciously "travel" to an inner world, such as the one I was now experiencing. ◌ "We would like you to perform the interviews with the Gemstone Guardians, for you have earned this privilege," he concluded. ◌ As the magnitude of what we were being asked to do began to dawn on me, it occurred to me that I should feel awe-struck. Yet, on the contrary, it all seemed quite natural. While I fully understood the significance of the task being presented to us, the idea of interviewing the Gemstone Guardians themselves seemed appropriate and even logical. Finally we were being given the opportunity to learn about gemstones from the individuals who knew them best. ◌ "Thank you. We are honored by your trust in us," I replied. Michael nodded in agreement. ◌ My mind raced ahead, and I began to wonder when the interviews would begin. As if he had heard my thoughts, the maroon-robed master said, "Select certain days and times over the next two months to conduct these interviews. Choose times when you know you will not be disturbed. Then sit in a comfortable position and close your eyes. ◌ "Spirit will lead you to the meeting place for each interview. Listen for the word of God. It will manifest as a current of music flowing from the source of life, through your heart, and back again. Follow that sound. Then open your eyes and behold the world that lies before you. The eyes you open will not be physical, nor will the worlds you perceive." ◌ True to his nature, Michael then proceeded to make the most of the opportunity at hand, asking the Guardians for suggestions and advice about the book. He spoke with nearly all of them—at great length with some and with others only briefly. ◌

As Michael talked with the Guardians, my gaze was drawn to a woman standing outside the circle. She radiated a brilliant white light. When this woman saw that the discussions had ended, she joined us in the circle. "This is the Guardian of the Mineral Kingdom and Overseer of all Gemstone Guardians," I heard someone say. ◐ "Before you begin your interviews, I would like to give both of you some advice," said the Overseer. "Don't try to remember everything a Guardian says in the hope that you will be able retain it and write it down afterward. If you do this, much information will be forgotten." ◐ Turning to me, she said, "Instead, surrender to Spirit and allow it to show you how to enter the aura, or field of energy, surrounding each Guardian. You will not lose consciousness or your identity, nor will you become the Gemstone Guardian. However, your physical voice will be able to speak the words that will flow from the heart of each Guardian. Have a tape recorder ready to capture these words. The Guardians will be able to draw upon the words and images stored in your mind. They will use language that is easily understood, so that as many people as possible may come to understand the true nature, purpose, and effects of their gemstones. ◐ "Michael, it will be your role to conduct and guide the interviews by asking questions of the Guardians. ◐ "The Guardians will not only speak of their own gemstones but will share the information needed to understand how all gemstones work. The knowledge that each Guardian gives will build on the knowledge given in previous interviews. Therefore, advise your readers to start at the beginning of the book and read each chapter in order. ◐ "By the way, some Guardians choose to further distinguish their gemstones with the names 'earthstone' and 'oceanstone:' earthstones are the rock of the planet, and oceanstones are treasures of the sea. You will first interview the Guardians of the gemstones, then the Guardians of the earthstones, and finally the Guardians of the oceanstones." ◐ "Do you have any other advice for us?" Michael asked. ◐ "Yes, there is one more thing. As you write the book, imagine yourself within the column of light you now see flowing through the crystal in the center of this circle. It is a pillar of love. Write with love and with light—and enjoy your work." ❍ Then the individual I now guessed to be the Guardian of Amethyst spoke once more. "I, too, have some words of advice. As you perform your task, you can give or you can take. If you choose to take, your options will vanish. If you choose to give, the number of options available to you will be infinite. Let life be the judge of the degree to which you are giving or taking, for the presence of options or the lack of them will be reflected everywhere. ❍ "The key to successfully completing your task, regardless of the number of options presented, is focus. Although I am referring to the completion of the book, this advice can be applied to any project." ❍ Then the maroon-robed master indicated it was time for us to leave the circle. We did so, and the Guardians returned to their discussion. ❍ "The first interview will be with the Guardian of Quartz," said the master. "Choose a time for the discourse, and remember to follow Spirit to the meeting place." ❍ Suddenly the scene vanished. Once again, my living room became the focus of my awareness. I sat without moving or opening my eyes for several minutes, trying to absorb the experience I had just had and to steady the rising excitement in my heart. ❍ Soon Michael and I would meet the Guardian of Quartz—and begin what promised to be one of the greatest adventures of our lives.

The
Guardian
of

QUARTZ

2

ATTRACTING LIFE FORCE

We met the Guardian of Quartz among billowing clouds. White mist surrounded us as far as the eye could see. The scene resembled the classic image of heaven, yet my heart knew we were standing somewhere on the Earth. Indeed, the ground felt firm beneath my feet.

The Guardian stood before us, wrapped in a softly glowing white cape. Energy flowed through him continually; like a waterfall, it entered his head from above and flowed into the ground through his feet. I studied his features carefully. He had shoulder-length, light blond hair and appeared to be about thirty years old. In his hands rested a large Quartz sphere. He placed this sphere beside him and, pressing his palms together, bowed to us.

Michael and I returned this silent gesture of greeting. Then, trusting the advice of the Gemstone Guardians' Overseer, I moved closer to the Guardian of Quartz. I looked into his dark brown eyes. As he gazed into mine, I felt for a moment I would be lost in the light that surrounded him. Then, without a word, I moved into his aura. From that moment on I was able to see what the Guardian saw, feel what was in his heart, and speak with my physical voice the words he spoke.

THE LIVING PLANET

To understand Quartz and other gemstones, *the Guardian began,* you must know that all crystals are alive. By "alive" I mean that they contain life force. This force is the divine energy that sustains, nourishes, and enlivens all living things. Sometimes known as the healing force, the life force is actually a current of light and sound which springs from the source of life itself. ☉ As the Earth was forming, the highly focused power of this light and sound was infused into the Earth's crystalline matrices. Much of this life force entered Quartz. Of course, other crystals were present in the young planet, and these too were enlivened by life force. ☉ The Earth is a complex living organism. Just as human beings need many different organs, all of which are necessary for their survival, the Earth needs many different kinds of crystals and minerals to survive. Each type of crystal performs a different function for the planet. ☉ As time passed and the clear Quartz crystals grew, some of these crystals were implanted with vibratory rates, or essences, that gave them color. These vibratory rates also defined the crystal's functions and imparted them with other characteristics. Thus, other Quartz derivatives were born to fulfill the Earth's needs. These Quartz derivatives are like Quartz's children: they all share similar qualities, yet each has its own personality. ☉ The early life of a planet is similar to the early life of a human being. When a fetus is in its mother's uterus, it grows and changes but does not yet have a life of its own; it shares its mother's life. So it was with the Earth: for millions of years when the Earth was forming, it did not yet have its own life. ☉ During those years the Earth shared the life of the universe. In human beings, as soon as a critical point is reached, the baby's Soul enters its body and the baby is born. When this critical point was reached for the Earth, a Soul was designated as the planet's Guardian. ☉ During a child's early years, it grows rapidly and seems to have endless energy. Similarly, during the early years of the planet, the Earth had so much energy that its crystals grew very quickly. Now the Earth is in her middle years, and, just as human beings in their middle years do things more slowly than a child does, the Earth's crystals grow much more slowly. ◌ You will find that the Earth is similar to human beings in many ways. Imagine all the textbooks required to explain to a medical student how the human body works. A similar number of textbooks would be required to describe the Earth's physiology and how it relates to the life living upon it.

PEOPLE, GEMSTONES, AND THE EARTH

People have always been powerfully drawn to gemstones. Indeed, gemstones are among the most beloved treasures of Earth. Gems are beautiful. Yet it is more than just their beauty that attracts people so profoundly. It is the radiance of life force contained in gemstones to which people are instinctively drawn. Deep within, people know that there is more to gemstones than meets the eye. ◌ Through the years, many have also sensed the potential for healing that a gemstone's life force can offer. So far, people have been mainly using the crystalline form of gemstones to tap this healing force. ◌ However, the days of primarily using crystals for this purpose are coming to an end. It is time for human beings to take the next step in their relationship with gemstones. We, the Gemstone Guardians, are giving these interviews, in part, to help you take this step—namely, to harness the much greater amount of healing energy that becomes available to people when gemstone crystals are fashioned into spheres. ◌ When a gemstone is cut into a sphere, the life force that is contained within its crystalline form—and that once possessed all the love and power of creation—is still present. A sphere represents wholeness and infinite potential. Cutting gemstone crystals into spheres unleashes their potential to heal and uplift the whole person.

"Why would you and the other Gemstone Guardians want to assist human beings, so many of whom seem to be destructive to the Earth?" Michael asked.

The reason is this: Human beings are not just destructive. In fact, human beings and the Earth give and take from each other. Many feel that people only take the good from the Earth and give back the bad. This is not so. A human being's greatest contribution to the Earth is his or her connection with the life force. ○ How does this apply to Quartz? To answer this question, I shall first tell you what Quartz does for the Earth: Quartz keeps the planet alive. Indeed, the mission of crystalline Quartz is to bear the Earth's life energy. Quartz attracts life force to itself and thus to the planet, brightening the Earth's aura and helping the Earth maintain balance. Quartz also collects, distributes, and absorbs certain energies from the atmosphere so that the Earth can use them for sustenance. ○ Yet Quartz can only collect and use the life force already contained within the Earth's atmosphere—whereas humans, in their capacity as spiritual beings, can consciously connect with the very source of this life force. When people wear a strand of Quartz spheres around the neck, the Quartz helps them become more balanced. This greater balance allows them to radiate even more life force into the Earth's atmosphere. The more balanced people are, the more life energy can flow through them. Therefore, one of the greatest gifts people can give to the Earth is to wear Quartz spheres. The more people do this, the more life force will be available to the planet.

TRANSFORMING LIFE FORCE

"Will you speak more about the effects of crystals and spheres on people?"
asked Michael.

Yes, *replied the Guardian of Quartz.* It is time that some truths be known. Let us begin with some basic principles of gemstone crystals and spheres. These principles apply to Quartz and many other gemstones on the planet. ⊙ Gemstone crystals not only contain life force, they also transform it into gemstone energy. Each type of gemstone converts life force into the kind of energy characteristic of that gemstone. In other words, a Quartz crystal transforms life force into Quartz energy, an Amethyst crystal transforms life force into Amethyst energy, and so on. ⊙ The Earth's crystals occur in clumps and clusters, with double terminations, and in all kinds of unique manifestations. However, the basic crystal has two ends: one pointed and one not pointed. Because of its shape, nearly all of a crystal's energy is compelled to flow through it in one direction: into the nonpointed end and out of the pointed end. ⊙ Sometimes, when people hold or wear gemstone crystals, they feel this energy. Specifically, they feel the life force that the crystal receives through one end, transforms in its crystalline matrix, and then expresses as gemstone energy through the other end. ⊙ Because energy moves through crystals this way, when a crystal is placed on a human body, it can pull energy out of or pour energy into the body. Specifically, if you place the nonpointed, energy-receiving end of a crystal over a disharmonious area, energy will be drawn out of the body, flow through the crystal, and leave through the pointed end. Yet there is absolutely no way of knowing for sure whether the crystal is pulling disharmonious energy or positive life force out of the body. ⊙ For this and other reasons, I must strongly caution you that placing crystals on the body can be extremely dangerous. ◐ How, then, can the healing energies of gemstones be safely and effectively used by human beings? Perhaps, by now, the answer is easy to guess: by shaping gemstone crystals into spheres. ◐ In a gemstone sphere, there is no giving or receiving end. Life force is continually drawn in from the entire surface of the sphere to the sphere's center. This means that a sphere has access to a much greater amount of life force than does a crystal. As life force is drawn toward the center of the sphere, it becomes highly concentrated. This concentration fuels the transformation process, causing the gemstone's energy to be unleashed with great power. A gemstone sphere radiates its energy constantly in all directions, like the sun. ◐ When gemstone spheres encircle the neck, as in a necklace, they essentially surround the core of one's being. This enables the gemstone energy radiated by the spheres to fill the subtle-energy field surrounding the individual. This energy field, also called the "aura," contains information about all aspects of the individual. ◐ As the aura becomes saturated with gemstone energy, the gem's energy is also drawn back to the spheres, carrying information from the aura with it. As long as the gemstone is worn, its energy continually flows into the aura and back again. In this way, the gemstone gets to know the wearer's needs and can adjust its energy flows accordingly. ◐ In contrast, most gemstones in crystalline form have little or no affinity for the human aura. In general, a crystal's energy is compelled to flow with great focus and force only in the directions dictated by the crystal's faces. Because of this, when a crystal is worn or used by a human being, the crystal's energy can touch only a small part of the person's aura. Very little, if any, information comes back to the crystal. The crystal has no way of learning the aura or the needs of the individual.

BALANCE AND THE LIFE FORCE

"In what ways can the spherical form of Quartz help people in their movement toward greater health?" Michael asked.

Some may wish to call Quartz a healing stone. However, in reference to Quartz, the word "healing" is misleading and vague. When Quartz is worn, it helps the individual make healthful changes by fostering balance in all aspects of life. When worn around the neck, Quartz balances the person's whole being; when placed on specific areas of the body, it balances those areas.* For example, if you place Quartz spheres on a disharmonious liver, the Quartz will promote balance in the liver, and this greater balance will help the liver become healthier. ◐ When an individual is more balanced, more life force can flow through that person to touch every aspect of his or her being. This increased flow creates even greater balance, which in turn brings even more life force to the individual. This process continues as long as the Quartz is worn. ◐ What does this mean for the individual's health? The more life force present, the less room there is for disease, for isn't disease anti-life? ◐ When Quartz spheres are worn, life force is continually drawn to the Quartz from several sources, though primarily from the unlimited source of life energy at the core of the wearer's being. As a result, additional life energy is drawn to the physical body. ◐ As life force flows from the core of one's being to the Quartz spheres around the neck, it also permeates one's inner aspects. By inner aspects, I mean the mind, memory, and emotions. This additional life force nourishes, balances, and aligns these inner aspects. This is important, because disease is usually more than just physical: it often manifests on the emotional and mental levels as well. ◐ Quartz not only helps

* SEE MICHAEL KATZ, *Gemisphere Luminary Therapy Guide*
FOR DETAILED DESCRIPTIONS OF NUMEROUS OTHER GEMSTONE 'PLACEMENT' THERAPIES.

balance its wearer's physical and inner aspects, it also helps bring into balance everything that comes into the person's life. If Quartz is worn continually, it will even work to deflect those forces that upset balance, and it will attract what is needed to maintain balance. ☉ When an individual gains balance, he or she handles all situations in a more dignified and balanced way. Because of this, Quartz seems to protect its wearers from the negative emotions of others. Actually, what happens is that the wearer is more able to place negative emotions in perspective and to maintain balance. Positive emotions appear enhanced, but only because the person experiencing the emotion wants to hold onto it longer and enjoy it more. ☉ As Quartz helps one achieve greater mental balance, it improves either analytical or creative thinking, depending on the needs of the individual. For example, to balance a particular individual's mind, the creative aspect may have to be stimulated and the analytical aspect quieted. This is the sacrifice one will make if one wishes to move toward a more perfect mental balance. Once this balance is achieved, both aspects of the mind will naturally be strengthened. Improved mental balance will also allow more life force to flow through the individual to the physical body. ☉ Often, as the planet strives for greater balance, it experiences earthquakes and volcanic eruptions. Similarly, during your own movement toward greater balance, you might experience eruptions and foundation shakings. This is one of the costs of attaining balance. The more out of balance you are on any level, the more upheavals you must experience before balance is established. Yet, because Quartz's nature is to promote balance, it will bring your entire being into balance in a balanced way—slowly and steadily. Nonetheless, upheavals may still occur. ☉ Before an earthquake occurs, a tremendous tension builds. The Earth wants to change and become more balanced and harmonious, but there is tension and resistance to the coming change. Of course, once the earthquake occurs, this tension is released. This is similar to what you might undergo when working toward greater balance. Tension will build somewhere in your life, and then there will be an "earthquake." During this time you may say, "Look what the Quartz is doing. It's certainly not making my life more balanced!" However, once the "earthquake" is over and you have attained greater balance and harmony than ever before, you may realize what has actually happened. ◐ The movement toward balance will occur in proportion to the mass and quality of Quartz you wear. The greater the mass and the higher the quality, the more effective the Quartz will be.

"How does Quartz foster balance?" Michael asked.

I have told you that Quartz attracts life force to its wearer. I have also explained that this life force, which enlivens and sustains all living things, is a current of light and sound. When we look more deeply into this current of life, we see that the life force itself is comprised of the seven colors of the rainbow. ◐ At a very basic level, you too are made of these color rays. In an optimally healthy individual, all seven colors are present in balance. Too much or too little of any color ray results in disease and disharmony. Thus, being nourished by a proper balance of color rays is essential to your health. ◐ Quartz gently attracts all seven color rays to its wearer. In the process, it corrects any color-ray imbalances in the wearer's physical and inner aspects. When one becomes more balanced on this fundamental level, all aspects of life improve.

EVOLVING CONSCIOUSNESS

Consciousness has been evolving since life began on Earth. Yet, only in the last few generations has the consciousness of the Earth's people been ready for the benefits of Quartz spheres. Before then, people simply weren't ready for the great upliftment that comes from the balancing effects of Quartz spheres and for the increased flow of life force it brings into the physical body. Now people are ready. ☾ As people begin to wear the spherical form of Quartz and as their inner aspects become more balanced, aligned, and able to accept a greater flow of life force, people's consciousness will awaken. As this happens, people will also become more aware of the greater functions of Quartz. They will discover new therapeutic and scientific applications as well as new ways to use Quartz in everyday living. It is my dream that Quartz spheres will become a common household tool. ☾ As people's consciousness expands, awakens, and rises, so will the consciousness of the Earth. Why? Because human beings will give more life force and spiritual energy to the planet. ☾ Remember, gemstones in crystalline form work for the Earth. Quartz crystals convert universal life force into the kind of energy that can be used as fuel by the planet. The process is similar to the way you convert food into fuel for your body. Yet crystals can only work for the Earth if they are still touching the soil; they cannot assist the planet directly if they are placed in the home or worn around the neck. If you return a harvested crystal to the soil, it will work for the Earth again. It doesn't matter how you plant it; you can bury it in the soil or simply lay it on the ground. ☾ Wearing Quartz crystals can make people feel good because of the crystals' energy. Crystals have concentrated, compressed life energy within them, and they give life, good feeling, and harmony to any environment or atmosphere. Yet, it is like smelling the aroma of fresh bread baking in the oven. It smells wonderful, but your body cannot live on the aroma, for the aroma alone cannot be digested and therefore help your body grow. ☾ Quartz spheres can take the energy in your aura, metabolize it, and return it to you in a more usable form. Quartz can call to itself the life force that exists all around you and in all your inner levels. It can bring this energy into the physical body in a form that the body can "digest" and use for its growth in consciousness. ○ As the spherical form of Quartz increases the flow of your life force, it will expand your awareness and might even increase your ability to communicate telepathically. This communication may occur among other wearers of Quartz who, along with you, might form a group of light-receivers for the planet. ○ Tomorrow night you will meet the Guardian of Lavender. He will explain in more depth what I mean when I speak of inner aspects. Lavender and Quartz work in both similar and different ways. Remember, Quartz's principal focus is for the planet. You will find that Lavender's focus is for the human being. ○ Until we meet again, may the blessings be.

"May the blessings be," replied Michael.

I slipped out of the Guardian's aura. He lifted the large Quartz sphere laying beside him, nodded his head and smiled. The white mist surrounding us gradually diminished until all that remained in my mind's eye was the memory of this unusual experience.

This was the first of our interviews with the Gemstone Guardians. We felt a mixture of inspiration, awe, and now eagerness—to meet the Guardian of Lavender.

The
Guardian
of

LAVENDER

3

AWAKENING TO SOUL

I closed my eyes and found myself, Michael, and four others sitting in a circle among the same soft clouds that had set the scene for our interview with the Guardian of Quartz. At the head of our circle stood the Guardian of Lavender.

The Guardian's hair was white and curly and fell to his shoulders. Viewed from the back, he might appear to be an old man, yet the rest of his features suggested someone in his early twenties. Beneath a dark lavender cape he wore simple, highly textured cotton clothing. His skin was fair. Most compelling were his eyes, in which deep lavender irises surrounded royal purple pupils. He did not focus his attention on any one individual, perhaps because his gaze would have been too penetrating and powerful.

I stood and moved next to him. He looked at me and nodded, and I was instantly drawn into his aura. He scanned his audience, focusing his gaze a foot or two above his listeners' heads and studying the light that entered each of them from above. Then he began to speak.

We are here for a purpose. You wish to learn of the gemstone Lavender. Indeed, I, as the Guardian of Lavender, am not Lavender. Lavender is simply the gemstone of which I am in charge. The Lavender gemstone encases the vibratory rate, or energy, it is my duty to protect. We will limit this discussion to the effects of Lavender on the human beings of Earth.

"Do you mean there are human beings on other planets?" asked a listener.

Yes. Would it surprise you if I said that I am one? Would it also surprise you to know that the Guardians of some gemstones may even have physical bodies on your Earth planet? A Gemstone Guardian need not only be from another plane of existence. ☉ Those of you who are attending from the planet Sarshauné may wish to wait for the next lecture, when I will be speaking about the effects of Lavender on your planet.

"Sarshauné?" asked Michael.

Yes, the people of that planet have been working closely with gemstones for ages. Regarding gemstones, Earth and Sarshauné have a strong connection. Both planets are Quartz-based, and it was the people of Sarshauné who introduced the Lavender essence to the Earth's Quartz. ☉ The Sarshauné's lifestyle is very different from yours, as is their climate. Their technology has made life simple for them. Technology has also provided them with what is perhaps their greatest challenge—how to prevent their minds from becoming as simple as their lifestyle.

"Why did they bring Lavender to Earth?" Michael inquired.

The ancestors of the Sarshauné mastered the Quartz crystal. It was they who taught the people of Atlantis how to use crystals. As you know, Atlantis was the home of an ancient civilization. The Atlantean continent was destroyed by earthquakes and now lies beneath the Atlantic Ocean. Of course, the Sarshauné were not the only ones who taught the Atlanteans; people from other planets influenced them as well. ☉ By working closely with their own Lavender, the Sarshauné developed a keen state of consciousness. The alignment of their inner aspects was so well managed that they could, at will, become clear channels for Spirit. This also made their inner guidance clear. ☉ Some followed their inner guidance more closely than others; these people knew that Lavender should be planted on Earth. They saw that the destiny of the two planets would one day cross, but only if the Earth also had Lavender. Others on Sarshauné resisted this idea. They were responsible for governing their planet and for upholding the law that prohibits people from indiscriminately planting gemstones on other planets. ☉ Nevertheless, those who followed their inner guidance knew what must be done. They began by trading the mature form of Lavender crystals with the Atlanteans. After much trading, the governing Sarshauné saw that Lavender was indeed harmonious with the Earth and gave permission for Lavender to be planted there.

IMPLANTING GEMSTONE ENERGIES

"How is a gemstone planted?" asked Michael.

To understand the process, you must realize that crystals are living things. They are like plants that grow from seeds. If you plant berry seeds indigenous to China in Canada—and the seeds grow—there will soon be Chinese berries in Canada. Similarly, if you plant seed crystals in a healthy environment on another planet, they will also grow. And, after a few thousand years or so, they will develop into mature crystals. ◔ Gemstones can also be planted within crystals that are already indigenous to a planet. Lavender's vibratory rate was planted in the Quartz crystal. Your scientists will say that the difference between clear Quartz and Lavender is a mineral component. But that is not the whole story. ◔ Before the vibratory rate of one gemstone can be planted in another, the minerals characteristic of the gemstone to be planted must be transformed into supra-physical energy. By this, I mean that its molecules must be made to vibrate at a higher rate than physical matter. Whenever you wish to make any physical change, it is always more effective to begin by making the change at a higher level of vibration. One reason is that higher vibratory levels, such as the supra-physical, are more flexible and changeable than the physical. ◔ It was not difficult to find the supra-physical veins and arteries of clear Quartz in the Earth. The Lavender, in its supra-physical form, was placed into this circulatory system. Since it was not the intention to transform all the Quartz on the planet into Lavender, it was planted only in certain veins. Quartz accepted the Lavender as a gift. It allowed Lavender's vibratory rate to travel along Quartz's network of veins and arteries to areas where the Lavender energy then concentrated. Once the Lavender vibratory rate was securely established in these areas, it reverted to its physical form. From then on, Lavender grew in these areas instead of clear Quartz. ◔ Now, why would clear Quartz accept Lavender as a gift? The Guardian of Quartz knew that it would benefit both the Earth and her people. He knew that when Lavender matured and was worn by people, it would open the flow of life force to a much greater degree than the clear Quartz could. As the Guardian of Quartz has explained, the more life force a human being can bring to the planet, the more life energy the planet itself will have. So the Quartz accepted the gift of the Sarshauné readily, happily, and gratefully.

SUBTLE BODIES AND THEIR AURAS

To understand my purpose, one must understand the concept of
subtle, or inner, bodies. The Guardian of Quartz referred to these
inner bodies as inner aspects or levels. One must also understand
energy centers, or chakras, since they are key to an understanding
of how I, as well as other gemstones, work. ◯ You are comprised
of more than just your physical body: you also have emotions,
memories, and thoughts. Whether or not you are always aware of
it, you also have an intuition which offers you guidance, especially
during times of danger and at other crucial moments. Indeed, you
are a spiritual organism comprised of many aspects. ◯ If you could
see beyond your physical body and into your inner aspects, you
would see that your emotions actually originate from another, subtle
body. I shall call this the emotional body, though it is sometimes
referred to as the astral body. The emotional body manifests an aura,
or energetic reflection of itself. This aura can be seen by sensitive
individuals as a layer of energy surrounding the physical body. ◯ If
you look deeper into your own being, you would see that you have
another, even more subtle body. This is the aspect of your being in
which your past experiences and patterns of stimulus and response
are stored. I call this the memory body, though some refer to it as
the causal body. Its aura can be seen as a layer of energy surrounding
the emotional aura. ◯ If you look even deeper, you would see yet
another body, which I shall call the mental body. This body is the
source of the river of thoughts that continually flows through your
mind. Its aura can be seen as a layer of energy surrounding the
memory, or causal, aura. ◯ Beyond the mental body is another
body, from which your intuitions arise. This is the intuitive body.
Its aura can be seen as a relatively thin sheath of energy surrounding
the mental aura. ◯ Just beyond the intuitive body is the aspect of
your being that is by far the most beautiful. It is not quite right to

call this aspect a body, because in essence it is pure Spirit. It is Soul itself. It appears as a beautiful, slightly golden, bright white light. ◌ Beyond Soul lies the infinite and divine source of all life—what some call the heart of God. This is where the life force—the current of light and sound also known as the healing force—originates. ◌ Together, all of your bodies' auras form what is commonly referred to as "the aura." The aura is not only a reflection of your bodies, it also contains information about all aspects of them. It is through the aura that gemstone energy usually accesses both the physical and inner bodies. ◌ Now, this concept of auras and inner bodies may be somewhat difficult to accept or even to grasp. However, it must be considered if one is to have any understanding of the way gemstones work with an individual's subtle aspects. ◌ Also, just as your physical body exists in the physical world, or plane of existence, your emotional body exists on the emotional plane, and your memory body exists on the memory plane. Your mental, intuitive, and Soul bodies also exist on their own respective planes. These planes exist in different dimensions, or at higher vibratory rates, than the physical. ◌ Since you have a physical body, your primary focus is on the physical plane. However, there are many beings, including a large number of Gemstone Guardians, who do not have physical bodies. They live and work on one of the inner planes. ◌ Nonetheless, the Guardians' spiritual duties often require them to put their attention on the physical and other planes in which their gemstones exist. Similarly, just because your primary focus is on a particular plane does not mean that you are limited to that plane. Michael, weren't you able to move your attention to this inner plane to meet me and obtain this information? ◌ Knowledge of the bodies' chakras is also essential for understanding how Lavender and other gemstones work. The physical and inner bodies each contain seven major chakras. On the physical body, these chakras are located down the middle of the front of the body, from the top of the head to the base of the spine.* ◌ The chakras act as doors through which the life force flows from its infinite source into the physical body. Ideally, the corresponding "doors" in each of your inner bodies line up with each other. When the doors are not aligned, the flow of life force through the inner bodies to the physical body is impeded and problems arise. For example, if the emotional body's doors are shifted out of their ideal positions, emotional difficulties may result; those with mental problems may find that the mental body doors have shifted to some degree, and so on. ◌ Blockages in these doors can lead to similar problems. For example, people who are caught up in the past may have blockages in some of the memory body's doors. Since blockages also inhibit the flow of life force to the physical body, physical problems may also arise.

MASTERING THE SUBTLE BODIES

When a strand of Lavender spheres is worn around the neck, Lavender's energy radiates into the entire aura and encourages all the chakras in all the bodies to move into better alignment. It does this by awakening the highest aspect of each body, so that each body becomes aware of its relationship with the next highest level. This inspires all the bodies to align and cooperate with each other. ◌ With each step toward better alignment, old issues come to the surface for resolution, and old blockages are released. Energies that have been stuck begin to flow freely, relieving the body of long-time burdens. With improved alignment, more life force flows through each of the bodies, nourishing and balancing them. ◌ As all the bodies become more nourished, balanced, and free from blockages, the individual becomes stronger, more creative, and more loving. In other words, the individual becomes a greater human being on all

---

* SEE MICHAEL KATZ, *Gemisphere Luminary Therapy Guide* FOR SPECIFIC CHAKRA LOCATIONS.

levels. ○ Indeed, Lavender helps people master themselves on all levels. One way it does this is by helping them gain greater awareness of their inner bodies. In fact, mastery of the inner bodies is the whole purpose of Lavender. Lavender also fosters awareness of one's spiritual Self and of one's connection with Spirit. ○ This awareness brings upliftment. When enough people are uplifted, civilization will be transformed. This is because, as awareness expands, people's needs and desires change. To fulfill these new needs and desires, there will be a natural evolution in technology, lifestyles, and the state of people's health. ○ As part of people's desire for spiritual advancement, many are striving to become perfected. This striving is expressed to some extent in the currently popular practice of cleansing toxins from the physical body. However, those who only put attention on the physical body and think that by cleansing it they can become more spiritual have it backwards. ○ If you wish to perfect the physical body, you must first work to align your inner bodies. Then life force can flow more easily through all the chakras to every part of your physical body. In this way you can become cleansed, balanced, and healed.

"How long does it take for one's bodies to become perfectly aligned?"
asked Michael.

It depends on how out of alignment your chakras are, as well as the size, quantity, and quality of Lavender you wear. Perfect alignment may never be achieved. However, the closer you come to perfect alignment, the better—because the more aligned you are, the more life and healing force will flow through you. ○ I would also like to say that the Sarshauné use Lavender for assistance with nearly every condition. Indeed, everyone on the planet uses Lavender at some time in his or her life. ○ The people of the Earth must start thinking and seeing beyond their own planet.

The time will come, as destiny has already ordained, that the Earth's people will become aware of civilizations from other planets. When this time arrives, the people of the Earth may wish that they had better prepared themselves to accept this awareness. Wearing Lavender is an ideal way to uplift oneself and prepare for the events of destiny. ◌ It doesn't matter what religion you practice, what spiritual teacher you follow, or what name you call God. Lavender transcends the divisions that Earth people have made between religions, because it fosters the conscious awareness of Soul, your own individualized spark of God. ◌ I have spoken of how I, as Lavender, bring the life force into the physical body. There is another who brings the healing force to imbalanced areas from inside the physical body. This gemstone is Aventurine. ◌

Come, let us meet the Guardian of Aventurine.

The

Guardian

of

AVENTURINE

4

PURIFYING THE PHYSICAL BODY

We left the clouds behind and entered an immense field of short grass. "In this field you will have the opportunity to attain greater wellness on all levels. Here you may ask for whatever you need to gain this wellness, and the answer will be immediately and clearly given," explained the Guardian of Lavender.

We walked across the field, covering what seemed to be a great distance. With the ground still firm under our feet, we entered an ocean of waist-deep green mist, which moved in rhythmic waves. These waves flowed back and forth, all around and through us. The energy propelling them was very great, and they stirred and soothed us.

Lavender spoke again: "We will walk toward the source of this energy. The closer we get, the nearer you will come to the truth about yourself and what you have done to make yourself who you are in a physical sense. Indeed, your thoughts, attitudes, and concepts of life, your feelings and the way you express them, and, yes, your memories, too, each influence the shape and stature of your physical self."

We neared a platform on which a man sat cross-legged, as if in meditation. It was from him that the waves of green energy were emanating. The man's eyes were closed and his hands rested comfortably in his lap. His round form reminded me of images of the Buddha. His skin was the color of Dark Green Aventurine and his clothing that of Light Green Aventurine.

"I would like to introduce you to the Guardian of Aventurine," said Lavender.

The Guardian slowly opened his eyes, and the whole land seemed to brighten. The white of his eyes contrasted sharply with his dark green skin, light green irises, and dark green pupils. He gazed at us, seeming to look through us, knowing exactly what we needed and exactly what he could give.

Then the waves of energy flowing from his being reversed direction and receded into him. He seemed to be gathering his energy as the waves compressed more tightly into his aura. The Guardian beckoned us to come closer and sit in a circle before him. He and the Guardian of Lavender nodded to each other respectfully, and then we all bid Lavender farewell.

The Guardian of Aventurine rose from his platform and joined us on the grass, completing our circle. Once seated, he used his hands to create an opening in the ground in the center of our group.

THE GREAT AWAKENING

Now you can see into the physical universe. There is your planet Earth. The continent you call Africa is now bathing in the sunlight. ☉ If you look at this planet with the eyes of knowingness, you will see that all over the Earth people are ready for an awakening. It is the awakening of the true Self. Some will call it greater spirituality, enlightenment, or Self-awareness. Some will call it a heightened sensitivity. And some will call it God's love shining upon them. Regardless of its name, it will be characterized by a renewed sense of Spirit and a greater understanding of all life, including oneself and one's relationship with God. ☉ I am here to help prepare individuals for this great awakening. My purpose is to heal the physical body, especially the most vital organs—for when the body is no longer ailing, one's attention can focus more clearly on this awakening. ☉ This is my function for the people of Earth. On some other planets, the people have already experienced this quantum leap. There I am used for many other purposes and in ways similar to those in which the people of Earth will one day use me. ☉ Aventurine has been a part of the planet for a long time. It did not form when the planet formed; instead, it evolved as the planet evolved. As the Earth prepared itself for human life, I was also prepared.

EXPELLING DISHARMONY

To understand my purpose, you must know how I work. You must also grasp the concept of vibratory rates. Unfortunately, the English language has limited means for describing the many and various forms of nonphysical emanations. In the context in which I will be using the term "vibratory rate," it has essentially the same meaning as the words "energy" and "frequency." ○ The Earth planet has two basic varieties of green Aventurine: Light Green and Dark Green. We will limit our discussion to these two varieties, for what good would it do to learn about what exists in other places? ○ The light green variety has few or no dark green flecks. The dark green variety is actually Light Green Aventurine so infused with flecks or particles of flecks that it appears dark green. Therefore, the light green variety that contains no flecks is essentially composed of one vibratory rate, and the dark green variety is essentially composed of two: the light green vibratory rate and the vibratory rate of the flecks. ○ Both the light and dark green vibratory rates focus their effects on organs. The light green uplifts and strengthens an organ by encouraging its healthiest cells to distribute their vitality throughout the organ. The dark green flecks expel the organ's low and disharmonious energies. ○ When either Light or Dark Green Aventurine spheres are worn around the neck, the Aventurine's vibratory rate fills the wearer's aura and enters the body through the breath. As with anything inhaled, the Aventurine vibratory rate first enters the lungs, then the blood stream, and then every cell in the body. This is how the whole body becomes introduced to Aventurine vibratory rate. ○ Although the "molecules" of Aventurine vibratory rate are distributed to every cell in the body, they maintain communication with each other. When enough Aventurine has permeated the body, it detects the organ with the greatest disharmony. When this occurs, all the Aventurine vibratory rate already in the body, plus any more that is breathed in, surrounds and begins to enter that organ. Once any amount of Aventurine vibratory rate—no matter how small—enters the target organ, it opens the door for more to enter. Then it gradually distributes itself as evenly as possible throughout the organ. ☉ What happens next depends on the variety of Aventurine being used. If a Light Green Aventurine necklace is worn, its effects will be those of the light green vibration—that is, it will encourage the organ's healthiest cells to distribute their vitality throughout the organ. ☉ You see, no organ has a homogenous vibratory rate. There are always some cells or groups of cells that have a higher vibratory rate than others. Cells with low vibratory rates are more susceptible to disease; indeed, they can act as the doors through which disease enters an organ. ☉ Fortunately, even diseased organs usually contain some healthy, vibrant cells. Light Green Aventurine focuses its vibratory rate on the healthiest of these cells. This compels them to spread their healthy vibratory rate to their adjacent cells, which in turn spread this vitality to their adjacent cells. As a result, the entire organ gradually gains more vitality and strength. ☉ If a Dark Green Aventurine necklace is worn, its primary effects will be those of its dark green vibration—that is, it will expel the organ's low and disharmonious vibratory rates. As more and more dark green vibration enters the organ, disease and disharmony will have no choice but to exit. In Dark Green Aventurine, the light green component takes on a supporting role: it helps make the organ more vital so it can more easily throw off the disharmony being expelled by the dark green vibration. ☉ Of the two types of Aventurine, Dark Green Aventurine can assist an individual most profoundly. Among other reasons, this is because the Dark Green Aventurine offers the effects of both the light and dark green vibrations. In other words, Dark Green Aventurine not only strengthens an organ, it actually drives out the organ's disharmony and disease. ☉ With both types of Aventurine, when the target organ is no longer the most disharmonious organ in the body, the Aventurine vibratory rate slowly leaves the organ. Then the Aventurine finds the next organ with the greatest degree of disharmony and begins working on that organ. The Aventurine continues this process for as long as it is worn. ◌ If Aventurine is worn long enough, it's possible that every organ will be treated. It is also possible that the original organ I worked on will again receive my attention. The longer I am worn, the stronger and healthier the organs will become. Naturally, this will lead to a strengthening of the entire body. ◌ The time it takes for Dark Green Aventurine to complete its work will depend on the size and quality of the Aventurine being worn. It will also depend on the degree of toxicity in the organ and the level of overall toxicity in the body.

NEUTRALIZING DISHARMONY

When Dark Green Aventurine expels disharmonious energy from an organ, a small amount of this disharmony is neutralized by the Aventurine's light green vibration. It is then up to the body to eliminate the rest—that is, unless Emerald is also worn around the neck. ◌ Emerald carries the green ray. The green ray is the aspect of the life force that focuses on raising the vibratory rate of the physical body. Aventurine encourages the body to relax and open itself to the green ray. ◌ When Emerald is worn with Dark Green Aventurine, the Aventurine focuses the Emerald's green ray on the target organ. The green ray then neutralizes much of the disharmony being expelled from the organ by the Aventurine. In this way, Emerald relieves the body of the burden of eliminating most of this disharmony. If Emerald is worn with the Aventurine, the time it takes for the Aventurine to complete its work may be cut in half. ◌ Because Dark Green Aventurine and Emerald work so powerfully together, I strongly recommend that people with diseased organs wear them together. Ideal would be a necklace of high-quality Dark Green Aventurine spheres and another necklace containing Emerald in rounded form. The gemstones' action should be supported with other therapies that boost the vitality of the entire body and support the eliminative organs, so the disharmony can exit the body more easily. ◌ One should continue to wear the Aventurine and Emerald, even if it appears that a healing has taken place. You see, once the vibratory rate of a disease has entered a body, it often lingers—sometimes for the rest of the person's life—even after the overt manifestation of the disease has been cleared.

RELEASING DRUG RESIDUES

Light Green Aventurine has a special role to play on your planet, where so much of your medicine is chemical. ◌ The physical body knows how to rid itself of most toxic foreign substances. Many of these substances will cause diarrhea or vomiting as part of the body's effort to force them out. However, when the foreign substance is not overtly toxic (as in the case of most drugs and some chemicals), the body doesn't know how to deal with it. It doesn't know how to pass the substance through the system in order to excrete it. This is especially true for certain drugs that are actually designed to be in harmony with the body and to have a specific effect on it; the body becomes confused about how to handle them. ◌ When the body doesn't know how to get rid of a drug (or, in some cases, its residue), it often encapsulates and isolates the drug after it has completed its work. More specifically, if a drug was targeted at a specific organ, the body's protective mechanism encapsulates what is left of the drug in that organ to protect the rest of the body from the drug's toxicity. ◌ I find it interesting that the pharmacologists and physicians of Earth who design drugs have perfected a healing system that is only halfway effective. They are ignorant—or choose to be ignorant—of the fact that although the drug may appear to be metabolized, some of the drug and/or its vibratory rate often remain in the body. ◌ If the organ with the encapsulated drug is the same organ being targeted by a Dark Green Aventurine necklace, the Aventurine vibratory rate will infiltrate the organ. It may then recognize these drug residues as disharmony and work to loosen and dispel them from the organ. ◌ Now, if the organ has been accumulating drugs for years, a potentially serious situation may arise when the Aventurine starts moving these drugs and their energies out into the body. The drugs and/or their vibratory rates will suddenly start circulating in the body, and the body will not know how to remove them. ◌ In this case, wearing Light Green Aventurine—especially if it contains some dark green flecks—is more appropriate than wearing Dark Green Aventurine. This is because the light green variety focuses more on uplifting the organ and loosening disharmonious energies than on dispelling those energies. Thus, the release of toxic energies into the body will be more gradual, and the body won't be overwhelmed by them. ◌ The process of moving drugs and their energies out of the body can be greatly enhanced if Emerald is worn with the Light Green Aventurine. To my knowledge, Emerald works only on natural toxicity—that is, the toxicity produced by a living organism. Therefore, the Emerald won't disintegrate the vibratory rate of the drugs themselves; instead, it will enhance the overall healing process by disintegrating the disharmony created in the body by the drugs' presence. ◌ Wearing the Light Green Aventurine and Emerald together will uplift the organ and encourage its surrounding area to become less disharmonious. This will help the organ, the area, and the whole body become stronger and more able to deal with the released encapsulations of toxicity.

GEMSTONE THERAPY

Where gemstone therapy clinics exist, a patient's time is respected. Patients receive attention as soon as they walk in the door and identify themselves to an assistant. The assistant then refers to the patient's file and gives the patient preliminary gemstones to wear. These preliminary gemstones are ordered by the gemstone therapist to prepare the patient for treatment. This practice also shows respect for the time of the therapist, who is in great demand. This demand will be created on Earth as well, because gemstone therapy works. ○ On an energetic level, gemstones work much better than most other medicines. One reason is that their vibratory rates remain constant. In contrast, if you take an aspirin or an herb, its vibratory rate changes as soon as it touches the tongue. Also, gemstones provide their wearers with a steady supply of the gems' healing energies. Perhaps most important, as a gemstone gets to know its wearer's aura, it continually adjusts and fine-tunes its actions to adapt to changes in the wearer. ○ However, only the highest quality gemstones are truly healing. Gemstones of lesser quality have significantly less, if any, therapeutic effect—and, indeed, can even have a detrimental effect on their users. Only therapeutic-quality gemstones allow the full range of a gemstone's healing properties to be expressed, and they alone should be used for the purposes and benefits the Gemstone Guardians describe. ○ For every gemstone there is a different set of criteria that makes that gem therapeutic. The characteristics that make Aventurine spheres therapeutic, for example, will not apply to other gemstones. ○ Information about the true purposes of gemstones is available to all. It is kept in libraries within the inner planes or is periodically given by the Gemstone Guardians in lectures such as this one. Those who wish to learn more about gemstones should study in these libraries or attend these lectures. I prefer not to be constantly interrupted with questions, so that I can keep my attention focused on maintaining and enlivening the flow of energy to all the Aventurine in existence. ○ Michael, to assist in my mission you must share the information I have given you. If information about a gemstone is given by its Guardian, you can be sure that it is as current and correct as possible for the conditions and consciousness of a particular time and place. ○ In the future, I will assist the people of Earth in greater ways than you can now imagine. However, I will not give you this information until you are ready. Look not to the gifts of the future. Enjoy and appreciate the value of the gifts you have today. Indeed, they are more valuable to you than any future gift, which you can neither use nor fully appreciate. ○ You, the people of Earth, are in the process of taking one of the greatest steps in your history. Use the tools that are already available to you to help you take this leap. These tools are gifts. They have already been given. It is up to each individual to unwrap and accept them. ○ It seems most appropriate that the next Guardian you meet will be the one in charge of Emerald, for we work so closely together. ○ May the blessings be!

The Guardian of Aventurine rose and returned to his platform. He sat down and closed his eyes, and once again the waves of green energy began to flow from his being.

I glanced down at our planet through the opening that the Guardian had made in the ground. His wave emanations poured through this opening and surrounded the Earth, touching and enlivening all the Aventurine on the planet. As my attention followed these waves, I realized that I too was moving closer to the Earth.

In the next moment, I regained the awareness of my physical body. I opened my eyes just as Michael was opening his. We smiled at each other, our hearts full of gratitude for the knowledge unfolding before us.

The
Guardian
of

EMERALD

5

HEALING THE PHYSICAL BODY

As I closed my eyes, I wondered what the Guardian of Emerald would look like. The sound I was hearing grew particularly loud, making it especially easy to follow. It led me to a small dark amphitheater where three others, including Michael, were already awaiting the arrival of the Guardian.

We stood in the center of this amphitheater, bathing in the glow of what appeared to be seven floodlights. Each of these lights showered one of the colors of the rainbow on us. The colors moved, as if dancing to the rhythm of music. My heart danced with them as I watched, awe-struck by their beauty.

Suddenly the green ray grew larger, and the other six rays receded to quiet flickers in the background. Within the column of green light, an Emerald crystal began to materialize. When it had fully formed, the crystal stood about six feet high and three feet wide. Like a magnet, the Emerald began to draw to itself all the green ray showering from above. The green ray moved faster and faster until it was pouring into the Emerald at a high velocity.

The transformation continued as the crystal took the shape of a tall figure wearing an emerald-green cape. The man who now stood before me had short black hair and a closely cropped black beard. He appeared to be in his thirties. As he opened his eyes, green rays of light shot from them, piercing the darkness that surrounded us. Then his eyes became a more familiar dark brown.

I looked up and noticed that the ceiling of the amphitheater had disappeared, revealing a midnight sky brilliant with stars. The seats in the amphitheater also vanished, and we found ourselves standing in the middle of a vast grassy field.

I approached the Guardian of Emerald. We looked deeply into each other's eyes, and again his eyes became green. The color overwhelmed me. Feeling somewhat intoxicated, I turned and stepped backward into his aura.

MOTHER CRYSTALS

I am glad all of you were able to make this inner-world journey to meet me halfway between your world and mine. Let us begin. ◌ When a planet becomes ready to support life, it is the duty of the Guardians of the Physical Universe to direct the implantation of the seven gemstones bearing the color rays. Emerald is one of these gemstones. As the Earth evolved and developed a capacity for life, it began to prepare matrices to encase that life. When the Guardians of the Physical Universe noticed this and saw that Spirit wanted life on the planet, they fulfilled their duty to direct the implantation of these gemstones. ◌ You will soon learn of the other six color-ray gemstones. Not all these gemstones were present when I was planted on Earth. This is because, at that time, some of the color rays were carried by gems other than the ones that carry them now. ◌ I was not planted in an existing gemstone, the way Lavender was planted in Quartz. Before I explain how I was planted, let me say this: Some wheat seeds are planted to produce flour for eating; other wheat seeds are grown specifically to bear higher quality seeds for replanting. Emerald crystals have similar classifications. ◌ A few coveted and highly protected Emerald crystals have a life energy so intense that only one race of people in the physical universe can handle the responsibility for them. These Emerald crystals are like the wheat seeds that are grown to produce more seeds. ◌ The Earth is a living planet. It contains supra-physical channels that fulfill a function similar to that of your blood vessels. Some people call the places where these channels reach the surface the "power points" of the Earth. ◌ When the Earth was ready, representatives from this race of people planted a cluster of these special Emerald crystals in a channel beneath a power point. This special cluster became the "mother crystal" of all the Earth's future Emeralds. The mother crystal gave the Earth a "blueprint" for making crystal line matrices to contain the Emerald's energy. ○ Once this mother crystal was planted, the Earth distributed the crystal's vibratory rate to other places in the planet. These birthplaces for future Emerald crystals were chosen by the Guardian of the Earth for the good of the planet. ○ The base of the mother crystal is somewhat circular. The cluster itself is about one-and-a-half to two feet wide and one foot high. These dimensions are only approximate and, ultimately, the actual shape and size of the mother crystal doesn't matter; it's just good for you to understand that it isn't a mile wide. ○ The race of people I referred to is responsible for planting mother crystals throughout the universe. These include more than just Emerald crystals. These beings have a technology and spiritual awareness far beyond anything even your science-fiction writers have yet conceived. Although they use spaceships, they are not bound by the limitations of the physical universe. They move from one end of the universe to the other in little time. This race works directly with the hierarchy of Guardians in this physical universe and in nonphysical universes as well. ○ When Spirit directs the attention of a Physical Universe Guardian to a planet ready to support life, the Guardian then notifies this race of people. When they are presented with a planet ready to support life—and thus ready to be implanted with at least the seven color-ray gemstones—they begin to research the planet. ○ These beings are like scientists. They scan the planet for its energy channels and power points; then they chart them. Because the planet is preparing to support life, all types of data about the planet must be gathered and stored. Of the millions of planets in the physical universe, many are preparing for life at the same time. Consequently, this race of people is kept very busy. ○ After the mother crystals are planted, certain members of this race continue to record data. One spaceship of these people, whose lifetimes span much greater lengths of time than yours, stays with this planet for hundreds of your Earth's years. Among the things they monitor are how the planet receives the gemstones, whether the planet is forming crystalline matrices as well as it can, whether the proper connections are being made between the mother crystal and its offspring, and how the planet is responding to the new light rays now available to it. ◌ By the way, you should know that when I refer to a light ray, I also mean the sound that accompanies the light. Gemstones carry light and sound. It is just tedious to say "light and sound" repeatedly. The word "light" is more easily understood by most people, since it is a more obvious quality of gemstones. ◌ Mother crystals still exist on the Earth. When your people have attained a certain level of technology and earned the responsibility, you may be able to locate mother crystals and dig them up. No mother crystals have yet been uncovered on the Earth planet.

"Do all gemstones have mother crystals?" asked Michael.

No. Lavender, for example, does not have a mother crystal; its vibratory rate was planted in Quartz. ◌ As a planet constructs crystalline matrices to house the vibratory rate of a mother crystal's offspring, mutations can form. This is one reason this race of beings monitors the planet for several hundred years or sometimes thousands of years. They also regularly return to observe each planet they have implanted with gemstones. Yes, some of these beings do visit the Earth once in a while. They do not walk the planet, because they are very different from the Earth's inhabitants and would be too noticeable. From their spacecraft, they scan the planet to monitor, for example, changes in life forms and power points, and, as always, they record this data. ◌ If a planet begins to develop mutations in a certain matrix, these people have ways to make sure the matrix does not continue to change. Of course, certain mutant crystals are not bad or undesirable; the Earth often creates them to help balance specific energies within the planet.

GEMSTONE WARFARE

During the Age of Atlantis, my powers were researched, and certain qualities of the vibratory rate of my crystal were discovered. You have heard of chemical warfare. There is also such a thing as gemstone warfare. I hesitate to speak of this. However, there are some things you must know even though they aren't pleasant. ☉ Most of the black inclusions one finds in Emeralds today are the result of foul play. When this foul play occurred, the black inclusions were not visible. Otherwise, it would have been obvious to the gemstone's recipient that the Emerald had been tampered with. This Emerald brought disease of the mind, emotions, and body. The Atlanteans responsible for this foul play were assisted by individuals from beyond your planet. Not all extraterrestrials have the best intentions. ☉ At the destruction of Atlantis, the Emerald on your planet needed serious attention, and many were called upon to assist. We devised a way to transform the destructive vibratory rate that had been placed within all the Emerald crystals on the planet. We transformed it into what appear to be black flecks. ☉ Today these black inclusions are no longer harmful, and there is nothing one could do to change them back into harmful energy. They are now a living part of the Emerald. Their vibratory rate continues to reproduce and grow within the Emerald crystals, somewhat like mutant genes. Although the flecks are now benign, they will always serve as a reminder that when powerful tools are misused, they can become highly destructive. ☉ Gemstones are powerful tools—more powerful than you may realize. Yet, when used with good intentions, an open and loving heart, and a clear and understanding mind, gemstone tools can yield astounding benefits.

COLOR RAYS

To gain a better understanding of my purpose, it will be helpful for you to have some knowledge of what color rays are, where they come from, and why they are so important to life. To explain the origin of color rays, I will use a simple image. ◌ Imagine that in an area of the intuitive plane, at the top of a towering mountain, lies an important crystal. Before the pure white light of Spirit can touch the worlds below, it must first flow through this crystal. As it does, the white light is separated into seven color rays: red, orange, yellow, green, blue, indigo, and purple. This process is similar to the way sunlight shining through a crystal hung in a window separates into the colors of the rainbow. ◌ Each color ray has a specific purpose, and all seven color rays are essential for life and health. A deficiency in any one of these color rays in an individual moves that person away from optimal health and an optimal expression of life. ◌ Every planet has a unique ratio of color rays. This ratio is essential for the life of that planet's inhabitants and the state of consciousness they are destined to achieve. The Earth, for example, has less of the red, yellow, and indigo rays than it has of the other rays. ◌ It is difficult to work directly with color rays in their pure form because they are not physical. The gemstones that bear these color rays are physical and therefore can be used as tools to enhance the flow of nonphysical color rays. ◌ In the past seventy years, people's consciousness has been rising rapidly. As people grow and expand in consciousness, they need increasing amounts of color rays. Individuals can fulfill this increased need for the green ray by wearing Emerald—and the more they wear it, the more effective Emerald can be.

EMERALD AND THE GREEN RAY

Emerald is found throughout the physical universe on every planet where life is evolving. Only planets that are just rocks in space and that support no life or only primitive forms of it have no Emerald. ○ My purpose for the Earth human who wears Emerald is the same purpose I fulfill for everyone in the universe who wears it: I provide the green ray. This ray is essential for the life of all plants, animals, and human beings. ○ Emerald has been the bearer of the green ray since the beginning of time. Since I am not bound by time as Earth humans understand it, Emerald is still in its prime. It will continue to be the bearer of the green ray for as long as your imagination can stretch into the future. ○ Emerald works on raising the vibratory rate of the physical body. When this upliftment occurs, the wearer's attention can more easily expand to include the other states of consciousness that lie beyond the physical. ○ In order to uplift an individual, Emerald resolves the weakest link in the chain. The weakest link is always the lowest vibratory rate in the body, and it is often the source of disease. Emerald's green ray disintegrates the disharmony that manifests as disease and discomfort. ○ It is not the green ray alone that does this. Rather, it is the green ray in combination with the vibratory rate of Emerald itself. For the sake of simplicity, I will refer to the combination of the green ray and Emerald vibratory rate simply as "Emerald energy." ○ Emerald energy also prepares the emotions and mind for the new state of consciousness that will arise when it has resolved the physical disharmony. Although my effects on the emotions and mind are secondary to my effects on the physical body, those who wear me can take comfort in knowing they are using a powerful tool to help heal the very cause of their physical conditions.

NEUTRALIZING DISHARMONY

It is not only physical-body disharmonies that manifest as physical illness. Disharmonies in the emotional and mental bodies usually lead to physical problems as well. Inner-body disharmonies block the flow of life force to the physical body and feed the body with disharmonious energy. Therefore, once you take care of the physical disharmonies, you must also resolve the inner ones; otherwise, these inner disharmonies will continue to manifest in the physical body. Perhaps they will manifest in a different location or as a different condition, but they will manifest. ◌ Between the physical body and the emotional aura lies a layer of supra-physical energy. This layer of energy is sometimes called the "supra-physical aura." The supra-physical aura appears to surround the physical body; the emotional aura appears to surround the supra-physical aura; the causal aura appears to surround the emotional aura; and so on. ◌ When Emerald is worn, its energy first floods the supra-physical aura and locates areas of physical disharmony. Then, like the eagle who has spotted its prey, it swoops down on these areas. The Emerald energy focuses on the disharmonious areas and enters them through the skin in a process similar to osmosis. It continues to do so as long as there is Emerald energy in the supra-physical aura. ◌ After the Emerald energy has saturated the supra-physical aura, it begins to saturate the emotional aura. There it works on any emotional disharmonies that may be feeding the physical condition. It takes more time and, in most cases, more Emerald to saturate the emotional aura than it does the supra-physical aura; and it takes even more time and, in certain cases, more Emerald to saturate the causal and mental auras. In these auras, Emerald focuses on resolving the causal and mental causes of the physical problem. ◌ This is one reason why people whose physical bodies are overburdened with disharmony should—probably for the rest of their lives—wear enough Emerald to continually saturate the supra-physical aura and to provide the other inner auras with enough Emerald energy to work on the underlying, inner causes of their physical conditions. This is also why people who wear Emerald and Aventurine necklaces together should keep wearing at least enough Emerald to saturate the inner auras for some time after it appears that the physical condition has healed. This will help resolve the condition's corresponding inner disharmonies so they cannot manifest again in the physical body. ☉ Now, you might wonder why, when an aura becomes saturated with Emerald energy, it does not stay saturated. One reason is that disharmony and the green ray are opposites, and in the process of neutralizing and disintegrating disharmony, the green ray gets used up. Indeed, if the disharmony is strong, the green ray is used up rather quickly. ☉ The size, quality, and quantity of Emerald worn determines its ability to saturate the auras and initiate healing changes. In other words, the higher the quality and the larger the overall mass and sphere size, the more effective the Emerald will be.

CANCER AND ALCOHOLISM

The effect of Emerald energy on cancer is one of shock. Cancer is like a living entity. It works to maintain its own life, which exists at the expense of its host. ☉ When introduced to the pure green ray and the vibratory rate of Emerald, the cancer entity becomes so shocked that it cringes and becomes a little more compact. If Dark Green Aventurine is worn at the same time, the Aventurine vibratory rate will be able to enter the diseased area more easily. This occurs for two reasons: first, the cancer will have become slightly more isolated energetically; and second, when the cancer entity is shocked, it will have let down its guard. ☉ When an Emerald necklace is worn along with a necklace of Aventurine, the

Emerald energy enters the body through the breath. In effect, the Emerald energy rides in on the Aventurine vibratory rate. Emerald and Aventurine energies work remarkably well together, especially after the Aventurine has entered a cancerous organ. Aventurine works from the inside of the organ to dispel disharmony and spread healthy, harmonious vibratory rate throughout the organ's cells. The Emerald stands at the gateway of each cell with a "hose," shooting green ray at the exiting disharmony and disintegrating it. This is the power of the green ray. It is the perfect opposite of cancer. ◐ Alcohol is a substance which leaves its mark on the liver. A liver which has been damaged by alcohol is different from a liver afflicted with cancer. Like cancer, alcoholism is an entity, but it doesn't latch onto the physical body like the cancer entity does. Instead, it clings to the person's aura. Alcoholism is actually an inner-body disharmony. ◐ That is why, when treating it, Quartz should be worn with Emerald. The Quartz will act like a window through which the Emerald energy can work on healing the areas in the inner bodies affecting the liver. The Quartz will accelerate the saturation of the inner bodies with Emerald energy, allowing it to enter those bodies even before the supra-physical aura has become saturated. ◐ By the way, the addition of Quartz would not be indicated in a condition such as liver cancer. The cancer is a malicious entity that will have grabbed onto the liver. In order to eradicate it, the individual will need to place maximum attention on the physical body. Only when the physical body has become stabilized should the focus shift to the inner bodies. ◐ Thus, if you want to focus primarily on the physical body, use Emerald by itself or with Aventurine. If your primary focus includes the inner bodies as well as the physical body, use Quartz with the Emerald. ◐ Do not underestimate the healing power of the gemstones that carry the color rays. Like some other color-ray bearers, Emerald is rare and precious, and therefore expensive. As a general rule, the more precious and the higher in quality a gemstone is, the more power it has and the stronger its effects are. Because of this power, less of the gemstone is needed on the planet. Therefore, it is naturally more rare. ✿ If all you had were a solid necklace of Emerald and a solid necklace of Aventurine, your gemstone "tool box" for physical-body healing would be almost complete. I do not wish to negate the importance of other gemstones and their significance for speeding up the resolution of certain isolated conditions. However, if you are working on healing a physical condition, Emerald and Aventurine are indispensable. ✿ There is still much to learn about Emerald. My nature is to assist in the upliftment of human beings. I do this by helping them resolve their greatest physical disharmonies. Once these disharmonies are resolved, attention can be placed on other aspects of growth, and spiritual evolution can accelerate. Emerald is ready to help. Now it is up to you.

Recognizing that the discourse had ended, Michael and the others thanked the Guardian of Emerald, who responded by nodding his head. As I turned to thank him, I found that I was no longer in his aura but was facing him. Again he looked into my eyes. Then he took my hands and gently laid in them a necklace of exquisite Emerald spheres.

The starry sky disappeared, and we found ourselves standing once again inside the amphitheater. The Guardian's body soon vanished, and the green-ray beacon resumed its previous form. Then the other six colored floodlights reappeared in their former positions.

We looked at one another, silently assimilating the experience we had just shared. Then, one by one, each of us walked away in separate directions.

6

PURIFYING THE EMOTIONAL BODY

Four individuals stood waiting for Michael and me beside a thick, pale pink fog. We joined them and acknowledged one another silently. Then we all joined hands and walked into the mist.

The fog quickly turned into a light pink rain. This gentle rain did not wet us but seemed to cleanse and soothe our emotions. Through the rain we saw a figure approaching us veiled in a swirling mist of pink light. Although the misty light made her features hard to see, I knew she was female by the quality of her energy. When she arrived, she placed her palms together and bowed her head in greeting.

I walked up to her and asked permission to enter her aura. She shook her head and stepped back. The rain seemed to stop in mid-air, and the swirling mist of pink light surrounding her became absolutely still. She stepped away from it and stood before us.

The Guardian had long, dark blonde hair. Her eyes were brown. Her simple clothes appeared loose-fitting and comfortable, and her shirt revealed muscular arms. She seemed as ordinary us anyone, yet the light in her eyes and the radiance of her body made her seem like no one from the Earth planet. The pink shell of misty light she had once occupied came alive again, and its energy began to swirl like a whirlpool.

The Guardian looked at us and smiled. Then she invited me to stand next to her and connect my consciousness with hers so that I could relay her words.

In many ways I am just like you. I have a family and I have children. But I also have a spiritual responsibility: I am the Guardian for Rose Quartz. ○ My name is Roselle. I would be grateful if you also called the spherical form of Rose Quartz "Roselle." This will help distinguish the properties of the spherical form from those of the crystalline form, commonly known as Rose Quartz. ○ I do not live on the Earth planet. I live on a plane with a vibratory rate higher than that of the physical plane. My world is unseen by physical eyes, yet it is as real to me and its inhabitants as your world is to you. Many people who see me every day have no inkling of my spiritual responsibility as the Guardian of Rose Quartz, nor do I advertise it. I only speak of this to help you understand the possibilities of who and what a Gemstone Guardian might be. ○ Before I give you an overview of my purpose for the Earth planet and for the human beings who live there, why don't we all sit down? The rain has stopped, and the sunshine is warm.

EMOTIONAL EVOLUTION

When I am in crystalline form, my focus is on the planet. I act like a magnet, drawing the Earth's vibratory rate upward toward the emotional plane. My magnetic influence pulls the Earth to a higher state of consciousness. This movement toward greater consciousness is part of the Earth's evolution. ○ You see, the planet's first life forms—single-celled plants and other organisms and, later, fish, reptiles, and animals—were physically oriented. Any thinking or feeling experienced by these life forms were directly related to the physical functioning of their brains and were mostly a product of habit and instinct. As human beings evolved, they could not grow beyond this purely instinctual state of consciousness until there was enough emotional energy on the Earth to allow this growth to occur. ○ So, when people became ready to grow beyond this state, the light ray that gives life to the emotional plane was directed toward the Earth in a great beacon. It enveloped the planet and began filling its aura. This light ray from the emotional plane was the pink color ray. ◌ Once enough pink ray had accumulated in the Earth's aura, its vibratory rate collected at the planet's power points. Quartz then directed this vibratory rate along the Earth's supra-physical veins and arteries to many places where Quartz was forming and growing. When this pink energy was accepted by certain Quartz crystals, it took hold and began to spread through them. ◌ In this way, Rose Quartz was born. My birth allowed both the Earth and the human beings living there to experience the emotional level of life. This gave the evolving human beings a conscious awareness of their emotions the animals did not possess. ◌ By the way, today most animals still react, feel, and think only on an instinctual level. However, those animals who have been touched and loved by human beings are given a special gift which most pet owners are unaware of. Because the pets' owners are in touch with their emotions, these pets become more in touch with their own emotions. Pets tend to encourage their owners to open their hearts and love them, thereby directing a stream of love and emotion toward the pets. This love raises the pets' consciousness and provides them with the gift of being more in tune with their own emotions. ◌ A tremendous amount of Rose Quartz has been born since the time of Atlantis, and it is still spreading throughout the planet. This growth is preparing the planet for greater consciousness. As the planet's Rose Quartz increases, the magnetic pull toward the emotional plane and the momentum of the upward spiral of energy in the planet will increase. The spread of Rose Quartz also serves to balance the downward spiral this planet is currently experiencing. We see this opposing spiral expressed as increased crime, corruption, and negativity. ◌ Since the Age of Atlantis, the positive and negative forces—the upward and downward spirals—have been struggling with each other. This opposition is the reason that most Rose Quartz has become so cloudy. The constant struggle between these two forces creates a conflict within the crystalline matrix and causes this cloudiness. ◌ Today, Rose Quartz in crystalline form can do little for human beings other than remind them of their emotions. Of course, if you have an affinity for a Rose Quartz crystal, if you like the way it feels and it has become a friend for you, I encourage you to enjoy it.

RELEASING SUPPRESSED EMOTIONS

When I am in spherical form, my mission is to help people move beyond their emotional limitations. I do this by helping people to express, release, and resolve suppressed emotions. These emotions—be they repressed, hidden, or simply unacknowledged—impede emotional health. They also block the experience of greater spirituality, self-awareness, and self-understanding. Indeed, they can act as great stumbling blocks to one's positive changes and growth. ◌ To accomplish my mission, I bring the attention of my wearers to their emotions. Specifically, I stir suppressed emotions, helping the individual to become aware of them. These suppressed or blocked emotions are like locked doors within one's being. I help the person open these doors. Then I gently stimulate the heart to open so the individual can express these feelings. In this way, I help my wearer resolve and let go of suppressed emotions. ◌ Be aware that the heart will open only if the physical body is ready to accept the feelings I have stirred; I will not force it to open. In other words, I help the individual's true nature to be stirred and felt; then, if the body allows, the door will open and this true nature will be expressed. ◌ I do not heal emotions. I simply help an individual resolve suppressed and other unexpressed emotions. These emotions include long-forgotten feelings that have been pushed deep within as a result of many kinds of conditioning. People often suppress feelings that are not in harmony with the religious, social, or cultural values they were taught as children or if they fear there will be negative consequences if they express such feelings. These suppressed emotions may even be positive ones, like love, joy, or happiness. ○ I accomplish my mission in two phases: In the first phase, I stir suppressed emotions, allowing the individual to acknowledge, understand, and then feel these emotions; in the second phase, I encourage the individual to express these emotions, resolve and let go of them, and move on. ○ Did you notice the numbers in this formula? There are two phases and four steps to each phase. The energies of numbers have great power and significance. The number two represents the emotional level, and the number four represents the physical. That these two numbers intertwine in this formula means that the emotions are provided with a greater connection to the physical body. This gives them an easier path for expression. ○ In general, you will find that I can assist women through these two phases more effectively than men. This is only because men have a more difficult time letting go of suppressed emotions. Naturally, most men easily express and let go of spontaneous emotions they don't want to suppress. A man who wishes to be helped by Roselle must be deeply willing to acknowledge and re-experience his suppressed emotions. ○ Women generally have stronger emotional constitutions than men. This means they can wear greater amounts of Roselle without feeling imbalanced. One might think that women are emotionally weak, since stereo-typically they cry more often than men. But, on the contrary, it takes great emotional strength to let go and cry. ○ Often people need to use their minds to understand certain emotions before they can resolve them, let them go, and move on. Roselle can help people better understand their emotions. Not only do I act like a magnet to draw the energy of the physical plane upward, I also pull mental-plane energy downward. As mental energy is drawn to the emotional level, a greater understanding of the emotions is gained. ☾ Some say I remind people of positive emotional qualities and that I promote feelings of goodwill, friendship, and love. This is the effect of my color. However, judging a gemstone's properties by its color alone can be misleading. A gemstone is not simply its color; it has other energies as well. I have a clear and specific purpose not defined by the vibratory rate of my color. It just so happens that the pink color ray is the most effective vehicle for my mission. ☾ I can assist people with many kinds of emotional conditions—from people with only slight emotional problems to those whose emotional state is so disharmonious that they are considered emotionally ill by society's standards. I can help the emotionally ill regain some emotional strength. I can also prepare them—or anyone else—to wear a gemstone such as Rhodocrosite, which has a strong ability to break up emotional patterns and to cleanse and rebuild the emotional body. ☾ Even if you don't feel that you have an emotional problem, imagine how enlightening it would be to discover what emotions you may be suppressing. It can be an interesting experience in self-awareness and self-understanding to wear Roselle and observe the emotions that start coming up and the ones that you try to suppress. The experience may also help you recognize which of your attitudes are causing you to suppress certain emotions. Because it can show people so much about themselves, Roselle is a helpful addition to any counseling or self-help program. ☾ Roselle is not a particularly strong gemstone, especially when you compare its strength with that of the color-ray bearers. However, Roselle is a tool that should not be overlooked, especially if one has any emotional disharmony whatsoever—for although my action is subtle, it is effective. ☾ You will find that some gemstones are more powerful than others. That is why some Gemstone Guardians must be Guardians full-time and always immersed in their work. Perhaps this is why I, as Roselle, am able to take the responsibility of being a Guardian and yet still have a family and lead a somewhat normal life. ☾ You may never know whether your next-door neighbor is a master of the life force or adept in the teachings of Spirit. Yet, as you ponder this possibility, you may experience a sense of wonder and curiosity and perhaps even a certain humility.

GEMSTONE SPHERE SIZE AND CLEANSING

It is probably best to begin by wearing a strand of either 8-mm or 10-mm Roselle spheres. People will be attracted to the size that is most comfortable for them. After several months—or when you feel that you have resolved certain emotional blocks and issues but still have more to work on—move on to the next larger size. In other words, when you are ready for even deeper work on your emotions, move on to either 10-mm or 12-mm spheres. ☾ In general, quality being equal, the larger gemstone spheres are, the more powerful are their effects. Nonetheless, one should not use spheres larger than 16 mm in diameter for medicinal purposes. Such large spheres do not resonate with human beings the way smaller spheres do. Single spheres larger than 16 mm, however, can be used for contemplation and to uplift the atmosphere of any indoor environment, such as your home or workspace. ☾ When people wear gemstones and start moving toward a healthier state of being, they release old, limiting, or other disharmonious energies. These released energies often become attached to the surface of the gemstones or collect in the gems' energetic field. These collections of negative vibrations hinder the gemstones' effectiveness by impeding their ability to radiate their own vibrations into the aura. For this and other reasons, therapeutic gemstones must be regularly cleansed of released negative energies.*

---

* See Michael Katz, *Gemisphere Luminary Therapy Guide* for specific instructions on how to cleanse each type of gemstone discussed in this book.

◐ Tomorrow I will introduce you to a special friend. I do not get to see her often myself. She is the Guardian of Ruby. The gemstones she and I care for can do wonderful things for the human being when they are worn together. ◐ If you are having trouble expressing and/or letting go of your emotions, it will be helpful to wear Ruby along with Roselle. Ruby's powerful love will give you the confidence you need. Ruby will help you know that you will still have love and be loved if you express the feelings you have been suppressing. ◐ Do not hesitate to wear Ruby with Roselle, for Ruby will give light and life to my effects. Ruby can help uplift the individual more than Roselle alone ever can.

Roselle smiled briefly. Then she stood up and re-entered the shell of pink swirling energy. We watched, amazed at her ability to do this. Then she placed the palms of her hands together, bowed her head to the group, and walked away.

7

HEALING THE EMOTIONAL BODY

We sat in Michael's living room and prepared to meet the Guardian of Ruby.
Already her presence was strong, as feelings of love and joy charged the room.
All the molecules in the air seemed to be turning themselves inside out, changing
into particles of greater and greater energy, and this energy was love.

I closed my eyes to become more attuned to these feelings of love I knew must be
related to Ruby. Indeed they were, for within moments I was standing before the
Guardian of Ruby in the same pink mist where we had met the Guardian of Roselle.

Red energy swirled around the Guardian's body, forming what appeared to be a
floor-length gown. Her hair was dark, almost purple-red. A red ray either shone
from her eyes or was reflected by them—I could not be sure which. Gloves covered
her arms. The only skin I could see was that of her face and neck, and it was
unusually white.

She extended one hand to Michael and one to me, and together we walked through
the pink rain and mist to the Guardian of Roselle. When the two Guardians met,
each held her palms together and bowed slightly to the other. Then Roselle turned
to us and said, "I see you have already met the Guardian of Ruby. Follow her.
Perhaps you and I will meet again somewhere in time. For now, farewell!"

Ruby led us to the edge of a cliff where about fifteen listeners were gathered,
awaiting her discourse. The wind was strong, yet curiously it did not ruffle our
hair or clothing. Peering over the edge of the cliff, I saw clouds below and,
hundreds of feet beneath them, the ocean. Despite the distance of the water,
the roar of waves crashing against rocks could be distinctly heard.

All attention was focused on Ruby. She seated herself close to the cliff's edge,
and the listeners gathered in a semi-circle around her. She started to speak, and
I remembered my duty. Feeling conspicuous, I stood and approached her.
She seemed to understand my intent and drew me toward her.
Then I fell into her consciousness . . . .

When each of you first felt my presence, you experienced what Ruby does naturally. Ruby placed anywhere in the atmosphere will begin to change the molecules around it. It turns them inside out, in a sense, to reveal the love that created them. And what is this love? It is the divine love that created all molecules and atoms. You can call it the love of God.

PLANETARY POWER POINTS

The chemical matrix of my crystals, known as corundum, formed when the Earth formed. At the birth of the planet, corundum was colorless and existed in pockets in many places around the planet. These pockets had a certain geographical relationship with the Earth's power points as they existed at the birth of the planet. ◐ If you study the major deposits of corundum and the power points of the Earth, you will discover this relationship. This is because corundum of any color strongly desires to be positioned at a certain distance from the power points—not too near and not too far. It will even cause shifts in the planet in order to achieve this distance. ◐ Power points have shifted several times since the birth of the planet. Each time the power points shift, the minerals and crystals that need to be certain distances from the power points are drawn to these positions like magnets. This attraction compels the plates of the Earth's crust to move, so that the crystals can realign and relocate themselves at the ideal distances from the power points. ◐ I am saying that corundum has the power to force the Earth's patterns to change. Do you think that a human being's patterns are hard to change? My friends, there is nothing harder to change than the physical matter of a planet. And if corundum can do this, it can easily change a human being's patterns. It is just a matter of applying it properly.

RUBY AND THE RED RAY

Red corundum, or Ruby, came into being when the vibratory rate of the red ray combined with the crystalline matrix of clear corundum. It was not until the Age of Atlantis that the people of Earth needed the strong vibratory rate of corundum behind the red ray. Prior to that, there was another carrier of the red ray. ◐ During the Atlantean Age, the reign of this previous carrier had begun to decline rapidly. This carrier had taken the responsibility of bearing the red ray for the Earth, but it faltered when it could not handle the long-term responsibility. Its crystalline matrix was too weak to handle the vibratory rate of the pure red ray over a long period of time, and this weakness caused an imbalance. This imbalance corrupted the gemstone and its Guardian, and the two became a negative influence on the people of Atlantis. ◐ Because of this corruption, a new carrier of the red ray had to be quickly acquired. So, the Guardian of Earth, the Guardian of the Universe, and whoever else was required to make such decisions focused the red ray like a laser toward specific deposits of clear corundum. ◐ The transfer from the old carrier to the new occurred almost instantaneously—by Earth standards, in about two hundred years. This was all the time needed for the corundum to change from clear to pink to a true red. So, if you wonder whether pink Ruby is an immature form of red Ruby, the answer is yes. On most other living planets, the red ray is planted in corundum at the same time the other six color-ray carriers are planted. I do not know why the Earth was different in this respect. ◐ When I was given the responsibility of bearing the red color ray for the Earth, the previous carrier resisted. It would not let go of the responsibility. Therefore, to protect and maintain my mission, I had to create a mask of power. This was necessary to keep my predecessor from influencing my work. Unfortunately, people soon noticed this mask of power and then misused it for themselves. I was meant to be a gemstone that taught the force of love. It was never my intent to carry the force of power. ☽ You see, as long as I was wearing this mask, I was unable to fulfill my mission as the force of love, which is the positive aspect of the red ray. Today there are other gemstones and earthstones that carry the element of power. The energy they bring to the Earth satisfies the need for power possessed by individuals in a certain state of consciousness. ☽ My predecessor's energy has greatly waned and does not fit the expanding consciousness of most people today. Because my predecessor's energy has weakened, my power mask is no longer necessary. It seems as though a cycle has ended and I can begin my reign all over again. This time I can do it right. Now the consciousness of human beings is ready for Ruby. ☽ Because I have experienced the apparent conflict between power and love and have resolved it within myself, I can assist others who are also experiencing this struggle. I can give them the strength to move beyond this conflict. ☽ The color red may always be a symbol of power, yet it is also a symbol of love. My predecessor allowed the red ray to enter the body principally through the root chakra. I bring the red ray in through the heart. Often the heart is so thankful for my presence and for the love I bring with me that it freely opens its door to me. ☽ I could continue discussing my past in greater detail, but it is my importance for the present that you really should understand. ☽ Contrary to some people's concepts about the meaning and symbolism of different colors, every color ray is a spiritual ray. Each color ray is simply a different vibratory rate or expression of their common source in God. When color rays enter the body, they provide a bridge from the inner worlds to the physical world. In this way, they bring spiritual nourishment and upliftment. Each individual is in greater harmony with one particular color ray than with any of the other color rays. This color may be called the individual's "main" color ray. When you wear the gemstone bearing your main color ray, you will have an easier time expanding your consciousness, becoming uplifted, and moving closer to the infinite source of all life. In other words, wearing your main ray gemstone can serve as a powerful tool on the road to greater spiritual growth. ○ As the carrier of the pure red ray of the life force, Ruby is not just the red ray or just the vibratory rate of corundum. It is a unique combination of the two. Thus, the way Ruby expresses the red ray is different from any another source of red ray, red color, or red light.

EMOTIONAL MASTERY

If one's body tenses at the discussion of emotions, this is a sure sign of a red ray deficiency. One may say, "I'm willing to learn about emotions," but the eyes will say, "I'm afraid. I'm not ready. I don't want to know." With this in mind, if you feel tension during this discussion, try to be aware of any other emotions you may be experiencing. ○ Emotional mastery implies emotional balance, understanding, and the ability to regulate how much emotion you want to exhibit in a certain situation. Yet this is not the kind of mastery that Ruby teaches; this is only the effect of the mastery. ○ The emotional mastery Ruby teaches is total awareness of the emotional body. The emotional body exists in an emotional world, just like your physical body exists in a physical world. The emotional world is very different from the physical world, yet in some ways they are similar. In the emotional world there are trees, mountains, oceans, deserts, jungles, birds, flowers, cities, and houses. There are also good people, bad people, and problems, just like there are in the physical world. ○ The emotional world is a more beautiful place than the physical world. There is more light, and colors are more vibrant. The sound current of the life force can be more easily heard, and energy or vibratory rates are more easily seen. Understandably, the founders of some religions who have glimpsed this world have called it heaven. ☉ The greater awareness and knowledge one has of this inner world, the more its tools, laws, and principles can be used in the physical world. If you are using Ruby, you will not need to consciously "travel" or project yourself in any way into this world in order to master it. ☉ I shall use an analogy to help you understand the potential of emotional mastery, for I see that this concept may be difficult to understand. ☉ Let's say that the physical world is like high school and that the emotional world is like college. Let's also assume that you are a high-school student who enjoys chemistry. One day you start to wear Ruby in its spherical form. Soon thereafter, whenever you walk home from school, an inner urge guides you to the nearby university. There you begin to sit in on a first-year college chemistry class. As a result, you start to realize that your high-school chemistry is much more basic than you had thought. ☉ Every day you still have to attend your high-school chemistry class. But the more college chemistry you learn, the easier your high-school chemistry assignments become. Your high-school chemistry becomes easier because you are seeing it from a broader point of view. You also begin to understand the reason you are in high school—to prepare for college. ☉ If you are still in high school, college-level information will make your high-school work easier. Similarly, if you are still in the physical world, knowledge of the emotional world will make your life much easier. It will give you greater perspective on your Earthly life. ☉ In this analogy, Ruby opened your awareness and understanding, thereby enabling you to accept college-level information. Without Ruby, you wouldn't have been ready for such information until you had completed high school. Ruby sped up the process. It allows "college-level" information to be understood by "high-school" students. ☉ You may be interested to know that, just as Ruby brings the emotional level to physical awareness, blue corundum—also known as Blue Sapphire—brings the mental level to physical awareness.

DIVINE LOVE

To better understand Ruby, you also need to understand the kind of love Ruby teaches its wearers. It is not human love, for human love implies needs and expectations. My love implies freedom. My love is a noble and powerful love. It turns your attention to that which is greater than yourself. ◌ Human beings need love. They need human love. Yet human love alone does not sustain them, because it does not provide their emotional bodies or their interpersonal relationships with enough nourishment. People also need divine love. Human love says, "I need your warmth. I need you to hold me and kiss me. I need you to tell me where you're going, so I'll know where you are and won't worry about you." ◌ Divine love says, "I love you regardless of what you do. I love you regardless of who you are. I love you even if you go someplace and forget to tell me where you're going, and I'll love you when you return. I love the Soul that is inside your physical body. I love that which gives you life. I love the part of you that is God." ◌ Divine love gives individuals the freedom to be who they really are and who they really want to be. This freedom nourishes them and their relationships. It gives them space to grow. Ideally, individuals in a relationship should be able to share both human and divine love. ◌ Unfortunately, most people today do not understand the difference between human love and divine love. Even those who understand the concept often have no real idea of how to open their hearts and express divine love. The necessity of divine love may make sense mentally, but when it's time to express divine love emotionally, few people know where to begin. ◌ Ruby teaches this. Ruby will open your heart and give you a taste of what divine love is. Then it will teach you how to be a vehicle through which divine love can enter your life. This love will then touch others around you, even if they're not wearing Ruby themselves. They will learn from your living example. ◌

Ruby's love is powerful. Divine love is powerful. An example may help explain what I mean. A husband may tell his wife from a human-love point of view, "Please stop smoking, because it's bad for your health, my health, and the kids' health." To return the human love, the wife will want to stop smoking and try to do so. However, because it's hard to let go of a habit, she may encounter one obstacle after another. Even though she wants to stop and realizes mentally that it's not good for her children's health, the struggle to quit may be too great. ◯ If the husband has divine love flowing from his heart and asks his wife to stop smoking, his words may be exactly the same. However, behind the words he will be saying, "Please stop smoking. Yet, I will love you even if you continue to smoke, and I will love you if you stop." If the husband is truly a vehicle for divine love and the wife sincerely wants to quit, the divine love flowing through her husband will give her the power to do so—for love is power.

CONNECTING HEART, MIND, AND BODY

Ruby has its greatest effects on the emotional level. The red ray exists on the intuitive, mental, causal, emotional, and physical levels. However, it seems to collect on the emotional level, where it forms a direct link, or bridge, to the physical level. This is part of the reason that Ruby can lead your awareness from the physical to the emotional level. ◯ The accumulation of red ray on the emotional level gives the area an overall appearance of pink. The color pink causes a stirring of the emotions. This stirring is important for maintaining emotional health, just as your blood circulation is important for maintaining your physical health. The emotional body contains little needle-like tubes, two- to four-inches long, which are similar to your blood vessels. It is along these tubes that emotional energy flows. ◯ When Ruby is worn, it gently encourages many of these tubes to point in the direction of the heart. This allows the red ray, the feeling of love, and an awareness of the emotional level to flow through the heart chakra and filter into the physical body. Ruby also gives the mind the power to orchestrate a greater relationship between the physical and emotional bodies. It empowers the mind to create the opportunities that will enable you to become more in tune with your emotions. This is useful, because the mind is primarily responsible for bringing things into your life or for removing them. For example, it is usually your mental processes that lead you to decide to change jobs, move to a different location, or perhaps take college-level classes when you are still in high school. ◔ When you begin to wear Ruby, your mind will see that your heart is opening. It will see that you are preparing to accept greater knowledge of your emotional world. When you are ready, the Ruby might, for example, encourage your mind to decide to attend a certain lecture. Perhaps this lecture will present techniques for becoming aware of your emotions, or it may present a healing method that the mind thinks is necessary to clarify the connection between your emotional and physical aspects. ◔ As Ruby gives its love and you accept and become accustomed to it, your heart will open more. The more your heart opens and the more love enters you, the more love the Ruby will give.

DISSOLVING EMOTIONAL CONGESTION

Emotional disharmony is often caused by congestion in the emotional body. Because this congestion blocks the flow of life force to the physical body and feeds the body with disharmonious energy, it can cause physical problems as well. When one wears Ruby, the heart begins to open and feelings start to flow, be felt, and expressed. This causes emotional congestion to loosen and dissolve. When this happens, more life force can flow both into and through the emotional body, bringing with it greater harmony and balance. ◑ When emotional congestion is dissolved, any condition it has caused in the physical body will cease to be fed. For example, if one has congestion in the area of the emotional body that corresponds to the stomach, it may cause chronic stomach distress. When the emotional-body congestion is resolved, the stomach will no longer be fed with disharmonious energy, and a true healing of the stomach's distress will be able to take place. ◑ Now, the congestion in the emotional body will not be the only factor contributing to the physical condition. At least two other aspects must be resolved if a physical condition is to be healed. Associated with the emotional-body congestion will be emotional patterns, and associated with the physical condition will be physical patterns. ◑ Both these kinds of patterns form when certain actions, reactions, or feelings are repeated over a long period of time. Like emotional congestion, the emotional patterns will continue to feed disharmonious energy to the physical patterns until the entire condition is resolved. ◑ Ruby first works on relieving the congestion. This brings more fluidity to the emotional body and loosens the patterns associated with the congestion, thus diminishing their influence. At the same time, the individual will need to work on changing the physical patterns involved. ◑ One of the most effective ways to change physical patterns is to change one's diet and exercise routine. These are things over which you have conscious control. By changing them, you can easily influence your other physical patterns. The more radically you change your diet and exercise routine, the more swiftly your other physical-body patterns can change. However, if you rely solely on changes in your diet and exercise routine to change physical patterns, you will probably make some progress and then reach a plateau. After some time, you'll probably start to fall back toward your original patterns. ◑ Again, this is because physical disease is always either reflected or initiated in the emotional body. Therefore, in order to resolve most physical conditions, you must change your emotional patterns as well as your physical habits; otherwise, your physical condition will never fully resolve.

"Are you saying that people who focus only on diet, lifestyle, and exercise and who don't wear Ruby won't resolve the cause of their physical conditions, no matter how radically they change?" Michael asked.

In many cases, yes. Of course, there are exceptions. For example, attitude is an important factor. If you are one of the rare individuals whose desire to change originates in your heart, from Soul within, then you will have the power of divine love behind your change. Such love can dissolve your emotional congestion, melt your patterns, and assist you in your changes on all levels. In that case, you will not need the assistance of Ruby. ☾ However, Ruby can be a great tool if you truly want to change and are willing to make the effort. Yet, even if someone is not willing to open up or has no awareness of Ruby's effects, Ruby will still give powerful love. ☾ Love is the force and power behind an individual's strength, willingness, and ability to make changes. Remember, Ruby opens people to the infinite source of divine love. This helps them make the changes they wish to make and grow into the individuals they wish to be, for my love also implies freedom.

A CURRENT OF LOVE

To receive the greatest benefit from any gemstone necklace or therapy, it is always best to open your heart to the gemstones you will be working with. Whenever you bring a gemstone into your aura, do so with gratitude. This simple yet important act will create an opening through which the gemstone's energy can more fully enter your being and begin to make its healing changes. ☾ It is wise to meet gemstones on the fertile ground of love. Gemstones are great blessings. They are gifts of love. Love is the current that runs through them. Connect with this current as you put on your necklace. ◌ The next Gemstone Guardian you meet will be the Guardian of Rhodocrosite. Rhodocrosite also works on emotional patterns by breaking them up, cleaning them out, and making new, more harmonious ones.

"Thank you for sharing your wisdom. May the blessings be," said Michael.

As I turned away from Ruby, I suddenly felt as though I didn't know her anymore, whereas only a moment earlier I had understood everything about her.

Ruby paid no further attention either to me or to the listeners. She seemed preoccupied as she turned her head to gaze beyond the cliff out over the sea. Something over the water had caught her attention.

The

Guardian

of

RHODOCROSITE

8

DEVELOPING INNER FREEDOM

Ruby's gaze was focused in the distance, where a tornado was forming. The other listeners and I had not yet seen it. Our attention was still on Ruby as we wondered whether she would continue her discourse.

Then we heard the sound. It was a thunder unlike any heard on Earth, and it grew louder as the tornado moved closer. I had a feeling this whirlwind was the manifestation of a Gemstone Guardian and wondered how I would step into its consciousness. How does one communicate with a tornado? I thought I should feel afraid, yet my heart was still so full of Ruby's love that there was no room for fear to take hold. So I watched patiently with the others.

As the tornado drew nearer, we could see that it was actually a swirling mass of translucent pink energy. It grew larger and larger, until it hid the entire horizon. Then suddenly it was upon us, and we were enveloped by it. The thunder was deafening. Flashes of white light in the pink whirlwind blinded me, forcing me to shut my eyes. The wind and storm did not disturb my clothing or hair. Instead, it moved through me, affecting me on inner levels.

Then the center of the tornado hit. The impact of the silence and calm was even more forceful than that of the raging wind. Beyond the stillness could be heard the distant sound of a single note. This sound was not a hum, nor a siren, nor a flute, and yet it was all of these. The pink and white whirlwind of thunder and light now spun around us. Standing next to Ruby, in the absolute center of the calm, stood a man with dark hair and deep olive skin. He wore white and pink robes.

"I am honored to introduce you to the Guardian of Rhodocrosite," said Ruby, as she stood and stretched out her hands to this man. The two held hands for a moment.

"He will discuss more deeply the patterns within the physical and emotional bodies," Ruby explained. "Whereas Ruby gives an individual the power, love, and desire to change patterns, Rhodocrosite actually changes them." Without warning, Ruby became a vortex of red energy. Then she disappeared.

The Guardian of Rhodocrosite waited until the group's surprise at Ruby's sudden disappearance subsided. A calm settled over the listeners. Then he looked at me and said, You know what you must do to relay my words to the people of your planet.

I was somewhat reluctant to approach him. Then his eyes caught mine, and I felt a flood of reassurance similar to the calm that had embraced the group.

It will be all right, *he said. I gathered my courage and walked forward to the Guardian. Then I turned so I was facing in the direction that Rhodocrosite faced. I kept my attention on the sound of Spirit, which I had learned to trust so completely.*

Greetings and welcome, *Rhodocrosite began. Then he turned to Michael.* I believe we have some focused business. I will do my best to answer your questions. You may begin.

"Can you give us a brief overview of your effects?" asked Michael.

Change. I cause change. But the changes I produce are not directed at the physical body. I am responsible for making changes in the emotional aspect of individuals. Nonetheless, these changes often result in alterations in the physical aspect of those who wear me.

There was a long silence. We wondered whether Rhodocrosite would continue.

You did say "brief?" *the Guardian asked.*

"Yes, I did," replied Michael apologetically. "Can you give us more detail?"

Yes. When I am worn, I make changes. I do not wait until my wearer becomes strong enough to handle me. If a change needs to be made, I make it. I do not wait for the person to get under an umbrella before I rain. ◯ The vibratory rate of my sound does one thing; the vibratory rate of Rhodocrosite itself does another. The thunderous sound I carry destroys the emotional patterns that restrict an individual's growth. It also cleanses any disharmony caused by the destruction of these patterns. Then the vibratory rate of Rhodocrosite rebuilds. These three functions—destruction of patterns, cleansing, and rebuilding—work together. I do not allow any work to be left undone. ◯ My work can be compared to playing with a puzzle. When an incorrectly assembled puzzle has been sitting around for a long time, dust settles between the pieces. If the puzzle is shaken up, this dust will fly into the air. ◯ Emotional patterns behave in a similar way. When unhealthy emotional patterns are formed, they tend to collect miscellaneous and undesirable energies in other words, emotional "dust." These energies further clog the emotions and prevent them from being expressed. When Rhodocrosite is worn, my thunder shakes up these unhealthy patterns and cleanses the "dust" from them. Then I rebuild the puzzle so that all the pieces fit together correctly.

"Can you tell us of your birth?" asked Michael. "Were you formed at the birth of the planet, did you evolve naturally, or were you brought here by others?"

When your body needs a certain chemical and it has the ingredients, tools, and energy to produce this chemical by itself, it will do so. For example, when you eat something, the cells in your digestive system begin to produce acids and digestive enzymes that were not present before the food was ingested. ◯ The Earth also has the power to manifest the chemicals or vibratory rates it needs when and where it needs them. Hence, Rhodocrosite was not brought here; nor was it formed when the Earth was formed; nor did it evolve with the planet. The planet manifested it, just as a human being manifests certain enzymes when the need arises. When the need arose, Rhodocrosite was born. ◐ There is something else you should know. Your scientists say that the Earth is so many millions of years old. That is because they measure time as a constant. Actually, time has slowed down since the early years of the planet. Today, it may take several thousand years for a crystal to grow from point A to point C. A hundred thousand years ago, time on the planet moved much more swiftly. Crystals did not need the same number of today's years to grow from point A to point C. ◐ What might take a year to happen now may have happened in a week back then. In other words, the Earth is much younger than you think. But time is an illusion anyway, so in the end what difference does it make?

HUMAN DISEASE/PLANETARY DISEASE

Within the Earth are secrets, powers, and abilities of which you are unaware. The Earth and human beings share a profound connection and similarity. Once people understand this connection, they will be better able to understand and master the forces of their planet. ◐ The Earth is a living entity, a living creature. Gemstones are also living beings. A gemstone is made up of one homogenous pattern; I will call it one type of "cell." The Earth, like human beings, is made up of many different kinds of cells: its "cells" are the gemstones, rocks, and other elements of which it is made. ◐ Why are human beings so similar to the planet on which they live? Because, among other things, they are born on the planet and have lived on it for thousands and thousands of years. The relationship of human beings and the Earth is so symbiotic it is uncanny. Everything the human race experiences is reflected in the planet, and vice versa. ◐ If you need to understand and cure a certain disease, look first to what is happening in the planet. In the future, physicians who dedicate their lives to discovering cures for diseases will need to spend many hours in the study of the planet's physics and "supra-physics." Yes, I am speaking of a new science: "supra-physics." ○ They will study this, because every human disease is reflected in the planet. Because the planet is so big, it is easier to see which planetary pathways need to be cleared to resolve a certain disease; it is also easy to see the relationship of these pathways to those in a human being.

"Can you give us a specific example of the relationship between human beings and the Earth?" asked Michael.

I am reluctant to speak. Yet I look to Spirit, and Spirit approves to a degree. So I will speak of this to a degree. ○ If you are thwarted in your attempts to reach a greater understanding of any disease, you must look beyond physical chemistry. Look to what is happening in the planet in a spiritual sense. When you look at the Earth this way, you cannot help but see the group consciousness of human beings. You can see how human beings and the Earth are related and the direction in which the two are going. ○ Also, you cannot help but notice patterns. Diseases do not just happen suddenly. They are the result of patterns. Every one of them from the common cold to AIDS to the most elusive cancer—is the product of patterns. Many patterns are the responsibility of the individual; hence, the currently popular philosophy that you create everything and are directly responsible for everything that happens in your life. However, many patterns affect you that are not the direct result of your own actions. They are the result of your relationship with your planet, society, and other factors over which you have only indirect control. ○ When specific locations in the body become the repositories for the body's toxicity, tumors are formed. Tumors are isolated encasements of toxicity. Often the rest of the body will seem healthy; hence, the idea that you can surgically remove the toxicity or tumor and the body will be healed. ○ Look at the Earth now. Are there any spots on the Earth that are like cancerous tumors?

"Yes. Toxic or radioactive waste dumps."

I was actually thinking of some cities, where the toxic encasement forms a cloud of pollution encompassing the city. Looking at the Earth from above, you can see that cities look like isolated pockets of toxicity, indicated by the cloud or dome of pollution surrounding them.

TOXIC WASTE DUMPS

Radioactive or toxic waste dumps are somewhat different, in that their effect on the Earth is different. Instead of forming a surface dome of toxicity, they act like an injection of a harmful substance into the Earth's body. The vibratory rate of radioactive or toxic waste is not limited by its containers, no matter what is used to encase it. Instead, it seeps into the Earth. ◯ Usually, when human beings inject certain chemicals into themselves, at first they feel very good and even experience a heightened sense of awareness. Then what happens? They fall. Often this fall is harder than they consciously realize. Sometimes they don't even think they have fallen. However, their vibratory rate falls, and that is disastrous, because maintaining a high vibratory rate is essential to the maintenance of life. ◯ When radioactive toxicity is dumped into the Earth, its vibratory rate is thrown into the surrounding "cells" of the Earth. For a short time thereafter, because of the nature of this material's vibratory rate, its radioactive energy acts on the planet like a hallucinogen. ◯ I was not going to speak about this. However, since you mentioned it, I will say that radioactive waste dumps are more dangerous to the people of Earth than the most polluted city. Why? Because a drug addict is unpredictable. A cancer patient is much more predictable than a drug addict, wouldn't you agree? ◯ Once you start injecting hallucinogens into a planet, you don't know what the planet will do.

This is not good, considering what only the slightest variation in a planet's orbit or in the tilt of its axis would do to the climate of the planet. The slightest falter or misstep in the Earth's rhythm could bring planetary disaster. ◌ Perhaps the only reason I began to discuss this is so that people will know what they are doing when they dump toxic wastes into their planet. Perhaps that was the whole point of this tangent. If I leave you with this awesome situation to ponder, perhaps it will give people more impetus to stop the injection of hallucinogens into the Earth. ◌ In any case, diseases are caused by patterns. My role is to change the patterns that eventually cause disease. It is certainly a diseased individual, or group of individuals, who would inject their planet with a hallucinogen.

"One more thing. Does the Earth have the ability to resolve the effects of radioactive waste dumps?" Michael asked hopefully.

Look at the human drug addict, *suggested Rhodocrosite.*

"Addicts often need to fall before they really come to grips with their lives."

Or the ones who love the drug addict help the addict before he or she falls. When a drug addict falls, you don't know whether the fall will just be a fall, or whether it will bring death. ◌ Many forces love the Earth planet enough to prevent it from falling. Many individuals are even willing to sacrifice their lives to stop the use of radioactive substances. Yet, in order for the efforts of these people to be truly effective, they must work on the actual cause of the problem. They must work on the patterns that cause people to want to promote the use of radioactive substances and related technology. ◌ Spiritual or positive forces that intend to make any kind of major change must work subtly. They must be in the door and working before the individuals who need to change even know that these forces are there. In other words, they must be established in the individual's consciousness before the person even realizes that the change is something to be resisted. This can also be true for changing diseases or for altering the course of conditions that are becoming diseases.

CREATING HEALTHIER PATTERNS

To understand how Rhodocrosite works, you must also understand patterns. Behavioral patterns manifest in the inner bodies as what appear to be very thin lines. A closer look reveals that they are made of "blocks" positioned one after the other. One block is a certain cause, the next block is the response to that cause. The next block is a cause, the next is its response, and so forth. The more often you respond in the same way to a particular cause, the longer that pattern line will become. ◔ As soon as you finish reacting to a certain cause, the circumstances surrounding the next cause will start to form, until a complete new cause block is formed. As soon as a new cause block is completed, it develops a magnetic charge which draws to it the response characteristic of that particular pattern line. The longer your pattern lines are, the more strongly they can affect you. ◔ Rhodocrosite affects the magnetic charge at the end of each pattern line, adding to it a small ball of energy resembling a little sparkler. Once the magnetic charge of the cause block has changed, ideally, a different response is drawn to it. ◔ Usually this new response is not drawn to the cause block immediately. Instead, the next time you respond to a particular cause, you may simply find you have a greater awareness of your actions—that these actions no longer feel like the most comfortable response you could make to that situation. It may seem like you have outgrown that response. Yet you will still respond in the same old way, despite your new awareness. It will be like wearing a shoe that fits a little too tightly but that you continue to wear because you have not yet made the effort to buy another pair of shoes. ◯ You might even respond the same way a second time; but this time the shoe will fit even more tightly, and the response will feel even less comfortable. By this time, you should be ready to buy another pair of shoes. "Buying a new pair of shoes" means deciding how you would like to respond differently the next time and practicing that response over and over in your mind. ◯ Here is an example. Your father has done a certain thing for years, and each time you have responded in a certain way. Now you plan to respond in a new and different way. If you wish to heal yourself and your relationship with your father, the new response should be more in harmony not only with yourself, but between you and your father, you and Spirit, and you and life in general. Once you have decided what your new response will be, think of your father's actions and mentally practice the new response you plan to give him. ◯ When you begin to react in a different way to a particular cause, you will form new pattern lines. Hopefully, these new pattern lines will be more uplifting and harmonious.

THE INFLUENCE OF PATTERNS ON HEALTH

I do not affect all patterns, because some are as simple and insignificant as the way, every morning for the past thirty-six years, you have brushed your teeth as soon as you woke up; then, before you did anything else, you washed your face and then brushed your hair. This same pattern, repeated again and again, is not negatively affecting your health. ◯ Rhodocrosite only focuses its energy on those patterns that have been highlighted by the mind. Your mind knows which patterns are adversely affecting you because it can look upon the emotional and physical bodies and see their needs. ◯ Emotional patterns feed energy into emotional and physical conditions like laser guns. The amount of energy fed depends on the amount of feeling connecting the cause block to the response block. Whether this energy is positive or negative depends on the attitude connecting the blocks. ◐ For example, there is little emotion in the pattern of waking up, brushing your teeth, washing your face, and brushing your hair. Because there is little emotion involved, little or no energy is thrown into the physical body. ◐ If the attitude attached to a pattern is one of harmony, goodwill, and happiness, the energy thrown into the physical body will be positive. If, when you were a child, your mother gave you a big hug every time you did your chores, a strong pattern full of wonderful feeling would have been formed. Therefore, this particular pattern line and the activities associated with it now throw wonderful, good feeling into the physical body. They have an uplifting influence on you. ◐ On the other hand, if the attitude connecting the response block to the cause block is one of hurt, anger, fear, or anything else negative, then this is exactly what will be thrown into the physical body. If enough of these negative emotional energies are poured into a weak spot on the body, physical disharmony will result. If unchecked, this disharmony will eventually manifest as an unwanted physical condition or disease. ◐ One can stop feeding the physical area with disharmonious energies by resolving its associated pattern lines and by creating new, positive patterns. Gem-quality Rhodocrosite will assist in this process. ◐ Another way Rhodocrosite assists is by making pattern lines more flexible or less stuck in the emotional body. When pattern lines are stuck, they restrict the flow of life force to the corresponding area in the physical body and thereby weaken that area. When people wear Rhodocrosite, their pattern lines begin to loosen until they move with the breath, like the ribs.

SELF-CONFIDENCE

As your patterns begin to change, you will become stronger. You will realize the great power you have within yourself. Perhaps you will also realize that Rhodocrosite is only a tool; that it is simply the force which mobilizes, encourages, and motivates. For it is you yourself who have allowed the changes to happen. When you realize you have the power to change your life and to change your emotions, patterns, and reactions, you will feel tremendous self-confidence. ☉ Some people who wear Rhodocrosite will feel greater self-confidence almost immediately. Others may start to behave differently before this new confidence is felt. Consequently, these people may be a little unsure of themselves at first. Continuing to wear the Rhodocrosite will eventually build their self-confidence. ☉ When a tornado comes, it breaks things up and dust flies. Similarly, when people begin to work on their patterns, their lives start to change. They start reacting to things differently. The self-confidence they gain from wearing Rhodocrosite may encourage them to do and say things they've never done or said before. ☉ As new emotional patterns are expressed, other people, in their surprise at this new behavior, may react unpredictably. If my wearer is affected by the behavior of others, my work will be disrupted. Therefore, I protect my wearer from the outside influences that would interrupt or inhibit my work. ☉ To counteract any disharmony created by my wearers' changes, I bring a harmonious force into the auras of those who wear me. This force touches their families, the people they work with, and anyone else close to them who might get caught in the possible dust storm. This harmonious force prevents a dust storm from occurring. Then it helps rebuild my wearers' lives by helping create even more harmonious and uplifting patterns. ☉ Rhodocrosite is here to support people's overall growth by helping them rid their emotional bodies of past impediments, accumulations, and emotional "tumors." Indeed, I can help people make these changes and rebuild solid, efficient emotional foundations. ☉ Rhodocrosite is a tool you can use to change your life. Conscious knowledge of how to use this tool will make its effects much more profound. Also, the more willing to change you are, the easier it will be for you to receive Rhodocrosite's benefits. Nonetheless, Rhodocrosite—like any gemstone—will work regardless of how aware you are of its effects or how willing you are to accept these effects.

"Can you speak about your future on the planet and how you will be assisting people? Can you give us a more expanded focus?" asked Michael.

Expanded focus! *the Guardian laughed.* That seems like a contradiction in terms! Yet one could say that the top of a tornado provides an expanded focus. ◔ Although people may know they need to change and that Rhodocrosite will assist them, Rhodocrosite will not be for the many. It will only be for those who are truly willing to change. Often these are the people who have a very special connection with Spirit. They see the purpose of changes and why mastery of the physical and emotional aspects is so important. ◔ It is not my choice that Rhodocrosite is for the special few. Each individual will have to determine whether he or she is one of these select few. This is because it takes a lot of strength to experience changes, and often this strength must come from Soul itself.

"Before we close, is there any other information you would like to share?"

I'm sorry, but nothing profound comes to mind. If you pay particular attention to what happens when I leave, you may receive some insights. ◔ I have spoken of the power of Rhodocrosite. Let it be known that it is with great love that I wield this power. It is a love for Soul's freedom. Patterns can enslave an individual. Yet when patterns are highlighted, worked on, and given perspective by Rhodocrosite, they can give an individual the lessons needed to master life. ◔ There is another who also has the mission of creating great change. We do not work together, yet our missions are parallel. This individual is the Guardian of what you call Purple Rainbow Fluorite. In order for you to understand the mission of this gemstone, it is best that you first interview the Guardian of Amethyst. Amethyst tends to come in his own time and in his own way, so I shall leave you now. ☉ It has been an honor to be included in these interviews.

"May the blessings be," said Michael.

May the blessings be, *answered Rhodocrosite.*

I slipped out of his consciousness gently, as if I were being held and supported.
Yet I wanted to hold onto this consciousness, for it was such a heightened one.
I had clearly seen the pattern lines of which Rhodocrosite spoke.
I had felt the Earth's pain when he spoke of radioactive waste dumps. And I had
seen the profound relationship between human beings and the planet; indeed,
we fit together like two perfectly matched puzzle pieces.

As the outer rim of the tornado was passing through us, I knew that this heightened
awareness would be gone as soon as the tornado departed, and I was filled with
sadness. Then Spirit reminded me that, by following Spirit and the light and sound
within me, I could again reach these states of awareness and even go beyond them.

Then the tornado was gone. The sunlight returned, and once again we could hear
the roar of waves and the song of birds.

"Let's see if Amethyst can top this performance," said one of the listeners.
We all laughed and felt more relaxed. The experience had strengthened our group
consciousness; somehow Rhodocrosite's presence had left us feeling as though
we were each part of a team on a quest for greater knowledge.

9

ATTAINING WISDOM

As the group sat and discussed when and how Amethyst might appear, the air grew uncomfortably cold. Clouds began to rise up over the cliff from the ocean below, obscuring the sun and engulfing us in a chilling fog. The sound permeating the air also changed. The single note became all notes, from the lowest to the highest, sounding all at once. The new sound was sweet and full of power.

At first I felt uneasy about the changing scene, but soon a serene calm began to fill me, rising from a source deep within my heart. It melted away my apprehension. In its place was the knowledge that everything was for a purpose, and that everything had its place and would occur in its own time. I knew that everything would be all right.

My perception of time also changed. I felt as though I had already experienced what was to follow. It was rather like being in a theater and getting ready to watch a familiar movie. I sensed the presence of someone approaching from behind me. It was hard to distinguish this presence from the feelings in my heart. I looked around and there stood the Guardian of Amethyst.

I recognized him from our first meeting with the Gemstone Guardians. He was an old man with white hair and a full white beard which reached almost to his stomach. His robes were of the deepest, finest royal purple. The Guardian supported himself with a tall staff of stark white wood. His eyes were also dark purple, but it was not until he placed his attention on us that a flood of life flowed from them, touching us all with love.

I did not have to ask permission to enter the Guardian's aura. I knew that Amethyst existed in the core of my being. All I had to do was place my full attention on that part of myself, and the words of Amethyst flowed freely.

I have come to speak to you of the wisdom of Amethyst, for of myself there is little to say. Come, let us move from this place to an area that will be more comfortable for us all, *the Guardian suggested.*

We walked through the cool mist until we came to a park.
There the sunshine was warm, and the thick green grass cushioned our steps.
Children were playing in the distance. Our small corner of the park, where we sat beneath a huge oak tree, was quiet and peaceful. As soon as we were all seated, Amethyst looked into the eyes of each of us, gazing deeply into our Souls.

I have known each one of you, and, indeed, each of you has known me. It is not necessary that you believe in past lives. Once you transcend your physical body, you will not have to believe—you will know that life does not end with the death of the physical body. ○ In a different time, in a different place, and in different physical bodies, each of you has worn Amethyst. You knew me when my power was in its prime and when Amethyst was at its greatest. That was in the Age of Atlantis. Now you have returned to learn more of Amethyst. Times are different now. I am no longer a youth, and my effects have changed as I have aged. Now you have the chance to know me once again. ○ During the Age of Atlantis, people used Amethyst in crystalline form. The Atlanteans knew how to harness the energy of the Amethyst crystal. At that time, people's consciousness was more physically oriented than it is now. Hence, crystals were more in harmony with the Atlanteans' vibratory rate. ○ Today the situation is different. Consciousness is rising planet-wide. People are becoming more spiritual and thus more balanced. Today they are learning to integrate all aspects of life. Now people are more in harmony with the spherical form of the crystal.

COLOR RAYS AND THE PLANET

At a fundamental level, all life forms are made of and nourished by light. This light is in the form of color rays. The color rays originate in the intuitive plane, where they are born of the pure white light of Spirit, and flow continually through all the inner levels to the physical plane. This flow is essential to our very existence. When it is blocked or constricted within an individual, that person's health and vitality are diminished. ○ Part of the mission of every living planet is to provide its life forms with all the elements they need for life and growth. Since color rays are the most essential element for life, a planet must provide vehicles for maintaining a constant supply of color rays to all its inhabitants. ○ These vehicles are the color-ray gemstones. Each of these provides a continual supply of its color ray. Each also ensures that its particular color ray is kept pure as the color ray makes its way to the physical plane. Amethyst is one of these seven vehicles. It carries the purple ray. ○ When the Earth was ready to support life, all the color rays were brought to the planet. It was by no coincidence that the purple ray was infused into the Quartz crystal, the most plentiful gemstone on Earth. That the purple ray was housed in Quartz, and therefore would be plentiful, hinted at the destiny of the planet and its people. It suggested that their destiny would be a spiritual one or that at least they had the potential for great spirituality. Of course, what people do with their potential is up to them.

EVOLUTION OF CONSCIOUSNESS

People's consciousness has been evolving and expanding ever since their birth on the planet. This growth in consciousness has accelerated in particular over the past few decades, and an even greater awakening is predicted in the next one to two hundred years. ○

Because of this growth, people will soon require a much greater flow of the purple ray. Amethyst will not be able to provide this flow. Its crystalline matrix is simply not strong enough to supply the greater amount of purple ray that will soon be required by the people of Earth. Instead, a new gemstone carrier will take the responsibility of providing the purple ray. The new carrier of the purple ray will have a crystalline matrix so strong that it will be able to provide as much purple ray as people require until the end of the planet's life. This new carrier will be able to fulfill the needs of the people no matter how great their spiritual growth. ◌ My successor is available on the Earth today. It has great potential. Still, it must earn the right to carry the purple ray because the responsibility will be enormous. You see, the life of a gemstone is reflected in its Guardian, who is responsible for containing the gemstone's life force. The Soul to be given the responsibility of being my successor must go through many spiritual tests to become strong enough to fill this role. ◌ The readiness of this successor will not be for me to determine. It will be the decision of several Guardians in the hierarchy. When this individual has gained enough spiritual strength and stamina, he or she will be ready to undergo the ceremony of being given the purple ray. Then the new Guardian will become responsible for distributing the purple ray through every one of his or her gemstones wherever they exist. ◌ I will be the carrier of the purple ray until my successor is mature enough to be given the rod of purple-ray power and to accept it in a responsible manner. ◌ The difference in the amount of purple ray I have brought to this planet and the amount my successor will bring is very great. Because of this, the Earth has provided the gemstone you call Purple Rainbow Fluorite to help people make the transition between the old carrier and the new. ◌ The recent acceleration in the growth of consciousness is reflected in yet another great change. For many ages people were closed and reluctant to change. People had hardened attitudes and opinions, because life was hard. In many ways people reflected the properties and characteristics of metals. Even the gemstones they wore were mounted in metal. Metal inhibits the power of gemstones; even gemstones that are in harmony with metal become more limited by any contact with it. ○ For centuries you have, in a sense, been living in an age of metal. As you are evolving toward the need for a greater amount of purple ray, you are also evolving out of what may be termed a "metal consciousness" toward what may be called a "gem consciousness." ○ The metal consciousness is characterized by rigidity, reluctance to change, and reluctance to accept new ideas and new things. ○ Gem consciousness will reflect the qualities and attributes of gemstones. Thus, people of the gem consciousness will be more radiant and giving, just as gemstones are radiant and giving. They will be able to accept much more of the light and sound of the life force. And they will have greater awareness of all aspects of themselves, since gemstones focus on all aspects of the individual: physical, emotional, mental, intuitive, and spiritual. ○ When a change is about to occur, people naturally cling more tightly than ever to that which is about to change. In the past several decades, gold and silver have been worn more than ever before. However, one should not stereotype those who cover themselves with gold as being stuck in metal consciousness. Have compassion, for it is these individuals who are closest to making a change away from the limitations symbolized by gold and other metals. It is these individuals who are clinging most tightly to what they know in their Souls they will soon be growing away from. ○ There is yet a third great change taking place today. This change supports the other two shifts I have described: the coming of a new purple-ray carrier and the change from metal consciousness to gem consciousness. This third change is reflected in increased communication. ○ For a long time, only a limited transfer of information was possible from one town to the next and practically none was possible from one country to the next.

Now communication is expanding in every aspect of your lives—not only among cities and countries, but also among the inner bodies of individuals. Soon enough, communication will expand beyond the Earth's boundaries to other planets.

AMETHYST AND THE PURPLE RAY

Today many people are strongly attracted to Amethyst. They sense that the purple ray I carry will assist them in their spiritual un-foldment. Indeed, Amethyst can help people let go of the metal consciousness and of their attitudes regarding limited technology and communication. ◯ I can help people let go of all that is old, all that holds them back, and all that is their destiny to evolve away from. I can give this help on every level and in every aspect of life. ◯ I can also help people prepare to let go of Amethyst, so they can accept the much greater flow of purple ray offered by the new carrier. Unfortunately, the memory of me and who I was during my prime only causes some people to cling to Amethyst more tightly. Yet, in a way, this attachment may be a good sign. Remember the spiritual principle I have given you: The closer people are to making a great change, the more tightly they hold onto what they know—consciously or unconsciously—they will be evolving away from. ◯ Amethyst can profoundly benefit people in other ways as well. Perhaps the most significant therapy Amethyst can offer is to help people understand and let go of anything that keeps them attached to a condition. For this, I simply need to be worn around the neck. From there I can affect all the inner bodies. This is especially important when working on letting go of attachments. ◯ I have a strong, overall balancing effect. When one's overall balance improves, more spiritual force can stream through the inner bodies into the physical body. This increased flow of life force can nourish every aspect of one's being. ◯ Once this force has flowed into the physical body, it must return to its source in pure Spirit. As it returns, I encourage my wearer's attention to return with it. In this way, I help my wearer's attention move toward the realm of pure spiritual knowledge. Then I help bring this wisdom back into clear, conscious thought. ○ Amethyst's purple ray reflects the highest aspect of the mind, which is also known as the intuition. I stir the intuition. This stirring helps the mind become aware of its own intuitive aspect and, ideally, of that which lies just beyond it—Soul itself. When the mind becomes aware of its highest aspect, the energy that the mind once fed its own undesirable tendencies is redirected. If the mind remains focused there long enough, these undesirable tendencies will dissolve. ○ When Amethyst is worn in a necklace that reaches the heart, my energy connects with the emotional body. I stimulate the area of the emotional body where emotions are born, and I uplift that area's consciousness. This upliftment provides a greater perspective on one's emotions. This broader viewpoint, in turn, reduces or balances emotional extremes. ○ Whatever emotion we send out eventually returns to us in one form or another. Therefore, as your emotions become more balanced and less extreme, a less intense energy will be returned to you. This is especially beneficial when the emotions you are expressing are negative. It is only in this sense that I can protect you from your own negative emanations. ○ If you are on the receiving end of someone else's negative emotions, you will be more protected from them, simply because your own emotions will be more balanced. This balancing effect on the emotions is cumulative. Therefore, if you are easily imbalanced by others, you should wear Amethyst continually, so that this balance can build and grow. ○ Amethyst should never be worn in a necklace that reaches much below the heart chakra. Necklaces of Amethyst that are too long will start to draw energy from the rest of the body to the stomach area, thus diffusing the necklace's focus and creating confusion. ○ When the necklace lies close to the throat, the purple ray tends to flow directly to the head and mind of the wearer, bypassing the emotions and increasing the amount of energy flowing in through the throat chakra. This gives energy to the voice. Therefore, those who must address a group but are afraid to speak will greatly benefit from wearing Amethyst around the neck near the throat. It will also benefit those who lack the self-confidence to express themselves or who speak too quietly or with uncertainty.

THERAPEUTIC QUALITY

"How does gemstone quality affect a gemstone's mission and effects?"
Michael asked.

The physical quality of a gemstone determines the degree to which a gemstone's true essence can be contained and expressed. Within the mineral kingdom is a wide range of qualities. Indeed, an infinite number of gradations exist between gemstones whose physical nature is so pure that they can express their energy freely, and gemstones that are so choked by inferior color, poor clarity, and contaminants that their energies are trapped, corrupted, or nearly nonexistent. ◌ Only the highest quality gemstones should be used therapeutically. Therapeutic-quality gems alone can express the life force in a way that is optimal for fulfilling a gemstone's mission. This quality allows such a pure and abundant flow of the gemstone's energy that its benefits will surely be received. ◌ Where is the line that separates therapeutic quality from that which is unacceptable? To be therapeutic, a gemstone's physical matrix must be virtually free of foreign matter. Yet, that is not the only requirement. As the Guardian of Aventurine pointed out, for every kind of gemstone there is a different set of criteria that makes that gem therapeutic. Therefore, to be therapeutic, a gemstone must exhibit all its own unique parameters for therapeutic quality, and these parameters must be present in proper proportion.* Anything less may distort the character of the gemstone's energy and make that gemstone unsuitable for medicinal purposes. ○ As Guardians of the Gemstones, we feel that a new standard for gemstone quality must now be set on Earth. It is logical that this be your responsibility, Michael. We intend to help you in this task by training you in the fine points of how to determine therapeutic quality so that you may share this knowledge with others. ○ The vast majority of gemstones available today are not therapeutic in quality. People often settle for these gems unknowingly. When someone wears these nontherapeutic gemstones expecting them to be therapeutic, an inner conflict will arise. The person will consciously expect the changes that the gems should initiate, but the person's inner knowingness will realize that the gems can't deliver. ○ This can have many effects. The wearer may unconsciously begin to reject or repel the gemstones, or he may lose faith in the effectiveness of gemstone therapy. In any case, the person will become discouraged, because the gemstones will not be producing the positive changes that therapeutic quality gemstones can initiate. ○ This is why it is so important for people to become aware of both the importance of using only the finest quality gemstones for medicinal purposes and of the difference between therapeutic and lesser quality gemstones. Then, as always, it is up to the individual to decide which road to take. ○ People have looked to Amethyst for wisdom for thousands of years. I say this: Look nowhere for wisdom but within yourself, for within the core of your being is the source and fountainhead of the greatest wisdom that can ever be known. Gemstones are merely tools. Many can help you look within to the truth that lies in the core of your being. They can also help you recognize and accept the truths you learn there. ○

---

* See Michael Katz, *Gemisphere Luminary Therapy Guide* for descriptions of the parameters each gemstone must display to be considered therapeutic in quality.

It is time for you to rest. Tomorrow you will meet the one who serves as the bridge between myself and my successor. He is known as the Guardian of Purple Rainbow Fluorite.

Amethyst stood up and looked again into the eyes and Souls of each of his listeners. Then he walked down the path that meandered through the park.

PURPLE RAINBOW

FLUORITE

10

EXPANDING CONSCIOUSNESS

The sun was just melting into the horizon when I placed my attention on Purple
Rainbow Fluorite. I had expected to meet the Guardian in the park where
Amethyst had delivered his discourse, but it was not to be. Instead, I was guided
to a place several hundred feet above a vast ocean. Below, I could see nothing but
water in every direction. Above, the stars were just beginning to sparkle in the
darkening sky. Michael's radiant inner form appeared next to me, and we waited
for the Guardian of Purple Rainbow Fluorite to join us.

Within moments we spied a robust male figure coming toward us. Brilliant streaks
of white and purple light spiraled around his body. Within the white light flashed
every color of the rainbow. The bright light stung my eyes, forcing me to look away,
but it was impossible to ignore the wall of sound now pressing on my ears.

We have met before. You know me as the Guardian of Purple
Rainbow Fluorite.

His voice was deep and soft. I opened my eyes and saw that now the streaks of
light flashed and swirled around me. Somehow I must have entered his aura,
but so subtly and quickly that I hadn't noticed.

When the Earth formed, a certain destiny was mapped out for it. Of course, this destiny is flexible, but it provides a guideline for how the life force is to be directed on this planet. The making of such plans is very important. ○ Destiny had preordained a certain window of time during which Purple Rainbow Fluorite would be planted into some of the Fluorite already existing on the planet. The exact time of the implantation would depend on the progress of the people's evolution. When the right time came, the Fluorite was infused with the vibratory rate of the purple ray. The way this occurred was similar to the way Lavender was introduced to clear Quartz. ○ I will be available only for a short time in Earth's history. When other races on other planets are ready for the transitions that Earth humans are now ready for, I will become available to them. ○ For the sake of comparison, let us say that if Amethyst's reign lasted ten years, my work will be required for six weeks. Amethyst's successor will provide all the purple ray needed by the Earth for the remainder of the planet's life. When this successor begins its reign, I will become less and less available.

INITIATING CHANGE

My effect on the Earth human is to assist in a fundamental change. It is a change in the way the physical body accepts the life force, particularly the purple and indigo rays. I prepare the physical body to accept a greater and more powerful flow of both these rays. ○ I have a two-fold mission. One aspect of my mission is to enable the physical body to accept more indigo ray. The second aspect is to help people let go of old patterns and to create newer patterns with fewer limitations. This, in turn, helps people gain greater freedom on all levels. ○ This second aspect of my mission directly concerns the purple ray and the transition from Amethyst to its successor. My purpose is to disrupt the old beaten path once taken by the purple ray. This will enable the new carrier of the purple ray to make its own path without having to follow the same grooves taken by the present carrier, Amethyst. ☉ Imagine a large hill of sand in which the purple ray flowing through Amethyst has carved deep grooves. The new carrier will not be able to follow these same grooves because it will possess much greater powers and abilities. I come as a whirlwind to scatter the sand and fill in Amethyst's grooves so that its successor can form its own path more easily. ☉ To help you better understand my purpose, we must discuss change—especially certain changes that are occurring in regard to the color rays. ☉ People resist change. As much as they want a change, in hope that it will bring something better, they often fear that the change will make life more difficult and uncomfortable. When people are faced with change—whether they want it very much or not at all—they itch and squirm. Even if it is for their own growth and benefit, people often find excuses, consciously or unconsciously, to avoid the change. This is human nature, and it is why I am here. ☉ I will make the change between Amethyst and its successor more gentle, less noticeable, and less recognizable as a change. A change made subtly will not be recognized as a change and therefore will not be resisted. ☉ That is my purpose on the grand scale. On an individual scale, Purple Rainbow Fluorite produces profound changes in the body. ☉ In a healthy body, energy naturally flows in through the throat chakra and out through the brow chakra. Purple Rainbow Fluorite strengthens this flow. It also raises the vibratory rate of the throat chakra, so that it will accept energies with higher vibratory rates. ☉ As a result, the vibratory rate of the energies leaving the brow chakra will also be higher. This means that experiences related to the brow chakra, or third eye, will be heightened. Thus, my wearer will have access to a greater arena of understanding, knowledge, and wisdom. This will lead to greater spiritual experiences, either during dreams, meditations, contemplative spiritual exercises, or daily life.

This is a fundamental effect of Purple Rainbow Fluorite and a very important one. ○ In the past, the indigo ray entered the physical body through the throat chakra. It entered this way for many reasons. One is that the indigo ray is extremely weak on the Earth planet; therefore, it could enter the body more easily through a chakra that has a naturally occurring inflow, rather than outflow, of energy. ○ When I am worn, the physical body becomes able to accept a greater flow of indigo ray. I am now entering my prime on the Earth planet. At the same time, people are becoming ready to accept more indigo ray and are ready or preparing to accept the indigo ray through the brow chakra. ○ Individuals who accept the indigo ray through the throat chakra are currently oriented more toward the physical and the Earth. Those who accept the indigo ray through the brow chakra have a more holistic, spiritual orientation with less emphasis on the physical alone. Those in whom the indigo ray enters both the throat and brow chakras are undergoing a transition. ○ I would like to clarify something I mentioned earlier. I said that energy naturally flows out of the brow chakra. If that is the case, how can a color ray enter the brow? The answer is: Although, in general, energy tends to flow either into or out of a particular chakra, in healthy bodies, the chakras breathe. They let certain energies in and certain energies out. ○ Many of the energies a chakra "exhales" are excess or those which have been used by the body and are no longer needed. It is similar to the process of physical breathing: When you exhale, you expel both oxygen and carbon dioxide—in other words, some air that is still useful and some from which all or most of its life force has been extracted. ○ Once the chakra exhales these energies, there is room for fresher energy to come in. On the "inhale," the chakra accepts energies that are harmonious with it and that will give it life and nourishment. By the way, the energies that nourish and strengthen the chakras and enable them to function efficiently are the color rays.

SPIRITUAL OPENING

I do not carry the indigo ray. My vibratory rate simply prepares the physical body to accept a greater amount and higher vibratory rate of indigo ray. I also prepare the body to accept the indigo ray's influence, which is to move the individual from a physical, materialistic viewpoint to a more spiritual, and thus holistic, viewpoint and way of life. ◯ I carry the purple ray to some degree. I prepare my wearers to accept a greater amount of purple ray, which in turn will bring them greater wisdom, divinity, and spiritual inspiration. ◯ If you study the effects of Purple Rainbow Fluorite, you will glimpse the capacities of the new carrier of the purple ray. For one thing, Purple Rainbow Fluorite opens your awareness to the worlds within you. Because the purple ray has the highest frequency of all the color rays, it is closest to the white light emanating directly from the divine source of all life. Thus, on the purple ray, you can soar beyond these inner realms to even higher states of awareness. ◯ Because it is so powerful, the new carrier of the purple ray will be rare in the first few centuries it is available. Therefore, even small amounts of it may be expensive. Later, as people can accept more of its effects without compromising their own balance, more of it will become available. People will be ready for it. At the same time, people will have a greater appreciation of the powers of all gemstones, particularly those of this new purple-ray bearer.

"Why do the Gemstone Guardians speak so much of spirituality and spiritual growth?" asked Michael.

You ask a good question. If Rainbow Fluorite can do nothing but prompt you to ask questions such as this, my mission is working perfectly. ◯ To answer your question: People are evolving. The next step in your evolution will be on the spiritual level rather than on the physical. This step must be taken because you have reached physical "walls" or limitations. You have the capacity to continue to grow physically; however, people's lack of understanding is making this physical evolution difficult. The food people eat and the air they breathe contain little nourishment and life energy. As a result, people's bodies are, in a sense, degenerating. Still, it is your destiny to evolve. If at this time you cannot evolve physically, you must do so spiritually. ◌ This is why gemstones are so important. Gemstones can assist people in their spiritual evolution. Spiritual development can enhance physical evolution by helping to bring about stronger, healthier physical bodies. By using gemstones, people will awaken to the limitations that they, as a race, have placed on themselves and on their own physical evolution.

"What is your purpose for the planet?" Michael asked.

The planet is a living entity. Just like human beings, the planet has an aura. It is experiencing a transition concerning the indigo and purple rays, just as you are. ◌ From my point of view, there is no distinction among the physical forms that Soul inhabits, be they planets or human beings. You are all going through the same transitions; it is just your physical forms that differ. I see beyond the physical forms. I see the energies, the auras, and the changes you are experiencing. I see how I can help you through these changes. ◌ In crystalline form I am necessary for the planet, because the crystalline form is more harmonious with a planet's state of consciousness. If you want Purple Rainbow Fluorite to affect you in the ways I have mentioned, you must shape my crystal so that the energy can touch all areas of the aura evenly. Rounded forms do this; the crystalline form cannot. The energy of the crystalline form can only flow in the directions dictated by the faces of its crystals.

THE SOURCE OF COLOR RAYS

"Some of the Gemstone Guardians have referred to a crystal on an inner-world mountain where the white light splits into the seven color rays. Can you describe how the light splits?" asked Michael.

It is easy for most people to comprehend that there is an area in the world of God where the pure white light and sound dwell. It is also easy to imagine a single stream of light flowing through a hole in the floor of this world and entering a mountain-top crystal below, where it splits into the seven color rays. ○ People are comfortable with this image, because they are familiar with the idea of hanging a crystal in a window to let the sunlight separate into the colors of the rainbow and dance on their floors and walls. Therefore, it is easy to comprehend how this great cosmic light is separated into seven rays of color and sound. It is also easy to imagine these rays flooding the worlds below and creating everything in them: the mind, memory, emotional and physical worlds, levels, or bodies, or whatever you wish to call them. ○ Now I would like to give you a somewhat different explanation. Before reading it, you may find it helpful to spend a few minutes centering yourself and opening your awareness to the concepts I will be describing. If you have some Purple Rainbow Fluorite, you may hold it to your brow chakra to assist in this process. ○ Close your eyes and take a few slow, deep breaths. Let your thoughts and concerns fall away, and allow your mind to become quiet and receptive. Then travel in your imagination as far away from the physical plane and its natural laws as you can. Allow your awareness to expand beyond the limitations of time and form. Linger in this vastness for a few moments, maintaining your awareness of it as you open your eyes and continue reading. ○ Here you experience a state of consciousness where you can know for yourself that time and space are illusions. In this state of awareness, you will see that there is no space. There is no division between the source of the white light and the "lower" worlds, which need the light to be divided into seven color rays in order to maintain life. All exists where time and space are illusory—right here and right now. And all that exists is life force and different vibratory rates—for within this spacelessness are only different states of consciousness. ◐ Within this spacelessness, too, exists every individual Soul. Herein lies a step in understanding how the physical and inner worlds are created. You see, it is a large collection of individuals' vibratory rates that creates a world. It's not the other way around. The worlds are created to meet the needs of the vibratory rates of the people who live there. This is why the physical world can change as people are uplifted. ◐ How does the white light split?

Now I shall speak of a macrocosm and a microcosm.

THE INDIVIDUALITY OF SOUL

Just as this spacelessness encompasses all Souls, within each individual Soul exists this entire, spaceless infinity. In other words, within each individual are an infinite number of vibratory rates. Yet, as you know, no two beings are the same. Each Soul has a different perception, understanding, and experience of life. What makes you different from anybody else, from any other Soul, is the particular pattern taken by the vibratory rates within you. ◐ To exist as a distinct individual, each Soul needs different and varying amounts of the pure white light and sound. In other words, to keep you alive, your different vibratory rates must be fed. Not all Souls can accept the pure white light and sound in its entirety. Most Souls accept and are nourished by one particular light ray more easily than any other light ray. This ray varies among individuals. ◐ Thus, within the white light, each Soul naturally and effortlessly accepts that part of the light that will give it life. It's as if you are given a fruit salad, and you only pick out the grapes, because you know that grapes are what you like and what you need for sustenance, whereas another individual may only pick out the apples. It happens naturally and without effort. ☊ The white light is willing to be divided and to give, because God is willing for you and all your vibratory rates to be alive. No doubt, you've heard this before: you exist because God loves you. God allows Its white light and sound to be accepted by all individuals as they need it. ☊ As each individual evolves and comes to realize the limitations of the parts, it is intended that his or her attention will turn toward the whole, toward the state of consciousness where the white light and sound is complete and can be accepted in its wholeness. In other words, the individual will realize that all the fruits in the salad are nutritious.

"From your point of view, why would the other Gemstone Guardians use the analogy of the crystal on the mountain. Is it just to provide a step in understanding?" asked Michael.

Yes, the image is a simple one, and so it can be easily understood. When people are learning new information, they usually need to take one step at a time. Do you want to look at it another way? A step beyond that step?

"Yes," replied Michael.

Then look at it this way. You realize that there is no floor to the "world" of God, nor is there just one little hole through which the white light and sound pour into the lower worlds. In its pure form, the white light and sound exist in infinite spaces; it is everywhere. Yet there must be something that differentiates the white light and sound from the lower worlds. It is not a floor, but rather an aspect of the life force that acts like a transformer. It differentiates that spaceless infinity (where the vibratory rates of individual Souls can accept the light and sound in its wholeness) from the lower worlds (where Souls have vibratory rates that need the white light and sound to be divided into color rays). This transformer is crystal-like in nature.

You can call it a layer of crystal, if it will help you understand.

"Yes, it provides a different angle," said Michael.

What I have described exists beyond the mind, and therefore words are inadequate to convey it. So don't be concerned if you don't fully understand this explanation. Purple Rainbow Fluorite will cause you to think more deeply about life. It will cause you to question that which perhaps you have held sacred for lifetimes. It will also bring you to the point where you are ready for greater truth. ☉ Also remember that, if there are a billion different Souls, there are a billion different viewpoints and a billion different ways of looking at truth. ☉ All I offer is the opportunity for you to become something far greater than you are now. Perhaps you will look at Purple Rainbow Fluorite as a challenge or as the gift for which you have been waiting for years. ☉ Purple Rainbow Fluorite may still be available in the distant future, but it will not be enlivened by its Guardian's concentrated focus for very long. When Purple Rainbow Fluorite is no longer needed and the indigo ray and the new carrier of the purple ray are well established, my attention will leave this planet. ☉ At that time, the Earth will no longer need my effects. My crystalline form may still exist, but my focus will be gone and the crystals' energy will be greatly diminished. It will no longer be effective because its effects will no longer be necessary. This process is similar to the way a fifth grader has little need for a first grader's schoolbooks; they just aren't needed anymore. ☉ I will leave when I am no longer needed, perhaps in another three or four hundred years. My reign on Earth will be short, but that is fine. I have undertaken my mission on so many different planets throughout time. When my focus has left the Earth, it will move on to another planet. ☾ Purple Rainbow Fluorite is for those brave and adventurous individuals who possess the strength and stamina to make changes. It is for those who are aware of the importance of changes, for I strongly initiate change. ☾ As you progress through your changes, do not hesitate to ask questions. Do not hesitate to feel the emotions that may also be changing. The more you resist on any level, the more difficult it will be for the changes to occur. Flexibility on all levels will allow for smooth sailing. ☾ Just remember to question and to find your own answers as much as you can. The answers anyone else gives you will be limited by their state of consciousness. Find your answers in that infinite source of wisdom within you. Then you will know that the answer you receive will be true, for you will also learn to recognize truth. ☾ The Guardian of Sapphire will meet you in a less spaceless space than this. It is difficult for me to feel comfortable in any one place because I am too busy changing. If my surroundings are void, then there are no manifestations of any kind, illusory or not, to resist my changes. This area of emptiness above the ocean may have seemed an unusual meeting place at first, but perhaps now you understand how appropriate it is for me and for the purpose of Purple Rainbow Fluorite.

"I thank you for sharing of yourself. May the blessings be," said Michael.

An unspoken flood of gratitude poured from this Guardian. As I felt these potent and formless words of thanks, I wondered if, indeed, formlessness has more power than that which is formed, since forms by their very nature are limited.

I slipped out of his aura on this flow of gratitude as easily, gently, and swiftly as I had entered it. Then the Guardian and the swirling, formless mass of purple and white energy receded into the distance.

11

HEALING THE MENTAL BODY

A gentle whirlpool of energy lifted Michael and me to a place filled with mist. The mist quickly dissipated to reveal a lush and grassy valley surrounded by towering mountains. I looked around. There appeared to be no easy way to leave this narrow valley on foot.

Several others had gathered with us. As we waited for the Guardian of Sapphire, we enjoyed the music of the many brooks and streams flowing into the valley. We stood in a circle, silently feeling each other's presence. We seemed to be forming a group consciousness, a shared energy more identifiable with every passing moment. This consciousness then took on a life of its own and became a dome of love and protection that settled over and around us.

The sound of the valley streams suddenly grew louder. It was then that we noticed a man walking briskly down a mountain path. He was dressed in layers of robes and carried a tall wooden staff. He had an air of determination.

We knew he was the Guardian of Sapphire. Even through his many layers of clothing, he radiated the blue ray. When he reached our circle, the Guardian looked at each of us. Then he removed his outermost, hooded cape. The man who stood before us seemed to be in his forties or fifties. His hair was dark and his face lined. The lines were not simply those of age but also told of great experiences.

Because he radiated so much energy, I was unsure how I would enter his aura. So I walked up to him, bowed my head, and inwardly asked for assistance. He understood and telepathically asked me to close my eyes. I had already left my physical body to come to this valley. Now I left another body behind. I met Sapphire in a radiant world where our forms appeared to be almost transparent and made of pure energy. We embraced, and the next thing I knew I was looking at the listeners through Sapphire's eyes.

When the physical, emotional, and mental forms are transcended, any individual from any planet looks about the same as anyone else. You are all Soul. You are all masses of spiritual energy. Yet you are also individuals, personified by your experiences. ◌ The time has now come for the people of Earth to know the truth about Blue Sapphire—about its mission, its effects, and what it can do for the human being. ◌ My purpose is to nourish the mind. Even the most brilliant mind needs to be fed or it will lose its vitality. I also balance the mind. This means that I put thoughts in order and perspective. When people's thoughts are in order and they are thinking clearly, their lives also fall into order. This is because the state of the mind is always reflected in the emotional and physical areas. ◌ Once there is order, doors will open and opportunities will be presented. If taken, these opportunities will lead to even greater order as well as experiences of greater spirituality in daily life. ◌ For the human wearer, I have two missions: one that is directly related to being the bearer of the blue ray and one that is the result of my vibratory rate. From one point of view, my two missions are parallel. From another viewpoint, they intertwine like grape vines.

LEARNING MENTAL DISCRIMINATION

Before I talk more specifically about Blue Sapphire's properties and effects, it will be good for you to understand something about the nature of the mind, since it is on the mind that I have my greatest effects. ◌ The mind is complex and comprised of many levels or areas. Thoughts are formed at the border of the highest level of the mind, the area closest to the purely spiritual aspect of the individual. They are generated continually; indeed, a new thought is born every moment. ◌ As Soul, you are the owner of your mind and have the power to discriminate and choose which thoughts you wish to have. This is an important choice, since your thoughts act as food for and otherwise profoundly affect your emotions and physical body. ◐ Consequently, mental discrimination is a good quality to learn. This is the ability to choose which thoughts you would like to put your attention on, express, and give power to. It is also the ability to choose which thoughts you would like to ignore so that they will flow out into the ethers and never manifest or affect anything. ◐ Mental discrimination may be difficult to learn. However, it does not take much thought to realize its potential benefits. Because mental discrimination gives great power, it also carries great responsibility—for, when one possesses such discrimination, mastery over physical and emotional conditions is an easy next step. And I mean all the implications of that statement. ◐ Blue Sapphire can effectively teach mental discrimination.

MASTERING THE MIND

Blue Sapphire can also be used as a tool to help one gain self-mastery. By self-mastery, I mean mastery of the mind, the emotions, and the physical body. To achieve this, the part of you that is bound and a slave to your body, emotions, and mind must be able to communicate with the part of you that is free. This part of you is Soul, your true essence. ◐ When you use the tool of Blue Sapphire, the first step I take is to bring some orderliness to the mind and thoughts. The way I do this can be compared to the way cowboys round up horses. Imagine that your mind is thousands of square miles of open range and your thoughts are the horses that roam it. Sapphire is like the cowboys who round up these horses and put them in a corral. Once this is done, the horses are no longer scattered and some order is introduced. ◐ When our thoughts are in order, our thinking becomes clearer and memory improves. Also, we give greater attention to genuinely important thoughts. The number of useless thoughts one has during the day is astounding. Sapphire promotes useful thoughts and useful thinking. When thoughts are in order, it is also easier to distinguish between true and untrue thoughts, complete and incomplete thoughts, and balanced and imbalanced thoughts—both in oneself and in others. ◌ Your mind has a profound effect on every aspect of your life. Indeed, one of the mind's functions is to control the emotional and physical bodies. Thus, when the mind is more orderly, this orderliness is also reflected in those bodies. Conversely, when there is a dysfunction in the mind, without a doubt a dysfunction will occur somewhere in the emotional or physical bodies. ◌ Your thoughts, attitudes, and concepts shape your physical body and all within it. They also strongly influence your emotions and emotional expressions, perhaps even more than they do your physical body. For example, if you think a certain situation will make you afraid, you will feel fear; or if it makes sense to your mind that a certain situation should make you feel loving, you will feel love. Consequently, when Sapphire puts the mind in order, the emotions naturally become more organized, more orderly, and more easily understood. It also becomes easier to express the emotions you want to express. ◌ You have heard that thoughts can cure. This is no tale; it is grounded in truth. The key lies in being able to determine which thoughts will act as medicine for a certain condition and which ones will feed the condition with disharmonious energy. You must also know which thoughts you must generate in order to cancel out and stop the flow of disharmonious thoughts. And you must know which thoughts will resolve the condition and raise you to the next level of understanding or health. ◌ When a physical body dies, in most cases the individual's emotional and mental bodies remain alive. My work is rooted in the understanding that life does not cease when the physical body ceases to exist. Therefore, and perhaps unfortunately, my work is not always directly related to preserving the physical body. As I open your understanding, you, as Soul, may conclude that the physical body has become too great a burden and that the lessons you must learn don't have to be learned in the physical arena. On the other hand, you may realize that you can retain the physical body and learn your lessons on an inner level. Indeed, you may even consciously come to understand why you have a particular illness and what is needed to heal the physical body. ◌ Blue Sapphire can open up all these levels of understanding, and these can cause fundamental changes in one's consciousness, attitudes, and outlook on life.

BLUE SAPPHIRE AND THE BLUE RAY

Now I wish to clarify my mission regarding the blue ray and the way it nourishes the mind. ◌ Today, with all the "garbage" thoughts that people have, it's a wonder they are not sicker than they already are. By garbage thoughts, I mean nonconstructive and negative thoughts, as well as negative attitudes, opinions, and prejudices. I call these thoughts garbage, because they offer no upliftment. The impulses they create only contribute to a downward spiral. ◌ When an individual is on a downward spiral, he or she is heading toward physical death. Death may not happen immediately. However, as one spirals downward, one experiences more and more unhealthy conditions and becomes farther and farther removed from the fountainhead of truth, the life force, and the healing force. ◌ On the other hand, one can be very ill and be on an upward spiral. On that upward spiral the individual will be moving closer to the life force and, therefore, to a healing. Unfortunately, a complete healing may not occur in the individual's current physical body. Nevertheless, that person will be progressing toward a healing, and that is ultimately what is important. ◌ When an individual allows mental garbage to flow through the mind, it often collects in the head, causing the physical brain and all the head's functions to become malnourished, strained, and stressed. It is no wonder that, in general, people's eyesight and hearing are deteriorating. Although this is not a direct effect of garbage thoughts, it is the effect of the congestion and malnutrition caused by the garbage. Too many garbage thoughts clutter the physical head and inhibit the flow of life force. ◌ I keep using the word "garbage," because it is such a good analogy. When you have too much garbage down your sink, your sink gets clogged. When too much garbage piles up in your trash can, it overflows, smells, and attracts disease. ◌ The blue ray I carry is nourishment for the head and the mind. It also acts as a disintegrating ray on any negativity or disharmony—in other words, garbage—existing in the head. This is parallel to the way Emerald's green ray disintegrates physical-body disharmony. ◌ The blue ray helps bring one's attention to the mind. The blue ray enters the physical body through the throat; then it rises and fills the head, nourishing the brain and the mind. The mind usually uses all the blue ray "food" it is given; whatever small amount the mind does not use flows out of the brow chakra. The more food it receives, the more the mind grows and expands in self-awareness. And the more expanded the mind becomes, the more food it requires. ◌ Blue Sapphire will also work on anything that is inhibiting the physical brain from working properly. I am not aware of all the names you have given to such conditions.

"Tumors, nervous conditions, blocked arteries, strokes," offered Michael.

These words mean little to me. Think of garbage and polluted waters. Think of the fluids in your brain and what diseases affect them; or think how the fluids flow and what diseases result from pollution in these waterways of the brain.

"Basically, when the brain is polluted, there is pollution throughout the entire body as well," said Michael.

Yes, but my concern is with the cause of the pollution. Gemstones work on causes. What caused the individual's brain or body to become polluted?

"Mental garbage?" suggested Michael.

Mental garbage, indeed. The person's negative thoughts, attitudes, and concepts have polluted the physiology. Every time you think thoughts such as, "Oh, I am so ugly, I am so fat, I can't do this, I'm so sick, I have this terrible disease, I'll never get well," you are throwing garbage into your system. You are perpetuating your disease and further removing yourself from the healing force. This also applies to negative thoughts about someone else. Every time you think anything negative about anyone, you yourself are affected, because that negative thought must flow through you from your mind to your physical brain. As it flows through you, it carries with it all the negativity, and that negativity is garbage. It collects first in your head and then circulates throughout your physical body. It collects there first because your brain is the transmitter of thoughts to your physical body, just as the heart is the transmitter of emotions.

"How long does it take Blue Sapphire therapy to be completed?" asked Michael.

With Blue Sapphire therapy, one never reaches a point where it can be said that the therapy is finished. There is always another step to take toward greater health and visual acuity. As your brain becomes more efficient and clearer, you will find that it can do more and more. Your brain has an enormous capacity, which people today have not even touched upon. And, of course, there is always room for more mental order. Mastery of the physical body, the emotions, and the mind is not a single achievement that occurs like graduating from school. Rather, it is an ongoing process.

FACETED GEMSTONES

"Many Sapphires are faceted. Are their effects different from those of rounded Sapphire?" Michael asked.

The ways that faceted and rounded gemstones express their energies differ in several respects. A faceted gemstone radiates nearly all its energy out through its top, or "table." Also, most of the energy radiated by a faceted gemstone is that which is already contained within the gem. Very little life force is drawn in through the base, transmuted into gemstone energy, and radiated out through the table. ◌ A gemstone sphere radiates its energy in a very different way. As the Guardian of Quartz has explained, a gemstone sphere continually draws in life force from its entire surface, transforms it into gemstone energy, and then radiates this energy from the sphere in all directions. A sphere also draws other energies from the aura back to the sphere. In this way, a strand of spherical gemstones not only fills the entire aura with gemstone energy, but also draws to itself information from the entire aura. This allows the gemstone to gain a more complete picture of what the individual requires for healing. A faceted gemstone cannot do this; it can only touch parts of the aura, and information from the aura is not drawn back to the gemstone. ◌ When a spherical gemstone is not being worn, it emits a very low amount of energy. When the gemstone is brought into a person's aura, it enters an environment which contains much more life force than the general atmosphere. Therefore, in the human aura, much more life force is available to flow into the gemstone and be converted into gemstone energy. The gemstone, in turn, can radiate a much greater quantity of its energy. ◌ Unlike gemstone spheres, faceted gemstones are not fueled by the human aura. They continually radiate their energy into the atmosphere, regardless of whether or not they are being worn. They are compelled to do so because of the way they have been shaped by the stone cutter. Furthermore, to wear a faceted gemstone, it must be mounted in metal. Metal confines the energy of gemstones. Because rounded Sapphires can be strung into necklaces which contain, at most, a metal clasp, the Sapphires' energy can be expressed without the limitations imposed by the energy of metal.

EASING THE COMING TRANSITIONS

The Guardians of Amethyst and Purple Rainbow Fluorite spoke of the many transitions that people today are experiencing. Blue Sapphire can help people make these transitions. One way I do this is by increasing mental flexibility. I loosen concepts and attitudes that are hardened, crusty, and stone-like. Because they are so ingrained, such concepts can keep an individual stuck in a certain state of consciousness. When these concepts are made more flexible, change of any kind becomes less traumatic. ◌ Another way Sapphire can help people make these great transitions is through the nourishment it brings the mind. This nourishment will help people comprehend these transitions and thus make them with more ease. Of course, these changes will occur whether or not any given individual is ready, for destiny has ordained them. ◌ Making these shifts will require a great deal of energy and clarity, and I can provide much of this. Actually, the word "shift" is not strong enough. The transitions of which Purple Rainbow Fluorite spoke— and the transition between the metal and gem consciousness that Amethyst described—are a total reconditioning or transformation of the vibratory rate of the planet. ☾ When these transitions are fully completed and society is on its feet, I will be replaced by another carrier of the blue ray. Then I will no longer carry the blue ray into the physical world. I will have relinquished this responsibility. However, I will have gained a greater understanding of the whole, and Sapphire will become a source of stability. ☾ Do not expect the new carrier of the blue ray for thousands of years. However, the transfer to the new carrier does have significance today. Because of the transitions that are now occurring, the time is right for the race of beings who plant gemstones to come and assist in the implantation of the seed of the blue ray's new carrier. The carrier itself will be needed in perhaps three to five thousand years. I am not sure exactly when the implantation will occur, since this is not under my control. However, the time is right for it to happen within this decade or the next or the next. Those of you who are interested may want to open your awareness to the possibility of witnessing it. ☾ Chances are good that the implantation will not hit the newspapers. Those who want to watch and who have earned the right and have the ability to travel in consciousness beyond the Earth's atmosphere will be invited to look down upon the ceremony. ☾ The process will not just happen in a moment. It will take several of your Earth's weeks, because this race of people must first research the planet. They must gather data and study the Earth's channels and power points. They will do this by circling the Earth in their spacecraft and by scanning the planet with special instruments. ☾ Then they will implant the vibratory rate of the new gemstone. I do not know whether they will implant this vibratory rate in an existing gemstone or whether they will plant a new mother crystal. In the latter case, a mysterious meteor may hit the Earth and become implanted beneath the surface. ☾ Regardless of how the implantation occurs, the Earth will respond in some way. It must respond in order to balance the powerful new energy that will be introduced. The Earth's response will probably be unique. It will not be an ordinary volcanic eruption, hurricane, or other weather pattern. ☉ My function and purpose is simple and basic. In fact, it could probably be covered in one page. Yet, I felt that to impart a better understanding of my mission and my effects on human beings, I had to share some knowledge of the mind as well.

"It has been an honor," said Michael.

There is someone I wish to introduce to you. You will have to follow me farther down into the valley, for he is playing with the other children. ☉ Although I am sure he is aware of his mission, I do not know what he will say. He is currently enjoying his boyhood as any boy would. You will know him as the Guardian of Indigo. ☉ Of course, if you call him across the field by that name, he will not answer you. He answers to a common name. It is a name which perhaps sounds foreign to you, but one common in the country of his ancestors.

I easily returned to full awareness of the lush valley and my fellow listeners. Then the Guardian motioned for us all to follow him.

12

DEVELOPING INTUITION

The Guardian of Sapphire led us down the grassy slopes to a playground where many children were playing ball. We could discern no order to their play, for there seemed to be no rules and no objective. Yet each child was playing with all his heart.

As the late afternoon sun began to set, we started to wonder why we were spending so much time watching these children. The sky darkened, and the children began to answer calls to return home for dinner. When the game finally ended, one boy looked up and ran to Sapphire. He appeared to be about twelve years old and had dark hair and light brown skin. Sapphire patted the boy's shoulder good-naturedly. I sensed a feeling of pride in the gesture, like a father would have for his son. Then the boy turned to Sapphire with a questioning look in his perfectly indigo eyes.

"They've come to learn about your mission," said Sapphire.

I know. I guessed that, said the boy. Shall we tell them now and then go home to eat?

"Yes," said Sapphire.

Okay, the boy said and then quickly trotted up the hill. We followed him and stopped just outside a village at a spot where the sound of pots, pans, and dinner dishes from nearby homes would not disturb us.

So, what do you want to know? asked the boy, as we all found rocks to sit on.

"Can you tell us how you affect human beings and what your relationship is with Sodalight?" Michael asked.

The Guardian of Sapphire glared at Michael. His look silently but unmistakably reminded Michael that Indigo was a boy and that he should word his questions appropriately. Michael got the message.

I think I understand what you want to know. You seem to have many questions. Let's sort them out and answer them one at a time. ◌ They call me Indigo. At night, I dream I am standing in space. Below me is the Earth. Then a light flows through me and touches rocks within the planet. In my dream the rocks listen to me, and I teach them how to become crystals. ◌ When I wake up, I don't remember everything I have taught the rocks. I do remember that they listen, they learn, and they move. Yes, their molecules actually move under my direction. ◌ The other thing I remember is the wonderful light that flows through me. I'm not sure where it comes from. It doesn't come from inside me. It seems to come from somewhere above and beyond me, from an unknown place I have yet to explore. It flows through my whole body, but especially through my eyes and my heart. ◌ This is what I do when I sleep. Yet sometimes all I have to do is close my eyes, and I find myself in this place above the Earth. ◌ I have heard of Sodalight. Sapphire is teaching me about all the gemstones on the planet. I know I have much to learn. I know that I'm special, because none of the other children gets to listen to Sapphire's talks. But I like to keep our lessons quiet, so people don't think of me as different. I think you understand.

AN INNER-WORLD TEMPLE

"Do you meet with any others who teach you about gemstones?" Michael asked.

Yes, there are others. I am taken to a nearby temple that sits on a high mountain. In the temple is a domed room. In the middle of this room rests the most beautiful faceted Indigo gemstone I have ever seen. I feel like I know this gemstone, that it is my friend, and I study it. From this gemstone pours a deep blue color they call indigo. This color flows into the room and beyond into the Earth's atmosphere. ◌ In the temple is a master with white hair, a white beard, and white robes. He is the Guardian of the Temple. The master stands next to me in front of this gemstone and directs my attention to certain aspects of it. He shows me how I should study it. ◊ During my dreams, I teach the information I learn from these studies to the rocks. I keep the vision of this perfect Indigo gemstone in my mind as I teach, so that the rocks will see this image and know what to grow into.

"Are your dreams only about the Earth planet?" Michael asked.

Yes, for this is my home.

"How do you get to this temple?" Michael inquired.

I've never really thought about it. I'm just there! One moment I am here, either looking at the mountains or lying in my bed looking at the ceiling. The next moment I am there. It's not strange and it's not hard. It just happens. Sometimes all I have to do is think about the temple and I'm there.

"Can you share some of the information you learn when you visit this temple—for example, what you teach the rock?"

I don't remember exactly what I tell the rock. All I know is that it's specific and involves patterns, numbers, sequences, and other things I don't understand yet. ◊ As I study the Indigo gemstone, I learn about things that are hard for me to believe. They're hard to believe only because, in my heart, I know that these things are also about me. I know that somehow I am connected more closely with this gemstone than I think I'd like to be. But they tell me that a lot of freedom comes with responsibility. I guess when I'm old enough, I'll also understand what that means.

"Can you tell us some of the things that seem unbelievable?" Michael asked.

The boy paused, apparently lost in thought. You're a stranger here. We don't get strangers here very often. I know you'll be leaving soon, for life is hard for people in this valley. Strangers never stay long. Although I've been told to expect visitors sooner or later, none has met me here before. I have been in classes in the temple where everyone gets a turn to lead the class, so I have already spoken in front of people. ☉ What seems unbelievable, *Indigo continued, returning from his thoughts,* is that they say I am helping certain rocks in the Earth to become gemstones. They say this will help the Earth and its people. This makes me feel proud. It means that I can touch the whole planet and everyone on it, even though I am stuck in this valley. ☉ Of course, I'm not really stuck here, because all I need to do is put my attention on the temple, or on any other place, and I am there. I don't know how many of my friends can do this. I haven't asked.

"What do your parents think of your experiences?" asked Michael.

I live with the Guardian of Sapphire. I call him Father. I don't think he's really my father, but he lets me share his dwelling. I think the villagers know that he isn't my father. Still, it's nice to have a father, and he takes good care of me. ☉ The villagers don't call him Sapphire, but you don't need to know his name. You don't need to know my name either. I am finding that teachings remain more pure when personalities are not involved.

"How old are you?"

Twelve, going on thirteen.

"Is there anything in particular you would like to do when you grow older?"

In a few years I will be old enough to go with other adults on long journeys outside of this valley. When traveling on foot, it can take many days before one comes to another village. Everyone who has ever returned from these journeys has such wonderful stories to tell.

This is what I look forward to doing.

THE INDIGO RAY

My first duty, as Indigo, is for the planet. I've been shown what can happen when the planet is given more of the indigo ray. It makes the air cleaner and it renews life. It allows the Earth to dream of what it would like to become, then it allows the dream to come true. ○ It is only now that there is enough positive influence on the Earth to encourage it to dream of becoming something greater than it is. Then when its dreams come true, the Earth will be something greater. In that way, the indigo ray can be rejuvenating. ○ I think this is what I, as Indigo, may also do for people. I have this idea that after I teach the rock to become a gemstone, I may teach people to become like gemstones. I may teach them to shine with the light already within them. ○ The more Indigo crystal there is on the planet, the more that the indigo ray can affect everyone who lives there. People should wear the Indigo crystal in a form suitable for human beings and that can influence the entire aura. In my imagination, I see the Indigo crystal accomplishing this when it is in a round form. ○ When enough indigo ray enters people's auras, they will see more clearly who they really want to be and what their true dreams actually are. If they continue to wear the Indigo, forces in their lives will work to make these dreams come true.

"Do you mean daydreams or night dreams?" Michael inquired.

Indigo stood up, as if to emphasize his answer. I mean the dreams of the people: their ideals and goals and the ability to take charge of their lives and say, "This is who and what I want to be, and this is what I want to know and how I want to express myself." When people wear the Indigo gemstone, the indigo ray will enter their auras and teach them what these goals can be and which goals they can reach for. I think that this teaching aspect is the most important part of my mission. It seems that I'm getting practice right now. ◌ I am a teacher. I teach the rock. I feel that, in the years to come, I won't only be teaching in my dreams. Soon I will begin working with people directly and teaching them about their potential. Then, by wearing the Indigo gemstone, they will learn how to achieve that potential. ◌ One time I got frustrated because I wanted to know more. I was instantly taken to the temple in the mountains. Somehow I found myself inside of that Indigo gemstone. Suddenly I knew everything about myself, about the inner worlds and the universe, and everything about the indigo ray. I knew about the white light, and the origin of the indigo ray, and where it leads. I wasn't ready yet for the knowledge. The information was so overwhelming that I was sick in bed for two weeks. ◌ *The boy laughed.* I'll never do that again! But it did teach me patience. There's so much I have to learn, but, from now on, I'll just learn what they teach me. And they do appear intent on teaching me. ◌ I seem to be good at absorbing information. It becomes part of me. I'm not sure exactly where it is stored, but I do know that it's not all stored in my mind. They're always testing me to make sure my heart is open enough to store the information in a place where it is eternally retrievable. ◌ You asked me about Sodalight. I have been taught a lot about Sodalight, and I have met its Guardian. I know I've avoided speaking of him. It's just that he's the sort of individual I would like to forget. For some reason, our personalities clash, and he makes me uncomfortable. Sapphire says that it's because we are so alike in many ways. ○ When I was with the Guardian of Sodalight, I just wanted to rebel. I felt like the typical teenager who wanted to be uncooperative and disagree with everything he said. I've never acted this way toward Sapphire. He is more like a friend than a parent, and we get along well. ○ I still don't understand why I acted the way I did toward Sodalight. Afterwards I felt foolish and wanted to apologize. Somehow I think he understood, because my actions didn't seem to surprise him much. In fact, I think he took my actions in stride. ○ Anyway, one of the things our gemstones have in common is our ability to absorb. The way I absorb is going to change as the Indigo crystals grow less and less like Sodalight. You see, the rock that I teach at night is Sodalight. ○ *Indigo again returned to his own thoughts and said,* Maybe that's why we didn't get along very well in person. It's different in the dream state.

ABSORBING INNER DISHARMONY

"Is it true that Sodalight absorbs pollution and any kind of negativity from the Earth's atmosphere?" asked Michael.

Yes. However, when Sodalight is able to form more perfectly into crystals, the crystals will absorb something different. Their primary focus will be to support the purpose and function of the indigo ray. ○ Then I, as Indigo, will be used to benefit people physically, emotionally, and mentally. I know I will be used this way in the future. I am not yet ready to do these things now. I've been told that I will grow to be a very strong man, and that the Indigo gemstone will also be strong. In the future Indigo will be called a healing stone, because it will absorb any disharmony in the physical, emotional, and mental areas that is keeping its wearers from achieving their potential and their dreams. ○ Actually, I think that the vibratory rate of the Indigo gemstone will make a disharmonious condition less stuck. Then more life force will be able to flow through the disharmonious area and spin around it. This will make the disharmony more apparent and therefore allow you to resolve it and be freed from it. Neither Indigo nor the life force will resolve things for you; you've got to do that yourself. But they can surely help. ○ This is what excites me. I'm looking forward to helping people more directly. Of course, I might never leave this valley. Instead, it might be like it is in my dreams when I teach the Earth—and that strange, powerful, and beautiful force flows through me and touches all the potential gemstones. I'm sure that, in the years to come, the same force will flow through me to touch those who wear the Indigo gemstone.

"What about the Indigo crystal that exists today?" asked Michael. "Is this Indigo different from the Indigo of the future?"

The Indigo available today is not yet transparent enough. The color ray hasn't quite set. The crystal still has more to learn, my friend. ○ To realize its dreams, the Earth works with the crystalline form of gemstones. If you want to help yourself realize your own dreams, you must work with a crystal that has been rounded into the shape of the Earth or the sun. Then the crystal will become like the sun and radiate its energy into your aura and touch every part of your being. ○ I was going to invite you to supper, but I can tell that Sapphire doesn't think it would be a good idea.

"Thank you for sharing information with us," said Michael.

I did my best. I hope you learned what you wanted to learn.

"Yes, and it was shared very well indeed."

Thanks.

"Until we meet again, may the blessings be."

Farewell. May the blessings be, *said the boy. Then, without hesitation, he turned and made his way up the hill in the moonlight.*

Sapphire watched the boy momentarily and then said, "I hope this information will give you a greater understanding of Indigo. I hope it will awaken you to the forces, perhaps even the unknown ones, that work on your planet."

"It is very helpful," said Michael. "It gives me a new perspective."

"Tomorrow evening you will meet with the Guardian of Carnelian," said Sapphire. Then he pulled his outer cape around himself and covered his head with its hood. "Good night, and may the blessings be."

"May the blessings be," Michael and I replied almost in unison. Sapphire waved to us in a half-salute and followed the boy up the hill.

When they were gone, the group began to discuss where we might meet Carnelian. Then we decided to wait and let Spirit guide us, since we could only guess where in all the universe the meeting place might be. We said our good nights, and one-by-one our forms disappeared from the valley. I, too, returned to my physical body, which was resting peacefully on the sofa.

The
Guardian
of

CARNELIAN

13

REVITALIZING YOUR BEING

`I closed my eyes and imagined Carnelian's orange light. The next moment I heard music flowing like a strong wind.

When I opened my inner eyes, the Guardian of Carnelian sat facing me. She was clothed in yards and yards of orange cloth, somewhat like an Indian sari but more voluminous. She appeared to be in her thirties. The reflective quality of her skin reminded me of fine white porcelain. Her eyes were dark brown, yet one could not miss the orange ray shining from them.

Michael and two others joined us, and Carnelian and I stood to greet them. Carnelian seemed aloof, yet I felt comfortable in her presence. I sensed her reserve, a quality I recognized in myself. Soon she too realized we had something in common, and a door seemed to open between us.

She asked me to stand next to her and enter her aura from the side. Never had this process required so much thought and calculation, and I was unable to take the step. Then her vibratory rate changed and she became less manifest and more obviously composed of energy. My body also underwent this transformation. Then, like two attracting magnets, we connected and I stood within her aura.

You wish to know about Carnelian. There is not much to say, for I am a simple gemstone, and the work I do is simple. My mission is to be the bearer of the orange ray for the people of Earth. I have little or no effect on the Earth planet; the Earth has its own ways of attracting the orange ray it requires. ◌ During the Age of Atlantis, certain wise beings in the inner planes noticed that the carrier of the orange ray could not adequately nourish the people. They saw that a new gemstone was needed to bear the orange ray. ◌ That is when I was given the responsibility of being the Guardian of this new gemstone. It is a unique responsibility. I was not just shown a gemstone and told, "Here, this is your responsibility." Instead, I had to work with the minds and hearts of certain human beings to inspire them to formulate a gemstone carrier for the orange ray. ◌ This first Carnelian was like a mother crystal. It was formed when Spirit, the Guardian of the Earth, and I worked with certain individuals in their dreams and inspirations. Since the orange ray is crucial to life, it was essential that its carrier be in absolute harmony with human beings. What better way to make it harmonious with human beings than for human beings themselves to have a hand in making it? ◌ What may be called "little miracles" also occurred. It was as though an orange picture was being painted—yet it was not until I, as the Guardian of Carnelian, touched it with my orange ray that it came alive. Then it was no longer just a painting but a living picture. Like this, the Carnelian gemstone became a living vehicle for the orange ray. ◌ The fact that today people transform Gray Onyx into Carnelian is a curious reflection of how the first Carnelian manifested on the planet. ◌ I also work on other planets. I teach the people there to form gemstones which bear the orange ray. Some planets have gemstones that bear the orange ray naturally. Since these gemstones are already in harmony with the people, I am not needed on those planets.

THE MAIN COLOR RAY

To better understand Carnelian, you should know more about the color rays. The Guardian of Quartz introduced you to the color rays, and other Guardians have spoken of them. Now I would like to give you more information about these rays. ◯ All individuals have one color ray in their make-up with which they are most connected. This ray can be used to balance deficiencies in the other color rays and to heal the conditions caused by those deficiencies. ◯ This ray is called your "main color ray" or your "strength ray." Indeed, it is your strength. It gives you energy. It provides a specific frequency of light and sound that enables you to grow beyond your current limitations. Your main color ray gives you the upliftment and strength you need to resolve all imbalances. ◯ Michael, your main color ray is blue. Therefore, the blue ray is your strength ray and your healing ray. It can be used to open the doors for all the other color rays so they may enter every aspect of your physical and inner selves. ◯ Each individual has a certain attribute corresponding to his or her main ray. This attribute is one of the greatest assets available to an individual. However, it can also act as an obstacle or trap. Interestingly, this trap can provide one's greatest opportunity for learning. ◯ Since your main ray is blue, your mind is your strongest attribute and one of your greatest assets. In other words, you tend to use your mind and draw upon its strength to overcome obstacles in life. Yet, if you were to use only your mind and place little attention on your other aspects, your mind could easily become your greatest obstacle. ◯ If you wear the gemstone that bears the blue ray, the blue ray will shine upon your mind. It will teach you how your mind can be a potential obstacle. At the same time, the nourishment it gives your mind will strengthen it and make it less susceptible to becoming an obstacle. ◯ Your main ray gemstone can teach you how to work with your strongest attribute and how to balance its power. You can then use your strongest attribute to help you resolve the karma and learn the lessons presented by the deficiencies in the other color rays. ◑ Those whose main color ray is red, consciously or unconsciously, draw on the heart chakra and emotions for strength. At the same time, the heart and emotions can be their greatest obstacles. ◑ Those whose main color ray is orange rely on a certain vitality or energy that gives life to ideas and to the cycle of cause and effect. The orange ray is a powerful, life-giving energy. It teaches the balance between the positive, negative, and neutralizing forces in life. The trap lies in using this energy, so naturally available to an orange-ray person, in an imbalanced way. ◑ Those whose main color ray is yellow draw their strength from their spiritual potential. For example, if a difficulty arises in the life of a yellow-ray person, the individual can easily remember his or her spiritual potential. That memory will be the strength or magnetizing force needed to move through the difficulty. The trap lies in the negative self-judgments that may arise when the individual perceives the contrast between this spiritual potential and his or her other aspects. ◑ Those whose main color ray is green draw their strength from the knowingness that there is just as much God or Spirit in the physical world as there is in any of the inner worlds. In other words, consciously or unconsciously, they know that God exists here and now. Their strength lies in knowing that the only difference between the physical world and the inner worlds is the degree of the illusion of materiality. The trap lies in becoming submerged in the physical to the exclusion of other aspects of life. ◑ Those whose main color ray is indigo rely on their intuition, their innate knowingness, or their sense about things. Often this knowingness baffles them, because they cannot determine exactly where it comes from. Their trap lies in neglecting the development of their other faculties to help them steer through life or in denying or disbelieving what their intuition tells them. ◑ Those whose main color ray is purple draw their strength from the current of wisdom flowing through them and through all of life. Their strength especially increases when they become aware of this flow. The purple ray has a frequency higher than those of the other color rays. The trap for people whose main color ray is purple occurs when these individuals believe that they are better than or above others. This attitude is an imbalance of the mind and can lead to serious mental aberrations. ◌ There are some individuals whose main color is white. All seven color rays have the potential to give these individuals strength. Their trap is in the confusion that often results when they try to sort out and balance the influences of all seven rays. These people are grounded in the higher planes. They possess physical bodies in order to carry out certain missions. It is only when they have mastered the balance of the seven color rays that they gain the ability to resolve their confusion and realize this true mission or purpose. These individuals should be aware that it may take many lifetimes before the confusion clears and this mission unfolds and becomes known to them. ◌ There are many concepts about colors. Therefore, it is important to understand that those whose main ray is purple are not necessarily more "spiritual" than others; those whose main ray is blue are not necessarily more "mental;" and those whose main ray is red are not necessarily more "emotional." For example, you can have a well-developed intuition without having indigo as your main ray. I am simply describing the primary strength upon which an individual draws, both during times of need and in daily living, if the channel for that person's main color ray is open.

COLOR-RAY GEMSTONES

Gemstones are powerful tools which can be used to open and balance this channel. Wearing the gemstone of your main color ray provides you with a continuous, pure, living flow of color rays for as long as it is worn or, in some cases, for as long as it is in your aura. Because this flow is alive and continuous, wearing your main-ray gemstone is much more effective than using any other form of your main color ray—for example, wearing a garment or eating foods of that color. It is true that food, like gemstones, possess life; however, once food is eaten, its color quickly changes. ◯ At this time, Ruby is the carrier of the red ray, Carnelian carries the orange ray, Citrine attracts the yellow ray, Emerald carries the green, Blue Sapphire carries the blue, Indigo carries the indigo, and Amethyst carries the purple.

"How can one determine one's main color ray?" asked Michael.

That is an important question. Soon you will be trained in this process with the intention that you will then train others.

"Would it be effective to use colored paper or colored lights instead of gemstones?"

Colored paper or lights do not work as well as gemstones, because they are not alive. Gemstones are alive. It is their life energies, or vibratory rates, that enable the color rays they carry to affect people profoundly. ◯ Staring at colored paper, for example, or shining colored lights on the body will teach the body to recognize colors. Colors exist everywhere, and these therapies may even teach the body to absorb colors from the atmosphere. However, if you are looking for a strong, effective tool that will make profound changes in your life, you should wear gemstones—and especially a necklace with your main ray gemstone in it.

"I asked that question because some people believe that a gemstone's essence is its color. There is little or no recognition of the vibratory rate of the gemstone itself."

If the color of a gemstone were its only essence, then orange plastic beads would work just as well as Carnelian spheres—and, of course, they do not. ◌ Remember, there is an intensely concentrated force of light and sound embodied in the crystalline matrix of gemstones. In the case of the color-ray bearers, this light and sound has the vibratory rate of a certain color ray. For example, Carnelian contains the compact, compressed vibratory rate of the orange ray and the sound the orange ray sings. ◌ There is a point I wish to clarify. Whenever a Gemstone Guardian refers to a color ray, both the light and sound elements of that color ray are implied in the reference. For example, whenever I refer to the orange ray, I am not only referring to its color, I am also referring to its sound. ◌ The original idea behind birthstones was to give an infant some form of the gem that bore the child's main color ray. Certain children were given gemstones that were not color-ray bearers but were otherwise associated with the child's destiny. Often these gifts were selected by masters of gemstone knowledge and wisdom. The birthstones established by the jewelry industry today have no correlation to a person's main color ray or destiny. ◌ One of the greatest gifts you can give an infant, child, or adult is a necklace of gemstone spheres bearing that person's main color ray. It is also one of the greatest gifts you can give yourself.

CARNELIAN AND THE ORANGE RAY

The orange ray enters Carnelian as soon as it is worn. More specifically, it enters when the Carnelian has been enlivened in someone's aura for an adequate length of time. A supra-physical chemical reaction occurs between the gemstone and the individual's aura. This reaction allows me to infuse the Carnelian with the life-giving orange ray. It is part of my duty to make sure that this infusion occurs. ◌ Carnelian acts as a bridge for the orange ray to enter the physical body. It radiates orange-ray vibratory rate into its wearer's aura, and from there the orange ray is breathed into the lungs and distributed throughout the body via the blood and lymph. The orange ray is a key ingredient for life, specifically for the life of the cells. Each individual cell bathes in glory in the presence of the orange ray. Cells need all seven color rays for life. However, when given even a little extra orange ray, cells react the way you might when you soak in a nice, hot bath after a hard day's work. You rest and relax, and although you continue to function, you let go of your troubles. ◐ Carnelian and the orange ray it provides help your cells let go of their disharmony and disease. They do this by stirring and dislodging the disharmony so the body can release it. The Carnelian spheres then absorb the disharmony the body has released. ◐ Carnelian can assist with any physical situation that is stubborn or not reacting favorably to other therapies. It is particularly helpful when the cells involved in the condition are reluctant to release their disharmony. As I said, it's as though I say to the cells, "Relax and forget your troubles. Release your disharmony. Enjoy the bath of the orange ray and enjoy life!" This effect will be magnified if I am placed over the disharmonious area under direct sunlight. ◐ The emotions also relax in the presence of the orange ray. This relaxation manifests as calmer, more balanced emotions. Negative emotions are not in harmony with the orange ray. Therefore, when Carnelian is worn, negative emotions are either dulled, dissipated, or canceled out, depending on the strength of the emotion and the amount of orange ray flowing through the individual. The orange ray acts like a ramp on which positive emotions easily ride into the physical body. Carnelian also helps positive emotions be expressed more easily. ◐ Carnelian stimulates, sharpens, and enhances mental functions. It improves mental clarity, memory, and the ability to see things from a higher viewpoint. However, these effects do not occur immediately. First, I stir up the clouds that inhibit mental clarity, and then I teach the body to metabolize these clouds. As more and more clouds are metabolized, mental clarity increases. As your body metabolizes and eliminates these clouds, you gain strength. This strength will help you accept the many changes that improved clarity will initiate in your life. ○ Sometimes when mental clouds begin to be stirred, it seems like mental clarity is actually decreasing. Your sinuses and lymph glands may also become somewhat clogged. However, this effect won't last long and is the result of all the body's processes becoming involved in metabolizing whatever has been inhibiting mental clarity. ○ Carnelian will benefit anyone who is deficient in the orange ray. A deficiency of orange ray frequently manifests as an imbalance between lower and higher energies. This imbalance is often recognized when people's dreams, thoughts, and aspirations point in one direction, but their lives seem to lead in another. ○ When you wear Carnelian, the lower and higher energies in your body will come into greater harmony with each other. This will encourage your aspirations and your current life path to come closer and closer together. Then, because your life will be moving more in the direction of your dreams and aspirations, you will have much more energy. ○ When Carnelian spheres are worn around the neck, my focus is on the higher chakras. However, in order to do my best work, I must first resolve imbalances in the energy flows of the lower chakras. This resolution involves creating a closed circuit in which energy moves in a circular motion into the body through the root chakra and out through the sacral chakra. This flow will become just powerful enough to feed and maintain life in these chakras. Then attention can be placed on opening and strengthening the higher chakras. ○ The lower chakras are not any less important than the higher chakras. Each chakra has a purpose, and one chakra does not have a greater purpose than any other. All are essential for life. If your goals and aspirations are of a spiritual nature, you will want to place attention on all the chakras. ☉ Before we end this discourse, I would like to reinforce the importance of the color ray gemstones as tools to help in every aspect of life. When you wear your main ray gemstone, your physical body, emotions, memory, mind, and intuition are all nourished with the light and sound of all seven color rays. As long as you have a physical body, your main ray gemstone can be one of your greatest tools. This is because the color rays are life itself. ☉ I would also like to say that anyone can wear any of the color ray gemstones and derive their benefits, regardless of whether that gemstone carries one's main ray. ☉ If you wear your main ray gemstone, you will not only enjoy the benefits that gemstone has to offer, you will also gain all the benefits of being supplied with your main color ray. Doors will open, allowing you to be healed and uplifted on all levels. You will also experience a greater creative flow on all levels. The ramifications of this are amazing. I will leave them to your imagination. ☉ I am sure you will not be surprised when I name the Guardian of Citrine as the next Guardian to be interviewed.

"Until we meet again, may the blessings be," said Michael.

Thank you for listening to my words.

"It has been an honor and a great privilege," Michael replied.

For me as well. May the blessings be.

I exited her aura the same way I had entered. As soon as I did, her form disappeared and nothing remained but a swirl of pure orange energy. We listened to the relaxing sound of the orange ray as we waited for the swirling energy to dissipate. Then an inner voice told me that this was the world of orange and this energy would never die down. We could leave whenever we were ready and return whenever we wished.

CITRINE

14

PREPARING FOR GREATER SPIRITUALITY

Citrine's energy was overwhelming. As soon as I sat and closed my eyes, I felt waves of its vibratory rate surging from the top of my head, down my spine, and up the sides of my back. It seemed to be readjusting and realigning my skull and all my vertebrae and their surrounding muscles. This energy then became a stream of pure yellow light which surged out of my body through my crown chakra. Its sound was incredibly loud. My attention followed this stream of liquid light as it flowed beyond the atmosphere and out into space.

The yellow current carried me through a tunnel into a world of brilliant yellow light. There I was greeted by a being clothed in a yellow robe. I knew in my heart that this was the Guardian of Citrine. The Guardian's head was almost entirely covered by the robe's oversized hood. Although I could not tell whether the Guardian was male or female, I glimpsed dark brown skin beneath the yellow hood.

Citrine led me past several golden domes. They were intensely beautiful, and I wondered what was inside of them. They are distractions, warned Citrine telepathically, Do not give them any attention!

Yet the domes were so beautiful and inviting that I began to wonder what was real and what was illusory. My heart told me that, to be safe, I must walk the path where the light and sound was most pure and intense. My curiosity about the domes faded when I realized the challenge of this exercise: the path of greatest light and sound was no wider than a razor's edge.

When we finally passed the domes, Citrine and I were met by my spiritual master. I wasn't surprised to see him there. I welcomed his presence in this land where the line between illusion and reality was so narrow. Because of the brightness and abundance of pure yellow light, one could easily think this place was the ultimate world, the true heaven itself. Yet somehow I knew it was only a reflection.

My spiritual master invited us to sit in a circle along with several other individuals. Then he stepped back to join two others who stood in silence a short distance beyond the circle. Although their faces were hidden inside the hoods of their robes, the light of their beings could not be contained, and it seeped through the seams of their garments. It seemed that they wished not to be noticed, though I couldn't help wondering who they were.

They are Gemstone Masters, *Citrine said telepathically when the Guardian saw me watching them.* You will learn more about them later.

Then Michael arrived and joined the circle, and I easily and swiftly slipped into Citrine's aura.

This discussion has a focus: to inform the people of Earth of my nature. Michael, I believe you have several questions.

"Would you begin by briefly describing your effects on the Earth human?" Michael asked.

It may be difficult to be brief.

PREPARING FOR THE YELLOW RAY

As Citrine, I assure the physical body—and, indeed, all the bodies—that it is all right to accept the yellow ray. The yellow ray is the aspect of the life force that prepares one for the coming of greater spirituality. It helps us release what isn't needed and accept what is needed to move to the next higher state. ○ I prepare all aspects of an individual to receive a greater amount of yellow ray. This is important, since the yellow ray in significant amounts is somewhat foreign to the physical body. Once the body is prepared for the yellow ray, I act like a magnet to draw the yellow ray to it. The yellow ray flows to the physical body through all the inner bodies from the place where the yellow ray manifests out of the pure white light and sound. ○ This task of preparing people for the yellow ray has been mine since the beginning. Every one of Citrine's effects is related to my purpose of preparing people for a greater flow of yellow ray. ○ Citrine does not actually carry the yellow ray. As I said, it draws the yellow ray to the physical body. Citrine is not strong enough to contain the high vibratory rate of the yellow ray. There is another gemstone that does this. Compared to that gemstone, Citrine is not very powerful; however, it is much more plentiful. It exists to make the light and sound of the yellow ray available to the masses. ○ Citrine is one of the vibratory rates that was brought to the planet along with the other original color-ray gemstones. At that time, the Earth's vibratory rate was not able to accept an amount of yellow ray equal to that of the other color rays. Therefore, only a small amount of the true yellow-ray gemstone was planted. ○ You see, my mission was and still is to prepare the Earth and its people for the power of the gemstone which bears the yellow ray. Currently, that gemstone is very rare. ○ My purpose for the planet is similar to my purpose for the human being. I prepare the aura of the planet to accept a greater amount of yellow ray. Your planet and its people will soon have to accept a greater amount of yellow ray because that is part of your evolution. Citrine can help you prepare for this. ○ The color rays are not present on the Earth in equal amounts. Indeed, the color rays are not present in equal amounts on any planet. Furthermore, their ratio varies from planet to planet. For example, on another planet there may be a deficiency in the blue ray, and on that planet there may be a gemstone whose mission it is to prepare the people for a greater flow of the blue ray. The particular balance of color rays found on any planet is determined by the needs of its people. It is determined by the lessons they must learn, the strengths they must gain, and the levels of awareness they must attain.

THE SOUND OF THE YELLOW RAY

At death, when your physical eyes close for the last time, your inner eyes will open to behold a world of brilliant light and beautiful sound. If, when you are alive, you can glimpse beyond the veil of death, the fear of death can be greatly calmed, resolved, or even removed. Then the inner sound you will hear and the light you will see at the time of death will be familiar. Citrine can help you become familiar first with the sound and then with the light. ◌ Citrine draws the sound aspect of the yellow ray more strongly than it draws the light aspect. Citrine's crystalline matrix is designed to amplify the sound of the yellow ray; therefore, it is heard more easily than the sounds carried by the other color-ray gemstones. Sound is equally as important to life as light, but subtle sounds are often difficult to hear amid the noises of daily living. Those who wear Citrine continually will find their ears becoming more familiar with the sound of the life force, and this life-giving sound will become more real to them. ◌ The more you listen to this sound, the more your inner ears will be cleansed and the more clearly you will hear it. This may allow your ears to open to the different sounds of all the gemstones. Each gemstone carries its own music, a unique and enchantingly beautiful sound. If one can hear the sound of a gemstone when one wears it, its powers will increase many fold. This is because the wearer will become more in tune with that gemstone's vibratory rate. What I am saying is that Citrine not only prepares one for the yellow ray; it can also prepare people to accept the greatest benefits that any gemstone can give. ◌ Wearing a necklace of Citrine along with a necklace of any other gemstone will not increase that gemstone's powers. However, your inner sight and hearing will be opened by the Citrine, and this will prepare you to become more in tune with the other gemstone you are wearing. This, in turn, will enable that gemstone to work more effectively and in greater ways than it could before. ☽ Possession of greater spiritual sight and hearing carries with it a certain responsibility. Before Citrine will work on opening your spiritual eyes and ears, its light and sound will bring into your life the lessons you need to earn that responsibility. To accomplish this, the Citrine must be rounded in some way; the crystalline form does not enhance spiritual sight and hearing. ☽ In general, the most effective learning occurs when lessons come from every direction and are somewhat unpredictable. When lessons are predictable, people can second-guess them and find ways to avoid the lessons. Citrine spheres reflect light in a predictable way. Therefore, spheres will not be as effective as the rounded yet irregular form you call "chips," which interact with light in a more unpredictable way. ☽ Wearing Citrine crystals, provided their color is pure yellow, can prepare the physical body to accept a greater amount of yellow ray. However, you are more than just a physical body; your inner bodies must also be prepared to accept more yellow ray. There is nothing wrong with wearing Citrine or other kinds of gemstone crystals. However, if you wish to work on all your aspects—physical and inner—you must work with crystals in rounded form. Rounded crystals will teach you about the worlds that lie within you. Wearing gemstones in crystalline form may help bring you to a certain point in your growth, but there is something more, something greater. In fact, there is much more. ☽ I find the relationship between the crystalline and rounded forms of gemstones very interesting. Wearing rounded gemstones will help consciousness grow and expand. This expansion of awareness will lead people to appreciate how important crystals are, what wonderful tools they are for certain physical applications, and the ways they can be used to improve technology. These technological advancements will provide people with more time and the right conditions to develop even higher states of consciousness. These higher states will then be supported by the rounded form.

HIGHLIGHTING AND UNWINDING DISHARMONY

"How else does Citrine affect the physical body?" Michael asked.

I highlight or identify areas of disharmony in the body. When worn alone, I focus the body's attention on these areas. When worn with a necklace containing a gemstone that affects the disharmonious areas, I focus that gemstone's energy on these areas. If Citrine is used for this purpose, it need only be worn along with the other gemstone for a few days. Then it should be worn for a day or two every two to four weeks. ☉ Wherever Citrine is placed on the body, it has a stirring effect. This is especially true when it is placed over the chakras. This means that Citrine will greatly benefit any chakra that is stuck or tightly shut. Its vibratory rate will gently massage the placement area and stir it open. Some individuals call this stirring effect "unwinding." Citrine will have this effect on the stomach chakra even when the Citrine is simply being worn around the neck. ☉ If the Citrine is held on or over the body with the left hand, there will be more of a calming, relaxing effect on the area. If the Citrine is held with the right hand, the stirring or unwinding activity will be emphasized, and the area involved will be stimulated to move into proper, natural alignment. ☉ Particularly sensitive individuals may experience somewhat uncontrollable movements or unwinding, as the body reacts to the Citrine's energy and moves into greater alignment. These movements are usually not uncomfortable. Those who are less sensitive will also experience the alignment, but the process will be more gentle and gradual. ☉ As a living organism, the body wants all its aspects to be in proper alignment. When any aspect is out of alignment, the flow of life force that keeps the body alive and gives it spiritual sustenance diminishes. Although food, water, and air are key ingredients for life, you are sustained by much more than these things. For example, your body accepts many life-giving energies through the chakras. Just as the body cannot live without food, water, or air, neither can it live without the energies that flow into the chakras; indeed, if all your chakras were tightly shut, you would die. ○ As the body ages, it grows more out of alignment and, as we all know, it draws closer to death. Citrine can help the body—at any age—to relax to the point where the life force can rush in, take hold of the individual, and move the physical body into a healthier state of alignment.

CAUSE AND EFFECT POINTS

"How does Citrine affect the emotions?" Michael asked.

All emotions are the result of something I call a "cause point." A cause point is something that initiates an emotional response. My function is to shine my spotlight not on the cause point, but on the "effect point," specifically the first effect point. The first effect point is the immediate mental reaction or first thought you have directly before you have an emotional response. ○ A cause point might occur when, for example, your child cleans the bathroom sink with your toothbrush. The first effect point may be a thought such as, "Hey, I have to brush my teeth with that!" This would be followed by your emotional response—probably anger. ○ I shine my spotlight on this first thought or effect point. This spotlight gives you a clearer view of what is happening before you respond emotionally. If you were wearing Citrine when this cause point occurred, your first effect point would be highlighted and, in effect, brightened. Then, instead of having a negative thought, you might think, "Well, perhaps my child was trying to help clean the bathroom but didn't have a scrub brush," or you might think, "Big deal. I can either wash out my toothbrush or get a new one." Such thoughts would tend to defuse an angry reaction before it occurs.

Of course, you might still choose to become angry if that's the most appropriate response to the situation. ☉ I take no responsibility for the emotion or the strength of the emotion you express. I simply highlight your first effect point and thereby increase your awareness of it. With greater awareness, your emotional response will tend to be more balanced. ☉ Emotions are often out of balance in those who have a deficiency of the yellow ray. If these individuals wear Citrine, they will become aware, although perhaps subconsciously, of an emotional center within them. In this way, Citrine can greatly benefit those who react in emotional extremes or who lack an emotionally balanced nature.

CHAKRAS AND THE COLOR RAYS

"How do color-ray deficiencies occur?" inquired Michael.

Each of the inner bodies has chakras, just as the physical body does. The color rays of the life force flow from their unmanifest source to the physical body through these inner-body chakras. ☉ Although ideally all chakras in all bodies are aligned, in reality no one's chakras are perfectly aligned on all levels. One chakra might be shifted a little to the left, another to the right, and so on. These shifts occur for many reasons, including the presence of various imbalances, patterns, or blockages. If a chakra in an inner body moves too far out of alignment, the flow of the color rays is affected. The misaligned chakra and all the corresponding chakras in the bodies "below" it will suffer from a life-force and color-ray deficiency.

"There is a belief among some people on my planet that each color ray of the life force enters the body through a different chakra—that red enters through the root chakra, with the other rays following the order of the rainbow up the body," Michael said.

Actually, all seven colors enter each chakra. However, one color usually enters each chakra more strongly than the other six. At this time in history, it is difficult to make a universal statement about which color enters which chakra most strongly. This is because some of the colors that predominantly enter certain chakras are moving to different chakras. In other words, the color rays that once entered certain chakras most forcefully no longer do so; they are shifting their focus to other chakras. These changes are a result of the transitions people are undergoing. ʘ The root chakra symbolizes the strictly physical state of consciousness people are moving away from. As people are evolving toward greater spirituality and wholeness, energies are moving up away from the root and sacral chakras. These two chakras are still crucial to life, and the color rays are not ignoring them. However, they are being nourished only to the extent that they can maintain their energy flows and support the higher chakras. ʘ The stomach chakra itself is also undergoing a change. It has always accepted the yellow ray as its primary color ray and will continue to do so. However, the stomach chakra is moving up the body, closer to the stomach organ. In some people it has already moved up; in others it is in the process of moving; and in others the change has not yet begun to take place. ʘ The Earth and her people are in a transition of great magnitude, depth, and significance. For the transition to be well established, all the changes I have described must occur slowly. ʘ I will continue my mission of preparing people for the yellow ray. It's as though my work will never be done. As soon as some individuals are prepared, others will be born who will also need the experience of being prepared.

AN INTERPLANETARY BEACON

During the Age of Atlantis, extraterrestrials used Citrine to keep records of their visits. They placed patterns of Citrine crystals in the Earth to mark where they had landed and where they should return. These configurations contained information on what they had done in a certain area and how the people there had reacted to them. The Citrine used in these patterns also acted as searchlights or beacons and served a purpose similar to that of airport landing lights. ☉ Although the general public of Atlantis was not aware of such things, some Atlanteans discovered the patterns of Citrine laid by the extraterrestrials. These Atlanteans then formed their own patterns that sent impulses into space and were quite effective in attracting spacecraft to their areas. ☉ I mention this only because I feel it might be fascinating to your people. I also wish to emphasize that crystals are tools and that their functions go far beyond that of being objects of beauty. ☉ When Atlantis was destroyed, a change in consciousness on the planet occurred. Citrine's power was transformed. I am no longer the beacon I once was. Now, when used in rounded form, I search for disharmonies within the body and, like a beacon, I highlight these areas. ☉ Still, there is something peculiar to the vibratory rate of Citrine that makes it easily seen from beyond the Earth's atmosphere. Nonetheless, people should not expect to be contacted by an extraterrestrial if they wear just one or two necklaces of Citrine, or even if they place a large amount of Citrine crystals in their backyard and wait all night. My power as a beacon has greatly waned. On the other hand, if you want to experiment, you could wear eight or ten necklaces of Citrine and place your attention on your hearing. The most effective time to do this would be at dawn or dusk. Doing this may enable you to develop communication with individuals beyond the Earth planet. ☉ By the way, not all extraterrestrials have the best intentions. You have the power to screen visitors by declaring that only those with honorable intentions are invited into your area. ☉ Before we end this discussion, I want to say that you do not need Citrine to prepare yourself for the yellow ray. You do not need gemstones for anything.

However, if you have a goal and you are wise, you will use the tools Spirit brings to your awareness, for they are here to help you. ◐ If you want to achieve your goal in this lifetime, I highly recommend using the tools with which you feel most comfortable and in harmony. As Citrine, I am available to assist. I am available to give. You have only to accept my gift.

"Is there anything else you wish to share?" asked Michael.

It makes no difference whether I am male or female, who I am, where I come from, or what I look like. My personality has nothing to do with my purpose. You should not place attention on these details. When my experience of being a Gemstone Guardian is completed and I have learned the lessons I need to learn from it, another individual will step into my place. Another individual will become the Guardian of Citrine, because the lessons and experiences that go with this job will be needed by that individual. This transition can occur at any time. Therefore, who I am is immaterial. After all, you do not wear the Guardian, you wear the gemstone. ◐ The next Guardian you'll meet is the one whose duty it is to experience and learn all the lessons required of being the caretaker of the gemstone Aquamarine. ◐ Thank you for meeting me here.

I slipped out of Citrine's aura easily. The Guardian immediately readjusted the bright yellow hood to cover his or her head more completely, knowing that I would probably want to sneak a look.

My spiritual master moved into the circle and motioned everyone to stand. Then, without hesitation, he walked away. I knew that he was going to the world of Aquamarine or to the place where we would find the Guardian of that gemstone. He did not look back. We all knew that if we wanted to meet Aquamarine, we must follow him without delay.

The
Guardian
of

AQUAMARINE

15

CONNECTING WITH
THE OCEAN OF AWARENESS

My spiritual master led us out of the land of golden yellow and through a tunnel
of enormous, transparent veils that shimmered with iridescence as we passed.
From there we entered a lush countryside where the colors of the thick grass and
abundant trees, flowers, and streams glowed brightly. The landscape before us was
unusually rich and seemed to vibrate with life.

We walked over a gentle hill and came to a small river. There we sat in a
semicircle in front of my spiritual master. After a few moments he walked behind
us and out of sight. I still felt his presence, but now my attention turned to the
melodic sound of the water tumbling against the rocks in the riverbed. Soon I
realized the air itself had a melody—a vibrant, golden hum. The more I listened,
the louder it became.

A woman approached us. Her light blue aura was so brilliant it seemed to be made
of Aquamarine itself. The Guardian appeared to be in her twenties. She had light
blonde hair, which was shoulder-length and very thick. Her eyes were pale blue.

She looked at me and gave me the telepathic message that she would not speak
until everyone could hear her. Only when I entered her aura could my physical
voice speak, word for word, what she wished to say.

Greetings to all who have come and to all who may read of this experience in the future. Each of you can come to this place and be here for this discourse at any time. Time is flexible here, and those who live here are not bound by it. ◊ My work is on the inner aspects. I know the inner worlds well, and my mission is to share this awareness with those who are in harmony with Aquamarine. ◊ Each of my children, each Aquamarine crystal, reflects the inner ocean—that vast area of liquidity, knowledge, and wisdom within each individual. I connect people with this inner ocean, so they may become aware of its knowledge and wisdom. ◊ My work is subtle and quiet. Rarely do I rage in a storm. I do so only when my wearer needs to be cleared of the dross that inhibits my mission and obscures the ocean within. ◊ Aquamarine has been manifested by Spirit as a source of spiritual nourishment. I bring upliftment, but not in the way Lavender does. My effect occurs directly as a result of the awareness I bring. This is an awareness of the truth and reality of every level of existence: physical, emotional, mental, and spiritual. ◊ I also open one's awareness to the ways in which the realities or truths on these levels seemingly conflict with one another. I bring awareness of these paradoxes, which exist because the laws of nature are different on each of these planes. Realities are different, the focus is different, the state of consciousness is different on each of these levels. ◊ I appeared on the Earth, not just as a product of its evolution, but as the result of a grand evolution constantly occurring on all levels. ◊ Pure Spirit is the fountainhead of the life force. It is also the source of another stream of energy which flows through the mental and emotional planes to the physical. As it flows through these planes, it changes color and consistency. On the mental plane, this stream is often referred to as the Healing Waters, the Nectar of the Gods, or the Fountain of Youth. On the emotional plane, it becomes somewhat more material. The people there fashion it into bowls and other objects that remind them of the source of life. When this stream finally reaches the physical plane, it manifests as the gemstone you call Aquamarine. A gemstone is the only physical manifestation that can contain the intense force of light and sound characteristic of my vibratory rate.

ILLUMINATING HIDDEN TRUTH

Just having Aquamarine in one's aura will begin to open one's awareness on all levels. To describe how Aquamarine does this, I shall compare the individual to a mansion with many rooms. The floors of the mansion are like the individual's inner levels, and each floor contains many rooms. Aquamarine works to open more and more doors in the rooms of this mansion. By the way, the doors I open are not the chakras. ◌ When the doors to these rooms open, my vibratory rate turns on the lights within them. In other words, my light and sound shine on all aspects of your inner bodies, increasing awareness in more and more areas. As a result, you become aware of things hiding in the shadows and recesses of your emotions, memory, and mind. You also gain greater insight and a fuller comprehension of who you are and what your potential is. ◌ Everyone reacts differently to Aquamarine because everyone accepts truth in different ways and to different degrees. Indeed, because I open the awareness so powerfully, many people feel uncomfortable when they first wear Aquamarine. This is because when the awareness opens, the truth revealed may be too much for the mind to accept immediately. If you're not quite ready to accept a certain truth about yourself, you may resist facing it, and, as a result, you may become uncomfortable or cranky. You may also want to remove the Aquamarine, and if you don't, you may become fidgety. ◌ At such times it might be difficult to see that what you are really resisting is your own growth. If this new awareness is too uncomfortable, you can regulate how much truth you want to see by adjusting the amount of Aquamarine you wear and how often you wear it. In any case, after wearing Aquamarine for some time, you will begin to relax. ☉ This relaxation occurs partly because of the vibratory rate of Aquamarine's color. The deeper the natural color, the stronger this relaxing influence will be. My color helps people let go of their resistance. When people relax, the truth can be accepted more easily. As one becomes more comfortable with increased inner awareness, this period of resistance, fidgeting, and crankiness will pass. ☉ As your awareness grows and you gain a greater understanding of yourself, several things will start to happen. Opportunities on all levels of life will present themselves. You will start to understand life better, and this will allow you to work in greater harmony with your true self and with all of life. Relationships will become stronger and more harmonious. If you are on a certain spiritual path, you may be awakened to its greater potential; on the other hand, your understanding may grow beyond the limits of that path, and you may be compelled to look elsewhere for spiritual succor and sustenance. ☉ Aquamarine is most beneficial to those who are on a path of awakening. It assists those who want to know more about themselves, their destiny, and their potential. I am especially helpful for those who have reached apparent plateaus in their spiritual unfoldment, for I can awaken them to new vistas and allow them to grow to much higher levels. ☉ I have patience. I am gentle, calm, and understanding. At the same time, I am painfully honest, truthful, and clear. My patience regulates my honesty. For example, when I am worn, I show you only enough about yourself to spur your growth. When this growth raises your vibratory rate, I will show you more. Again you will grow and reach yet a higher level, and again I will show you more. ☉ I will continue this cycle for as long as I am worn. The amount of truth I show people at each stage is only limited by the depth of my true color. Therefore, the deeper and brighter my natural color, the more I can give.

DISCOVERING THE CAUSE OF ILLNESS

In order to experience greater physical healing, people today must not only pay attention to their physical bodies but must also focus on their inner aspects and on developing awareness. When someone has a physical condition, it may seem that the life force is only being physically obstructed, when in fact the obstructions that cause most physical diseases usually occur on the inner levels. ◯ I do not remove physical symptoms or heal the physical body directly. However, when consciousness is uplifted, the body will change. In some cases, when this upliftment of consciousness occurs, the forces causing a certain physical condition will simply cease to exist. ◯ Aquamarine can help you become aware of why you have a specific condition and what caused it. Once you can acknowledge and accept the reasons for your condition, you will be halfway to a cure. People often blame their conditions on something in the environment or on something someone else did. It is easy, for example, for people to blame an illness on a certain disease-causing agent, such as a chemical. However, the truth is that if it were not for your own inner patterns and state of consciousness, you would not have developed your condition. ◯ On both inner and outer levels, you have set up the circumstances that have brought about your condition. You have done this because you need the experience of having your condition in order to grow and to master the lessons that accompany that condition. Every physical situation is the result of inner conditions, blockages, or patterns. These inner patterns act like guideposts for Spirit to lead you to your physical situation, because you, as Soul, need this experience. You need to experience the effects of your creations—what you've caused by certain actions, reactions, thoughts, or emotions in your past. ◯ Let's say, for example, that in this lifetime you are a miner and contract lung disease. It would be easy to blame the lung disease on your occupation. You might blame it on management for poor working conditions or on your father and grandfather for being miners and convincing you to uphold the family tradition. However, the only thing for which you can honestly blame others is acting as the vehicles through which Spirit worked to give you the experience you have set up for yourself. ○ The reason you are having this experience is to help you take responsibility for the effects you have caused. Eventually, you must take this responsibility; you must reap the karma for what you have created throughout your lives, past and current. This experience of lung disease—or any experience—could be resolving much karma. At the same time, it is giving Soul the opportunity for its mind, emotions, and physical body to learn the lessons involved in resolving, curing, or perhaps even dying from this disease.

CREATIVE INSPIRATION

One can use Aquamarine to enhance any creative process. I say "use" Aquamarine, because one "uses" a tool. Aquamarine is a tool. ○ This technique involves focusing Aquamarine's ability to promote awareness on a creative activity of your choice. Let's say that you are an engineer and you are designing a mechanism of some sort. If you wear a strand of Aquamarine around your neck and are willing to awaken to the inner levels where ideas and inspirations are born, the Aquamarine will open your awareness to possible designs for the mechanism you are working on. ○ This technique can be especially helpful if you are experiencing problems with the design. The Aquamarine can open your awareness to greater possibilities and to the insights needed to solve these problems. It can also help you move past a creative block or plateau. ○ This technique will help anyone who works with the creative flow. For example, it can be useful for a physician with a patient whose symptoms are unclear or not responding to therapy. Aquamarine can help if the physician is unsure about what course to take. The next time the patient in question has an appointment, both the patient and the physician should put on a strand of Aquamarine. The physician should explain the powers of Aquamarine and why they are wearing it. Then both the patient and the physician should focus their attention on opening their awareness to what should be done for the patient. ◯ When Aquamarine is used for these kinds of applications, it should not be worn continually. If it is, the focus will be lost. For example, artists should only wear the Aquamarine when they are painting or sculpting. They should remove it if they are interrupted for any reason, such as a need to go to the bathroom, answer the phone, or get a snack. This requires discipline, yet it is necessary for maintaining a pure focus—in this case, on the artwork in progress. ◯ Students could wear Aquamarine when they are taking an exam or during a particular class. Of course, it would be unwise to wear Aquamarine for more than two or three classes in a row, since focus would be lost as awareness opens and shifts in many directions. ◯ Remember, when using Aquamarine this way, focus is the key to enlivening its greatest power and effectiveness.

GEMSTONES AND THE GROWTH OF AWARENESS

I am eternally young. I bring youthful energy wherever I go. It is a characteristic of youth to want to know things, grow, and become more aware. There is no end to the growth of awareness. Therefore, there will be no end to Aquamarine on this planet. As long as there are people on the planet, there will be Aquamarine. ◯ As the awareness of people all over the Earth expands, people will recognize those things on the planet that are powerful forces for healing. People will become aware of the power of gemstones. Gemstones are the strongest, most concentrated containers of the healing force, or life force, on this planet. Once people know how to unleash and use this healing energy, they will make huge advances in the field of medicine and in other healing arts, as well as in their own spiritual growth. ◑ Gemstones accelerate spiritual unfoldment and the growth of awareness. Once you awaken to the powers of gemstones and use them to accelerate your evolution, you will become aware of even greater uses for gemstones. This, in turn, will further hasten your unfoldment. ◑ I, as Aquamarine, present a challenge. I present a door through which you can go to see the truth about yourself. Aquamarine is only for those who have the courage to walk through the door and confront themselves. Aquamarine is for those Souls who are brave, whether or not they are aware of their own courage. ◑ I feel I have said enough. I have not said all, but for now I have said enough. Now you must return to the physical plane. Too much work and too much attention out of the physical body is not in balance. The next Gemstone Guardian you meet will be one with a more physical focus. You will know him as the Guardian of Green Tourmaline. I can introduce him only by name, for we are from two different worlds. Spirit will make sure you find each other when you are ready to meet him.

"It has been an honor to hear your discourse," Michael said.

It has been a pleasure and a joyful opportunity for me to clarify Aquamarine's mission and effects. I thank you for this opportunity. It is my wish that I am worn by as many people as will accept me; the more people who wear me, the more I can be of benefit. It is time that Aquamarine be used on your planet for its proper purpose. It is time for its potential to be realized. ◑ In awareness, may the blessings be!

"May the blessings be," Michael replied.

I slipped effortlessly out of her aura. She smiled graciously and most gratefully.
I had never seen such pure gratitude, mixed with love and understanding.
If Aquamarine teaches these qualities, then it is surely a special gift from the
planet to its people.

The listeners remained silent, enjoying the beauty of the countryside. I looked
around and realized that ever since Aquamarine had begun to speak, the local
wildlife had been moving closer and closer to our circle. It was apparent that we
were in a world where companionship, understanding, and love for all life softened
the air. Here the animals lived among the people, and no fear came between them.

Several deer were grazing next to us, and a badger had nonchalantly waddled up
to the river for a drink, paying us no mind. Rabbits, birds and many other
woodland creatures surrounded us, apparently there just to listen and drink in
the sweet feeling radiating from Aquamarine's aura.

With reluctance, I returned to the awareness of my physical body. Yet I drew
consolation from the thought that this place exists somewhere within me
and—as Aquamarine said when she began—I can return whenever I wish.

The

Guardian

of

GREEN
TOURMALINE

16

BALANCING THE MALE

I looked within and placed my attention on Green Tourmaline. Immediately I felt a surge of its powerful energy. Although this energy felt somewhat uncomfortable, I knew I must find its source. Cautiously, I allowed the energy to lead me there. Moments later I found myself next to a tall, tropical waterfall.

I stood in a small clearing next to the cascade, surrounded by lush jungle foliage. A cloud of green spray rose from a pool at the base of the towering column of water. There was something unusual about this waterfall. I studied it more carefully and realized that the column of water wasn't water at all. It was a Green Tourmaline crystal! And the mist rising from the pool below wasn't water vapor but a cloud of Tourmaline's vibratory rate rising into the atmosphere. The pool itself was a seemingly bottomless hole filled with nothing but this mist, swirling and folding into itself.

Suddenly someone appeared at my side. It was the maroon-robed spiritual master who had accompanied Michael and me during our first meeting with the Gemstone Guardians. Four others, including Michael, also appeared. Finally, the Guardian of Green Tourmaline arrived. He had come by a footpath that led from behind the giant Tourmaline crystal

The Guardian appeared to be in his fifties. He wore a dark green, long-sleeved robe that hid what seemed to be a tall, slender, and muscular body. His forest-green hair had streaks of gray and framed an angular face. The Guardian's light-green skin looked surprisingly healthy despite its unusual color.

Then I knew why the spiritual master was there: I personally did not feel in harmony with Green Tourmaline. The presence of the master ensured that I would not become imbalanced by the great volume of Green Tourmaline energy radiating from its Guardian. I focused on relaxing completely and suddenly found myself within his aura.

I give power and strength to those whose molecular structures have a vibratory rate of a certain nature. Only the male vibratory rate has this nature and is compatible with Green Tourmaline. ◌ My mission is to balance the male and help him reach his full potential. I broaden the viewpoint of any man who wears me and maximize the life force flowing through him. Indeed, I strengthen the vibratory rate of every molecule within a man's body. ◌ I do not recommend that women wear Green Tourmaline without the gemstone you call Pink Tourmaline. If a woman wore a necklace of only Green Tourmaline, her masculine nature would eventually overwhelm her feminine nature. One imbalance after another would manifest. Her emotional strength would be crushed, and eventually hormone imbalances would occur. The addition of Pink Tourmaline would cancel most of Green Tourmaline's power—unfortunately, it would also nullify most of Pink Tourmaline's benefits.

THE MASCULINE AND FEMININE RAYS

The Green and Pink Tourmalines represent the positive and negative forces, both of which must be present for physical matter to manifest. They also represent the male and female energies and how both of these energies are required for life to exist. Green Tourmaline is the carrier for the male energy, the north pole, and the positive force. Pink Tourmaline is the carrier for the female energy, the south pole, and the negative force. ◌ The neutral force is the third ingredient required for manifestation. This third force was not manifested in the Tourmaline crystal, although it is hinted at in clear Tourmaline. Actually, there is no such thing as clear Tourmaline. If it were chemically analyzed, some molecules of the Green, Pink, or other color would probably be detected. ◌ The masculine and feminine energies were placed within crystals so the males and females who would eventually inhabit the planet would have energy sources to make each gender independent and strong. The crystalline matrix of Tourmaline was chosen to carry these energies because Tourmaline is strong, resilient, and steadfast. ○ Masculine and feminine energies exist throughout the universe. Tourmaline crystals in the Earth—even deeply buried ones—attract these energies. Green Tourmaline acts as the Earth's receiver for the masculine energy. This energy flows toward the crystal, filling the Earth's aura with a defined vortex of masculine energy. As I said, Pink Tourmaline acts as the receiver for the feminine energy. ○ When one gender dominates another, lessons are to be learned by both. Soul has important lessons to experience on both sides of the situation. Now, in the past several decades, a very curious thing has occurred. Both genders are demanding equality. One might think that only women are demanding equality, but this is not so. Men are striving for equality as well, whether or not they are conscious of it. ○ The dominant gender often dominates only to hide its weaknesses. It wants to hide its vulnerability, so it pretends to be strong. This impulse is natural for men, because their physical bodies are generally stronger than women's. This strength is due to the vibratory rate of their molecules. ○ The secret is that the equality sought by both genders is not the equality between the millions of women and men on this planet. That is only the outward appearance. What is really happening is not the "battle of the sexes"—it is the war between each individual's feminine and masculine natures. Whether you have a female or male body, both masculine and feminine energies exist within you. It is just that you have slightly more of one type of energy than the other, depending on the gender of your physical body. The true conflict is occurring between these two types of energy within you. ○ As I said, during this century both genders have begun to demand equality. There are probably many reasons for this highly unusual behavior. You may not believe that what I am about to tell you has anything to do with it, but the amount of Green Tourmaline on the planet directly affects the balance of masculine and feminine energies. It does this by influencing the amount of masculine force that exists on Earth.

STEWARDSHIP OF THE EARTH

In the past, much larger quantities of bright, clear, emerald-green Tourmaline existed on the Earth than do today. This variety of Green Tourmaline is the strongest and therefore carries the greatest amount and purest form of masculine energy. Very little of this kind of Green Tourmaline remains on your planet. ○ During the past seven hundred years, most of the highest quality Green Tourmaline has been taken from the Earth by individuals from other planets. The effects of the dark green crystals still abundant on Earth are not as strong, because much less light can flow through them, and their color is not as pure and bright as the green of the rainbow. ○ This situation is somewhat analogous to that of a farmer who does not know the boundaries of his property. To illustrate, let's assume that you are a farmer living on twenty square miles of land with no fence around your property. You probably don't know exactly where your property ends and your neighbor's begins. ○ Let's also assume that you have crystals growing on your land and you don't understand their value. Your neighbor, on the other hand, understands that they are very valuable indeed. Now, if your neighbor took these crystals from your land, you probably wouldn't consider it stealing. For one thing, because you're unaware of your exact borders, you can't be certain that the crystals are located on your land. For another, you don't think the crystals have much value. ○ One day you hire a surveyor to clearly stake your land. You learn exactly where your borders are, and you claim all the land within them as your own. You also declare that all resources on this land are yours. After that, if your neighbor took the crystals growing on your property, you would consider it stealing. This is because he would now be taking without permission something that belongs on land you have claimed as your own. ◐ It is time that the people of Earth do the same. It is time that you claim your planet as your own. You must do this to stop people from other planets from plundering the Earth's resources. ◐ Now, I am neither for nor against this plundering. However, it is my duty to benefit man (and woman, indirectly) in any way I can. If you claim the Earth as yours, those from other planets who have honorable intentions will not intentionally steal from you. ◐ You Earth humans need your resources. You may think you have plundered the Earth. However, what you have taken from the Earth is perhaps ten percent of what people from other planets have taken. To stop this plundering by outsiders, enough Earth humans must consciously claim stewardship of the Earth planet. To do this you must consciously state, "This is my planet, my home, and my land." This should not just include what lies within the boundaries of your own backyard. It should include the entire planet. If enough people adopt this attitude, the Earth will be protected from those with honorable intentions. Then, if these outsiders still want what the Earth has, they will have to open other avenues of negotiation. ◐ How does this help you understand my purpose? Indirectly. I give men motivation, courage, and self-confidence. I give them these qualities so they can become confident and strong enough to allow other feelings to develop and be expressed. These qualities also help them strengthen their weaknesses and become more balanced. In other words, I allow their masculine and feminine natures to work in greater harmony. ◐ One can begin to change his life by staking a claim: "This is my life. I have the power to take charge of it, and I am going to take charge of it. But I could use some help. I will use Green Tourmaline as one of my tools for attaining self-mastery." ◐ One can stake a parallel claim for one's planet: "This is my planet. I take responsibility for it. But I need the help of other individuals. Then we, as people of the Earth, can live in greater harmony and work together for the benefit of the whole."

STRENGTHENING THE WEAKEST LINK

Green Tourmaline promotes balance on the physical, emotional, and mental levels. However, the way I do this is very different from that of other gemstones with balancing effects. I promote balance by strengthening the weakest link in the chain. ◑ First, my energy fills your aura and gathers information about all your aspects. Then I identify and focus my energy on the weakest area of your physical body. When the physical body has achieved a certain degree of balance, I move to the weakest area of your emotional body. Finally, I move to the weakest part of your mind. ◑ Green Tourmaline works in stages. First the physical body is brought to what I shall call "stage one." Then the emotional body is brought to stage one, followed by the mind. At that point, Tourmaline's focus returns again to the physical body to bring it to "stage two;" the emotional body is brought to stage two, and then the mind. This process continues as long as the Tourmaline is worn. ◑ The first movement in the physical body from "zero" to "stage one" will probably take the longest to accomplish because physical matter takes a long time to change. Consequently, Green Tourmaline's focus is frequently on the physical body. ◑ Even after wearing Green Tourmaline for only one day, you may feel physically stronger. If you continue to wear it, you'll find that you also become emotionally stronger and then mentally stronger. ◑ Before the weakest link can be strengthened, it must be recognized. It takes much courage to recognize one's weaknesses and to face them. Therefore, when men first put on Green Tourmaline, my initial response is to give a feeling of strength, courage, and self-confidence. This occurs as soon as Tourmaline touches a masculine aura.

GREEN TOURMALINE AND WOMEN

When Green Tourmaline touches a feminine aura, an entirely different effect occurs: the Tourmaline pulls backs its energy. I hold back my energy as much as I can, because I don't wish to imbalance any human being. However, I cannot hold back completely. ○ When a woman wears Green Tourmaline, her body recognizes that she is not in harmony with it and will start to put up resistance. To some, this resistance may appear to be an aura of protection created by the Green Tourmaline. However, what is actually happening is that her body is protecting itself from an invader—a disharmonious vibratory rate. Therefore, what may appear to be an aura of protection is really the woman's own defense mechanisms at work and the Tourmaline's efforts to protect her from its energy. ○ When people encounter disharmony and must engage their defense mechanisms, they are faced with a choice between "fight" or "flight." The protective aura a woman creates when she is wearing Green Tourmaline is the fight response. This response is designed to last for only short periods of time. If a woman wears Green Tourmaline continuously, her fight mechanisms will be compelled to work constantly and will quickly become exhausted. Once her reserves are spent, imbalances will occur. ○ For women, it may be best to wear a fairly large quantity of Green Tourmaline. I say this only because it might help them get the message sooner that the Tourmaline is not right for them and that they should stop wearing it. ○ I, as Green Tourmaline, am providing you with knowledge about a powerful tool. However, power is a double-edged sword. You may use it to great advantage or misuse it to great disadvantage. I am a gemstone that must be used with respect, self-discipline, and understanding. I must also be used without ego, vanity, or concepts regarding my effects on women.

CREATING HARMONY BETWEEN MATES

Disharmonies often arise in relationships between mates. Many things can cause these problems, including alcohol, the kids, money, or another woman or man. ☯ Whatever the cause, a wonderful therapy for ailing relationships is for the man to wear Green Tourmaline and the woman to wear Pink Tourmaline. When the man wears Green Tourmaline, it will give him strength. He will learn to balance his masculine and feminine natures. Because Green Tourmaline's vibratory rate will fill the atmosphere in the house, it will affect the woman's aura as well. This will nourish the woman's masculine aspect. Since she herself will not be wearing the Green Tourmaline, she will experience an indirect effect that will benefit her and create no disharmony. ☯ When the woman wears Pink Tourmaline, it will greatly nourish her feminine nature. She will learn from the Pink Tourmaline how to balance her feminine and masculine aspects. At the same time, Pink Tourmaline's vibratory rate will touch and affect her mate's aura. Pink Tourmaline is a strong protector for both genders. When its vibratory rate enters an aura, it transforms the aura into a shield. When the man begins to feel this protection, consciously or not, he will feel safe and therefore comfortable enough to work on balancing his own feminine and masculine natures. ☯ Pink Tourmaline opens lines of communication between masculine and feminine, thereby creating balance. When a man and woman each wear the appropriate Tourmaline, rather than the Tourmalines canceling each other out—as happens when both Tourmalines are worn by the same person—each person benefits from the other's Tourmaline. The result is an opening of communication between the man and the woman and an increase in balance between the masculine and feminine energies within each of them. ☯ Therefore, if a man and woman wish to resolve problems in their relationship, they should try wearing Green and Pink Tourmaline. If they are not having problems, this will strengthen their relationship. However, if the individuals want to end their relationship, the woman should wear Green Tourmaline, and the man should wear Pink Tourmaline. If they do this, I guarantee the relationship will be over within weeks.

The man and woman will not be able to live with each other.

GEMSTONES AND THEIR GUARDIANS

"As a Gemstone Guardian, are you aware of all Green Tourmaline and the way each Tourmaline gemstone is acting on the person wearing it?" Michael asked.

No, I am not. Gemstone Guardians are to their gemstones what your brain is to all the cells in your body. Your cells give your brain information about their needs, and your brain directs the life force to the cells as they need it. In a similar way, every Green Tourmaline crystal relays information to me, and I direct life force and nourishment back to each crystal. However, both these processes occur on an unconscious level. ☉ You are not conscious of what every cell in your body is doing. Generally, your attention is called to particular cells only when they are experiencing a great challenge or when they are trying to accomplish something noble. This is also the case with Gemstone Guardians and the gemstones for which they are responsible.

"How does the gemstone get to know its wearer?"

I shall answer this question in simple terms. ☉ Your aura contains all the information about your physical body, emotions, memory, mind, intuition, and, to a degree, Soul itself. It also contains information about how your nonphysical aspects relate to the physical body. ☉ This information is stored in the aura in patterns or sequences of vibratory rate, sequences of light, and varying densities and concentrations of energies. These patterns contain specific information about the past, present, and future. By future, I mean the potential future as it is being created by conditions in the present; if you change the conditions in the present, you will change your future. ☉ The energy or vibratory rate that radiates from a rounded crystal fills the aura and touches these patterns and sequences of information. With most gemstones, the vibratory rate then returns to the gemstone, carrying this information with it. This is how these gemstones learn about their wearers. ☉ Green Tourmaline is slightly different. Tourmaline in rounded form knows all of its vibratory rate intimately. It's as though every "molecule" of vibratory rate thrown into the aura is still a part of the Tourmaline around your neck. ☉ On an energetic level, what essentially occurs is that the gemstones around your neck expand to the size of your whole aura. It's as though the gemstones themselves fill your aura. The gems' relationship with your aura becomes like your brain's relationship to the cells in your body or a Gemstone Guardian's relationship to the crystals of which he or she is in charge. The Tourmaline gemstones around your neck know what each "molecule" of their vibratory rate learns when it's in your aura. ☉ It is the nature of gemstones in rounded form to know the one who wears them, just as it is your nature to know the people with whom you live. The longer you live with them, the better you get to know them. ☉ One of the reasons I have shared this information about Green Tourmaline is to see how Earth humans react to such knowledge. Are they self-disciplined? Will they take the responsibility to use this powerful tool properly? Or will they ignore the gift and let it sit unopened in the box? ☉ Any man, even the healthiest on Earth, can benefit from wearing Green Tourmaline, because there is no such thing as perfect health. Something is always out of balance, or some weakness exists on some level. As far as health is concerned, there is always another step to take. ☉ As people attain greater health, their attention will naturally turn away from their physical problems to encompass a greater understanding and awareness of themselves. This will eventually lead to self-mastery. ☉ Before one can become a spiritual master, or a master of Spirit, one must first master one's physical body, emotions, memory, mind, and intuition. I help people master these physical and subtle aspects. To learn about spiritual mastery, look to the spiritual masters. ☉ If you walk down the path I took to get here and continue to the other side of the mountain, you will find a waterfall of pink and gold. There you will meet the Gemstone Master Rubellite. Rubellite is another name for high-quality Pink Tourmaline. ☉ I will lead you there. Before I do, have you any more questions?

"I only wish to know if there is anything else you want to share," Michael replied.

There is still much to share about Green Tourmaline. I could tell you about many specific ways that Green Tourmaline can be used, but this will wait for next time.

"Thank you," said Michael and the others, almost in unison.

May the blessings be.

As difficult as it was to remain in Green Tourmaline's aura, it was equally hard to leave. Even after I had finally wriggled out, I still felt his powerful effects. I sensed that they would be with me for many hours. Without saying another word, the Guardian walked down the footpath. We knew we were expected to follow, but I waited until everyone but the maroon-robed master had filed behind the Guardian. When I could barely see the others through the foliage, I started down the path. The master followed me. I decided not to hurry. As we walked, I let my senses drink in the balmy, fragrant tropical beauty surrounding me.

PINK
TOURMALINE

17

BALANCING THE FEMALE

The scene surrounding the second waterfall was almost a mirror image of the one we had just left behind. The mysterious pool, the lush foliage, and the small clearing were all before me again. The only difference I could discern was the color of the crystal waterfall and the mist rising from the pool. The mist was pink, and the mammoth crystal itself was a combination of light and dark shades of pink mixed with pure golden light.

The Guardian of Green Tourmaline had waited with the other listeners until I arrived. He introduced the Guardian of Pink Tourmaline with a simple nod of his head. She returned his nod, and then the Guardian of Green Tourmaline retreated down the path.

The Guardian of Pink Tourmaline was dressed in layers of sheer pink fabric, which draped her body like cascading water. She was about six feet tall and appeared to be in her late thirties. The Guardian had suntanned skin, rich golden eyes, and brown hair which fell just below her shoulders.

She smiled and reached for my hand. As I took her hand I knew I would slip instantly into her aura and the discourse would begin.

Greetings, everyone. My name is Rubellite. Rubellite is also the name given to the finest quality Pink Tourmaline, the gemstone for which I take responsibility.

"The Guardian of Green Tourmaline referred to you as the 'Gemstone Master Rubellite.' Is your mission different from those of the other Gemstone Guardians?" Michael asked.

I will speak of the Gemstone Masters, because I have great respect for them. However, I can only do so because I have not yet been fully initiated into this order of masters.

THE GEMSTONE MASTERS

You have already met many Gemstone Guardians. You have learned that they do not all come from one place, nor are they all the same age. You have also discovered that not all the Guardians are required to devote all their time to the gemstones for which they are responsible. Some Guardians, whom you have not yet met, are even in charge of more than one gemstone. ◊ What we Gemstone Guardians do in our spare time, if indeed we have any, is entirely up to us. I believe it is the same with you. My personal interests lie beyond the energies, powers, effects, and properties of the gemstone Pink Tourmaline. Although Pink Tourmaline is my focus, I am deeply interested in all gemstones. I am interested in their purposes, their effects on different people from different planets, and the ways in which they can be used. ◊ I am in training for initiation into the Order of Gemstone Masters. I have declared this intention, for it is the path I have chosen for my personal unfoldment. It is the way I choose to be a co-worker with Spirit. ◊ The Gemstone Masters do not work as the Guardians work. You might call these masters the keepers of gemstone knowledge, since their purpose is to collect, record, file, and keep safe all the available knowledge and wisdom regarding gemstones. This includes knowledge from all the universes and worlds where gemstones exist. One of their duties is to keep this information up to date. As gemstones grow, mature, and evolve, their properties and effects change. Similarly, as people experience their own individual and collective growth, their reactions to gemstone energies change. ⊙ The Gemstone Masters work directly with Spirit. They know what gemstones really are. I will tell you what gemstones really are, but know that my description is superficial. ⊙ Gemstones are embodiments of the light and sound of God. Your physical body also contains the light and sound of God. However, a one-carat gemstone can carry a thousand times more light and sound than your entire physical body can. This is simply because the crystalline matrix of the gemstone can handle more concentrated energy than the cellular matrix of your physical body. ⊙ When the Gemstone Masters are working, they often wear a black robe and a black hat. You might call this outfit their uniform. Black reminds them to be neutral and not partial to any one color or gemstone. Since black tends to absorb all colors of light, it also reminds the Gemstone Masters that it is their duty to absorb and gather information. The presence of the black uniform presents an interesting opportunity for those who meet a Gemstone Master. Unless you can let go of all concepts surrounding the color black, you will not be ready to learn or accept what these masters have to offer. ⊙ It is not the purpose of these masters to change people's attitudes, concepts, or opinions about gemstones, nor is it their purpose to raise people's consciousness about them. These things will occur in time. Therefore, anyone who says he or she has "channeled" a Gemstone Master has not communicated with a master of this particular order. You may find it interesting to know that, just as there may be a Gemstone Guardian with a physical body living on your planet, there may also be a Gemstone

Master with a physical body living there. ⊙ When an individual has earned the right and proved that he or she can be responsible for the information a Gemstone Master imparts, that individual will be given certain knowledge by these masters. It will seem as though that person has gained this awareness on his or her own, because the masters do not communicate directly. That is not their way. The Gemstone Masters take no credit for their work. They are beyond ego or vanity. They work with complete humility as co-workers with Spirit. ⊙ When my attention is not on Pink Tourmaline, I focus on learning and teaching some of the information the Gemstone Masters have gathered. I assist them in their research. Consequently, to some I may appear to be a Gemstone Master. However, I have not yet achieved full initiation into this order. I consider myself an apprentice. It was an honor to be called a Gemstone Master. It was Green Tourmaline's way of recognizing and affirming my direction and potential.

LIGHT, SOUND, AND SOUL

"Can you tell us why light and sound are contained in gemstones?" Michael asked.

Gemstones are vehicles Spirit uses to radiate a concentrated form of the light and sound of the life force into the physical and inner worlds. If there were no gemstones or crystals, planets would not be alive; and if planets were not alive, they could not support life. Like organs in the human body, crystals carry out specific functions needed to keep planets alive. ⊙ Metals and certain rocks are so physical and dense that there is no way for the life force to penetrate a planet made of nothing but these elements. A planet comes alive only when it is imbued with a Soul and its crystals are infused with life force. A planet gains its Soul in the form of its Guardian. Only then does it possess the three key elements needed for life: light, sound, and Soul. ◌ The more of these three elements available to you, the richer your life will be. This is why gemstones are available to human beings. Gemstones offer you the opportunity to gain a greater connection with your Soul. They also nourish you with a greater influx of light and sound. ◌ Actually, it is not correct to say you have a Soul. You are Soul. You, as Soul, have a mind, emotions, and a physical body. The point of having these physical and inner aspects is to gather experiences, learn lessons, gain strength and stamina, and become aware of Spirit. These lessons and experiences will then allow you to fulfill your true purpose, which is to regain awareness of your true nature as Soul. ◌ Eventually you will gain the awareness that, among other things, you live to become a co-worker with Spirit. I have chosen to do this by working to become a Gemstone Master. You can also do this by becoming an artist, engineer, teacher, homemaker, salesman— or whatever is your heart's desire. ◌ One way to describe Soul's path and purpose is to say that you, as Soul, originated in the heart of God; as you moved further and further into manifestation, you collected a mind, emotions, and a physical body. As Soul, your ultimate goal is to return in full consciousness to your source in the heart of God. ◌ It takes a great deal of awareness, experience, strength, and lessons learned to gain the impetus or power needed to return. Moving into manifestation is easy; it is like flowing with the force of gravity. However, just as a rocket needs a tremendous amount of fuel to defy gravity and leave the Earth's atmosphere, people need a tremendous amount of spiritual "fuel" to return to the heart of God. ◌ Gemstones are packages of concentrated light and sound "fuel." They can act like booster rockets, giving you the extra energy you need to help lift you in the direction of your goal. How a gemstone does this depends upon its mission, purpose, and effects.

NEGATIVE GEMSTONES

Not all gemstones give this boost or extra fuel to help Soul return. Only those gemstones beneficial to man and woman will do this. The gemstones whose Guardians you are interviewing for this book have only beneficial effects on their wearers. However, there are some gemstones whose duty it is to divert your attention from your goal. ☉ These gemstones often cloak their negativity, so that people with shallow insight will only see positive benefits from wearing them. Of course, if people saw their true nature, these gemstones would be shunned and not mined. Because they must be mined in order to carry out their missions, these gemstones create a false front. ☉ In a crude way, these gemstones temper men and women. They make people strong but only through negative experiences. These gemstones keep people on a downward spiral. If and when their wearers finally become aware of the ways in which they have been affected, they might also discover that they have gained strength. However, this is only because awareness is strength. ☉ In this rather harsh way, wearers of negative gemstones may come to understand the power of gemstones and may remove the negative ones from their lives. Then they may look to uplifting gemstones or to some other focus of light and sound to help them change the direction of their lives. This will help them evolve toward their ultimate goal. ☉ There are many ways or paths to this goal. Gemstones do not take the place of religions or spiritual paths, nor do they take the place of spiritual guides or masters. If I or any other Gemstone Guardian has given you that idea, I apologize. It is the wrong idea. ☉ Gemstones are not the "path" or the "way." They are only tools, though powerful ones. Their power is often proportional to the wearer's state of consciousness. The more spiritual energy flowing through the wearer, the more enlivened the gemstones will be. In other words, the more spiritually aware you are, the more powerfully gemstones will work for you. ◐ The purpose of gemstones is not just to heal the physical body or to make it feel better. When worn, gemstones gather information from and work on both your inner and your physical aspects. Holistic in the truest sense of the word, gemstones' work involves your whole being, the life force which sustains your being, and the energies that created your conditions. No other therapy can promise this—unless, of course, it includes gemstones or is one that involves working directly with the light and sound of Spirit.

THE LAW OF SILENCE

When I am initiated into the Order of Gemstone Masters, I will not be able to speak as freely as I just have. As an outsider of sorts, I still have the right to speak freely about gemstones and Gemstone Masters. On the other hand, I have only been given information that can be shared freely. When I am initiated, I will gain wisdom, information, and knowledge so vast that I might not know what can be shared, what needs to be shared, or what should be shared. ◐ You can well imagine that one of the prerequisites of Gemstone Mastership is mastery of the law of silence. Besides knowing when to keep silent about certain information, masters of this law know how to teach in silence. ◐ Indeed, it is much more effective to teach silently. Then the learner is not just given information by an authority with whom he or she can agree or disagree. When teaching is done silently, individuals learn through their own direct experience. They truly know what they have learned, and no one can take that knowledge away.

"When you become a Gemstone Master, will you still be the Guardian of Pink Tourmaline?" Michael asked.

No. Another will be given the experience of being the Guardian of this gemstone.

"How many individuals have been initiated into the hierarchy of Gemstone Masters?"

It is a relatively small order. I have never counted, and perhaps no one will ever know exactly how many are involved. You were correct to call this order a hierarchy, because the masters who have belonged to this order for the longest time are the most wise and have access to the most information. They are also the most silent.

"Do these masters store information in crystals?"

The information appears to be kept in large books and is impeccably neat and well organized. In order to extract information stored in crystals, a certain process is involved. It is easier to scan the pages of a book or the titles of many books, since there is no need for an information retrieval device. Nevertheless, the actual material of which the pages are made is illusory, for it is close to being pure light and sound. It is just for the sake of convenience that it manifests in a form which looks like a book. ⊙ These books have manifested only for recording purposes and for those of us who are apprentices. Often, when the Gemstone Masters need to know something, they expand their awareness to the level of infinite all-knowingness and perceive the answer. This source is beyond any kind of manifestation, be it in the form of books or crystals. My fellow apprentices and I are still unable to access this source of infinite wisdom whenever we wish. ⊙ By the way, although each discourse you hear will comprise one chapter in this book, know that enough additional information about each gemstone exists to fill an entire volume. As you research each gemstone more deeply, you will discover that the discourses you are hearing are actually introductions, for the Gemstone Guardians have been speaking in general terms.

BALANCING FEMININE AND MASCULINE ENERGIES

I have two missions. One is to give woman the power, understanding, and awareness to realize her full potential. I help her realize how her feminine and masculine natures coexist and interact, and I encourage them to come into greater harmony. ◯ My second mission is to provide protection by transforming the aura into a shield. This shield protects people from external disharmonious influences, be they mental, emotional, or physical. My two missions intertwine. This is because women often appreciate and can benefit from a certain level of protection when they are undergoing the changes required to realize their full potential. ◯ In the past, civilization was not ready for women to have the power and awareness I bring. If women had gained this awareness, history would have been different. Men might not have retained the dominant role. ◯ Only in recent times has equality come to be recognized as a virtue. Only now is it something that both genders, but particularly women, are working toward. The equality for which men and women are striving is not equality between the genders. The true equality they seek is the balance between the masculine and feminine energies within each individual. Once this inner balance is achieved, or at least approached, the harmony between the genders will increase. It will occur naturally. ◯ I am not saying that when masculine and feminine energies become more balanced that conflicts between men and woman will cease, nor do I mean that everyone will be in agreement with each other and that marital spats will be a thing of the past. Not at all. Men and women will bounce their energies off each other for eternity. It is the nature of their vibratory rates and their magnetism to do so. ○ For centuries, the feminine aspect of the dominant male was suppressed and therefore weakened. Because the male's feminine aspect is part of him, by dominating the female, he only weakened himself. Meanwhile, as the male was dominating, the female was learning to become strong. The method by which she acquired this strength is similar to the way negative gemstones teach strength—the hard way. It is true that sometimes this kind of lesson is remembered best, but it is certainly the most painful. ○ And so it was, that while man was weakening himself, woman was slowly, slowly becoming stronger. ○ Centuries of suppression have taught many women that their masculine aspect is wrong; or it has taught them that males in general are wrong, shortsighted, egocentric, and not as strong as they think they are. And I am sure that if you include three or four blank lines in your book, many women who read this list would be happy to fill in more adjectives. ○ I notice that some men in this audience did not find that humorous. ○ Women consist of both masculine and feminine energies. Therefore, until a woman releases her concepts about male energy, she will not be in harmony with herself. Pink Tourmaline will help a woman understand both her male and female aspects and improve communication between them, thus creating harmony. ○ If a woman can master both her masculine and feminine aspects, there is nothing she cannot do. She will only be limited by how far she wishes to go. Women who reach this state of strength, self-confidence, balance, and power tend to see more of the whole picture of life. Among other things, they may begin to understand that one of their greatest blessings is the power of motherhood and the preservation of the family. Some may realize that they can best use their power and abilities to preserve the family rather than to enter the workplace and assume a typically male role. Of course, there is nothing wrong with taking either avenue. ○ It is the male's purpose to carry the strength of the family's group consciousness through the generations. This manifests as the custom of passing family names from father to son and of women taking their husbands' names. Similar customs are practiced in societies on other planets. ◔ It is the female's purpose to provide the force of change. She broadens the family's group consciousness and therefore strengthens it. When a daughter marries, she steps away from one family unit and enters another family's group consciousness, broadening and strengthening it as she enters. ◔ If a woman refuses to take her husband's last name or chooses to change her last name after she has taken her husband's name, it is an indication of imbalance. Yes, I know that this statement will ruffle some feathers! ◔ I could speak for hours on this subject. However, that is not the purpose of this discourse. Besides, I feel I have already given you enough information to upset many people's concepts about male-female relationships. ◔ Pink Tourmaline can give a woman the self-confidence to stand on her own as her own individual being, separate from her husband. Yet in her recognition of the importance of family preservation, she may see the importance of having one identity, or name, for the family unit. When you wear an identification bracelet, the bracelet is not you; it is only something you wear for identification. Likewise, when a woman wears her husband's name, it is not her. But she can use the name to identify the group consciousness she is forming in her family. One family name strengthens the group consciousness of the family unit. ◔ In any case, a name is only a temporary identity. Who you are as Soul will not change if your name changes. Nonetheless, names can be tools. For example, if you wish to release an old identity and take on a new one, you are free to change your name. I have come to realize that it doesn't matter what my name is or what people call me. I am who I am.

PINK TOURMALINE AND MEN

Pink Tourmaline will not imbalance men in the same way that Green Tourmaline can imbalance women. When worn by a man, Pink Tourmaline will produce the same protective effects it does for a woman. Wearing Pink Tourmaline will also encourage a man, consciously or unconsciously, to recognize his feminine nature. Often, when this happens, a man will not like what he sees or will not be able to accept it—especially if his feminine nature needs attention and healing. ○ Therefore, one of the greatest gifts a man can give himself is to give Pink Tourmaline to the woman with whom he is sharing his life. As the Pink Tourmaline vibratory rate fills the woman's aura, it will also affect his aura. This indirect effect may help him balance and heal his feminine qualities more easily, because the Pink Tourmaline's influence will not be as overpowering as if he wore it himself. The aura of protection created by the Pink Tourmaline around the couple will also enable the man to feel safe enough to allow his own healing changes to occur.

CREATING A PROTECTIVE SHIELD

Pink Tourmaline protects its wearers from external disharmonious thoughts, emotions, and energies, including electromagnetic radiation and microwaves. I do not protect you from your own inner disharmonies. If you already have a certain disharmonious vibratory rate within you, it is difficult to protect you from external forces of the same disharmony. For example, if you have greed within you, I cannot protect you from greed. I can protect you most effectively from disharmonies that are foreign to you. ○ When you are protected from external disharmonies, you have the freedom to be braver and more adventurous than you would otherwise be. You also have the freedom to think new thoughts and feel new emotions. ☉ If you travel to foreign countries or to foreign parts of your own country, you will be protected from the stresses of travel. No matter where you are, you will be protected from the energies and influences that are foreign, disharmonious, and potentially harmful to your body. ☉ You have been told how the white light differentiates into seven color rays. You may be surprised to learn that, even though I manifest in several shades of pink, the color-ray vibratory rate which flows through me is actually blue. ☉ The vibratory rate of my crystal pulls the blue ray into the physical world with such force that the pink ray of the emotional world is pulled along with it. This force is so strong that particles of pure white light are also pulled into the physical. By the way, the pink color ray—which gives Pink Tourmaline its predominant color—is a dilution of the red ray. ☉ When a person wears Pink Tourmaline, the light rays that are pulled toward the gemstones collect in the aura. This makes the aura so strong that it is nearly impenetrable to many energies. ☉ I must also warn you about Pink Tourmaline: Its power should not be underestimated. Tourmaline crystals take a long time to grow. They are built carefully and precisely. As each molecule is added, it is done with an understanding of Tourmaline's responsibilities. ☉ Because of Pink Tourmaline's power, it should not be worn as a solid necklace unless the wearer will be doing something potentially dangerous or will be entering an environment that is very disharmonious. Only in these situations should Pink Tourmaline be worn alone. It will allow you to focus less of your personal strength on self-protection and more on the task at hand. In other words, Pink Tourmaline should only be worn in a solid necklace when your natural defense mechanisms may be so overburdened that your well-being would be compromised. ☉ Pink Tourmaline's energy enters the body through the lower four chakras and sometimes through the throat chakra. It only exits in a gentle flow through the brow chakra. Wearing even one solid necklace brings more Pink Tourmaline vibratory rate into the body than the body can express through the brow chakra. ☉ Therefore, if an individual wears a necklace made entirely of Pink Tourmaline, the pressure of its vibratory rate will soon build in the head. (Consequently, a headache is a sure sign that you have been wearing too much for too long.) A solid necklace of Pink Tourmaline can distort the balance of mental energy and accentuate negative thought patterns. If the individual continues to wear this much Pink Tourmaline, the emotions will soon exhibit the same imbalances. ☉ For everyday use and protection—and to experience all the other benefits I have described—Pink Tourmaline should be combined with other gemstones in a necklace. However, one must be sure that these other gemstones do not impede, confuse, interfere with, or cancel out my work. For example, Green Tourmaline should not be included with Pink Tourmaline, because it will have negative effects on my work. ☉ My protective properties can also have an indirect healing effect on the body. When outside influences bombard a particular part of the body, they often prevent or inhibit it from healing. These influences may include the energies of the thoughts, feelings, attitudes, concepts, and prayers that friends and family may be directing toward the person or the diseased part of the person's body. Not only must that part of the body focus on healing, but it must also contend with these outside influences. Despite good intentions, these influences may or may not be positive, welcomed, or in the best interest of the individual. If the individual wears Pink Tourmaline, the affected organ or area will be able to relax its defense mechanisms. It will be able to place its full attention and energy on healing, cleansing, or rejuvenating itself.

TOOLS FOR HEALING

Gemstones are not to be used in place of physicians. Gemstones are tools. If I had a certain condition that was inhibiting me from attaining my goal, I would certainly see a physician with whom I felt comfortable. At the same time, I would use my intuition to select the most powerful and appropriate tools I know of to help me resolve and remove the obstacle. ○ The most powerful tools I know of—and that are available on the Earth planet—are gemstones. Some may argue that drugs are more powerful than gemstones. Drugs appear to work faster and provide results almost immediately. My question is: do they work on the actual causes of the problem, or do they only work on symptoms? Remember, gemstones work on the actual causes of conditions. ○ Herbs are different from either drugs or gemstones. Herbs, like gemstones, can greatly benefit human beings; yet there are important differences between gemstones and herbs. For example, although herbs grow much faster than gemstones, their life spans are much shorter. Also, because therapeutic-quality gemstones are rarer and more difficult to obtain, they cost more. Yet gemstones contain a more concentrated healing force, and, unlike an herb, the value of a gemstone and its giving properties will not wane. The life span of most gemstones will exceed your own, no matter how often you use them. An herb cannot promise that. Nonetheless, I have great respect for herbs. They are very beneficial, and one can use a vast variety of them. ○ It is probably no coincidence that I, as an individual, was given the responsibility of being the Guardian of Pink Tourmaline. I may be the first woman ever to be in line for initiation into the order of Gemstone Masters. If there is a woman who has already attained this initiation, her vow of silence is impeccable. I have not yet met her, nor have I heard of her. I am doing something that, as far as I know, no other woman has done. I know that, in addition to all the requirements demanded of any applicant, it takes something extra for a woman to do this. ○ As I look at each of you sitting comfortably in this lush jungle garden, I realize you have not caught much of what I have said. I have been given a chance to share myself, but from what I see, at this time only a small piece of my discourse has taken root in your hearts. This observation only supports my growing understanding of the law of silence. It confirms the value of using the silent method of teaching to convey information. If I had taught you in silence, each of you would have gained a knowingness of what I said. Of course, that would have been impractical for the purpose of this interview. ○ Next you will meet the Guardian of the earthstone Sodalight. You will find that some Earthstone Guardians are similar to the Gemstone Guardians, while some are quite different. The vibratory rates of the earthstones greatly influence the appearance of their Guardians. Just as gemstones work on inner planes, so do their Guardians. In general, the work of most earthstones is directed primarily to the physical and/or emotional planes. Therefore, the attention of many of the earthstones' Guardians is focused on those areas. Do not expect to hear as much about Soul or the inner bodies in their discourses. ○ Thank you for the joining me here today.

"Thank you," I heard Michael reply, as I slowly began to move out of the Guardian's aura. For several moments, I remained suspended halfway out of her aura. In this state I knew all that she knew. At the same time, I was aware of what the listeners had experienced. Only a fraction of what she had said had taken root in their hearts. I only wished that my own heart could be fertile enough and my experience profound enough for her words to become my own knowledge.

Then I completely slipped away from this Gemstone Master-to-be. We watched her body slowly fade until her vibratory rate became one with the mist rising from the pool.

The
Guardian
of

SODALIGHT

18

PURIFYING THE AURA

The Guardian of Sodalight and I had made an "appointment" to meet. Now, as
our meeting time approached, I was feeling a pull toward the Guardian. I tried to
move into the inner worlds where we usually met the Gemstone Guardians but had
no success. I soon concluded that I was struggling because I was looking in the
wrong direction. Sodalight was an earthstone. Therefore, I should find him
on the Earth.

I turned my attention toward the Earth, scanned the planet for the source of this
attraction, and then let go. In the next moment I found myself in the rocky
foothills of a mountain. The Guardian of Sodalight sat waiting on a boulder.

He had short dark hair and deep blue-gray eyes. He appeared to be in his thirties.
His royal blue pants and shirt were so loose-fitting that they could have been
mistaken for robes. He looked quite human. I guessed that if he were dressed in
less unusual clothing, I probably wouldn't pick him out in a crowd. He also
appeared burdened, as though he were carrying a great inner weight.
Nevertheless, I felt refreshed in his presence.

Michael soon joined us and took a seat on another large rock. No other listeners
arrived. I asked the Guardian if I should enter his aura as I had been entering the
auras of the Gemstone Guardians. He told me just to sit down next to him and
close my eyes. I did what I was told and began to imagine what it might be like to
see what Sodalight saw, feel what his heart felt, and know what he knew.
Then I felt our auras slipping into each other and the Guardian
beginning to speak . . . .

Greetings, my friend. Your partner is using a different technique to relay my discourse. This is necessary because my vibratory rate is different from those of the Gemstone Guardians. ☾ When un-cut Sodalight is exposed to the atmosphere, it makes the Earth a cleaner, more enjoyable place to live. It does this by absorbing unnecessary energies that collect in the atmosphere and impede life. ☾ In spherical form, Sodalight assists human beings by making its wearer's aura a cleaner and more harmonious place to live—for, indeed, just as a planet lives within its atmosphere, so do human beings live within their auras. ☾ You might gain a better understanding of my purpose if I could somehow convey to you my love for this planet. As I look at the blue-green valley stretching below us and the bright blue sky dotted with clouds above, love fills my heart. ☾ You have been told over and over that the Earth is a living entity. As the Earth grew and recognized a future need for something to maintain balance in its atmosphere, it started to formulate the chemical composition of the earthstone you call Sodalight. Sodalight grew in many places around the planet. It was as rock-like as rock can be, since at first the Earth only needed it for itself.

PSYCHIC POLLUTION

As people evolved, they began to use their minds and emotions from a less instinctual and physical viewpoint. This new way of thinking and feeling gave people greater freedom of expression. However, they had not yet developed the sense of responsibility that must accompany such freedom. As a result, people's thoughts and emotions became unruly and negative. As they manifested, these negative thoughts and emotions were released into the Earth's atmosphere. ☾ The Earth noticed its atmospheric balance was being upset by the negative energies people were irresponsibly, though unconsciously, throwing off. It also knew that Sodalight had the potential to cleanse negative thoughts from people's auras before they were released into the atmosphere. To do this, the Sodalight would have to be fashioned into spheres. However, the Earth also realized that it would be thousands of years before the consciousness of the people would develop to the point where they would be ready to do this. ○ In the meantime, the Earth had to do what it could to protect and balance its atmosphere. This meant that Sodalight itself had to change. It had to raise its vibratory rate so that it would be closer to the vibratory rate of people's thought emanations. Consequently, Sodalight started to become more gem-like and less rock-like. This change increased its power to absorb negative thought emanations and disharmony released into the atmosphere. ○ As Sodalight evolved, another need arose requiring yet another change in Sodalight—that is, people began to require more of the indigo ray. To fulfill this need, a certain amount of the Earth's Sodalight began to evolve into a true gemstone. Indeed, the more gem-like it became, the more indigo ray this new gemstone could carry. The vibratory rate of this new gemstone continues to move further and further away from the vibratory rate of the Sodalight earthstone. As you know, this new gemstone is named Indigo. ○ Currently, the Indigo gem still absorbs negativity and disharmony from the atmosphere like Sodalight does. However, this ability will decrease as Indigo begins to carry the indigo ray more purely. The Indigo gemstone will become more responsible for the changes that the indigo ray brings to people, and it will also support them through these changes. ○ At this time, I am still in charge of the gemstone Indigo. The Guardian of Sapphire is in charge of training Indigo's Guardian. The Guardian of Indigo is only a boy. However, as soon as he is ready, a split will occur. Then he will take complete charge of the Indigo gem, and I will focus my energies exclusively on Sodalight. ○ The earthstone Sodalight continues to undergo its own evolution—one that is quite distinct from that being experienced by the gemstone Indigo. The vibratory rate of true Sodalight is becoming stronger and more effective both for the planet and for the people who wear it. My powers for absorbing disharmony and negativity from the atmosphere and from the human aura are increasing, because the Earth needs this to help maintain its balance. ○ By human standards and needs, the indigo ray carried by true Sodalight is almost insignificant. Yet, if human beings gaze upon it, my indigo color might inspire them to share my dream of maintaining a clean blue sky. Then perhaps human intuition will open and certain people will be inspired to mine more Sodalight. Increased mining of Sodalight is important, because only when Sodalight touches the atmosphere can it work on cleansing the air.

"Are you referring to air pollution?" Michael asked.

Yes, but remember that air pollution includes disharmonious thought energies as well as disharmonious physical molecules. ○ I work to maintain the clarity and health of the atmosphere through my ability to absorb and through the indigo ray that I carry. I do not absorb physical pollution directly. First, the air must break it down and process it. It is similar to the way your body can digest food much more easily after it has been chewed. The air begins to work on its pollutants immediately, drawing on a variety of natural resources to help the process. For example, the Earth sometimes uses ingredients in forest fire smoke or in volcanic gases to break down pollution and correct imbalances; there are even occasions when the Earth uses radiation emitted by sunspots. ○ Uncut Sodalight also absorbs people's negative thought emanations; however, the air must "chew" them even longer than physical pollutants. The air must work on lowering the vibratory rate of human thought emanations to a point where uncut Sodalight can easily absorb them. Thus, it takes the air longer to break down thought forms than it does to break down physical pollutants, such as carbon monoxide.

CLEANSING THE AURA

Just as a clean atmosphere is important for planetary health, so is it essential to human health that one's aura be as clear as possible of disharmonious energies. A clean aura supports balance and harmony in the individual, while an aura clouded with negative and disharmonious energies burdens the individual. Indeed, the more disharmony the mind emanates into the aura, the more imbalanced and burdened the mind itself becomes. If the mind is relieved of the burdens it has created, it can more easily find balance. ○ When an individual wears Sodalight spheres, I remove the clouds of disharmony emanated by that person's mind. I do not absorb or remove the cause of the disharmony; I only remove the clouds. This new clarity frees the mind to see what it has done and why it throws off negative energy. ○ Once the clouds are gone and these reasons are known, it is hoped that the individual will make the changes needed to stop producing such disharmony. If the person does not make these changes and stops wearing Sodalight, eventually the aura will become as polluted as it was before the Sodalight was worn. ○ In addition to negative mental energies, the aura tends to accumulate various other energies that are unnecessary for survival. These energies can bog down one's mind and inner workings. Sodalight absorbs these accumulations so the light of Spirit can shine more brightly through the individual's inner bodies to the physical body. This effect is comparable to the way the sun shines on the Earth more brightly when the clouds have dissipated. ○ When your aura is cleaner, you can see yourself more clearly: who you are, what your strengths and shortcomings are, and in what direction your life is headed. Once these things are better known, you can choose to enhance your positive attributes, work on your shortcomings, or more clearly define your life's direction. These are all secondary effects of Sodalight's cleansing of the aura. ○ Those who benefit most from wearing Sodalight are people who continually feel overwhelmed or burdened, often for no clearly defined reason. Because I clear "garbage" from the aura, individuals who wear me can more easily recognize their true thoughts, feelings, goals, and dreams. Therefore, I am also especially beneficial for those who have difficulty distinguishing between their own thoughts, emotions, goals, and dreams—and those projected onto them by others. ○ I can also protect individuals from negative thoughts, emotions, or other energies directed toward them by others. This includes unwelcome prayer or black magic. When worn, I can soak up these energies as they enter the aura. ○ Sodalight's aura encompasses an area several hundred times the size of its physical form. Sodalight's aura acts like a sponge. It possesses a strong magnetic attraction for the disharmonious mental energies in your aura. Because of this attraction, negative energies easily flow from your aura into the stone itself. By the way, my wearer is not consciously aware of my work. Only the results of my work are felt consciously. ○ Remember that my primary purpose is for the Earth. Yet, as I have explained, when people wear Sodalight in spherical form, many of the negative energies in their auras are absorbed before they can be released into the Earth's atmosphere. Therefore, the more that people wear me, the less pollution the Earth will have to deal with.

"You are called an earthstone. Does that mean you are indigenous to the Earth?"

Yes. I, as the Guardian of Sodalight, work only for the Earth planet. I have enough to do to maintain balance on this one planet without being concerned about other planets as well. It is not possible to mine too much Sodalight. In fact, it would be wise to prepare for possible surges of disharmonious thoughts, vibratory rates, or conditions that one day may enter the atmosphere. It would serve my mission to be widely and evenly distributed among the people of Earth, because when I am evenly distributed around the planet, I can serve the planet most effectively. ○ Sodalight is often overlooked because of the brilliance of the gemstones. Yet Sodalight is crucial to the life of the planet and therefore too important to be overlooked. This will be especially true if humankind continues to deplete the atmosphere and if scattered mental energies remain largely negative. Without the help of Sodalight, many forces could assault the planet, impeding human life and, consequently, the life of the Earth. ○ Fortunately, time seems to expand for the busy person. I say this because I see myself only becoming busier in the future. As far as I am concerned, I have not yet reached my prime. I only hope that the growth in strength I am bound to experience will occur as rapidly as the Earth's need for me.

THE POWER OF GEMSTONE SPHERES

Only recently has human consciousness risen to the point where people are ready to accept the powers that gemstones unleash when they are not confined to the crystalline form but are fashioned into spheres. ○ In essence, Michael, you and I are pioneers, exploring the effects of the spherical form of gemstones. It is just that my pioneering efforts are sharply focused on Sodalight. As far as I know, no one knows every application of the sphere. Spheres radiate their energy in an infinite number of directions; the possible applications of a sphere are probably just as infinite. ○ I myself am unaware of all the effects that Sodalight spheres may have on the human being. It is my responsibility to become aware of these effects as they become apparent and are felt and recognized. My duty as a Guardian includes collecting, recording, and cataloging data about Sodalight. This data includes the ways in which Sodalight's vibratory rate changes under different atmospheric, astrological, and spiritual influences. ☉ Earthstones are more affected by the position of the sun and the planets than are the gemstones. This is because the earthstones have a greater affinity with the vibratory rate of the physical plane. Gemstones, on the other hand, may not be at all influenced by the movement of planets and their magnetic energies, because the scope of the gemstones' effects reaches far beyond the physical. ☉ I also work in the dream state with individuals who are either ready for Sodalight's effects or who are already wearing Sodalight.

"What is your opinion about gemstones and earthstones being worn in their natural form?" Michael asked.

Be careful when using the word "natural." I know you are referring to the shape of gemstones and earthstones as they are found in the ground, yet it is very natural for human beings today to wear spheres. Their consciousness is ready for spheres. Once a gemstone or an earthstone is shaped into a sphere, its energies can be unleashed on its wearer in a way that would be impossible if it were in its crystalline or rock form.

"Many people think that it is wrong to change the shape of gemstones or earthstones," Michael said.

The information the Guardians are giving you is on the crest of the wave. This means that not everyone on the planet is ready to accept the powers of gemstones in spherical form. Fortunately, enough people are now ready to accept this information, work and experiment with it, learn from it, and grow from it. ◯ People often hold on dearly to what they know. They cling to what has worked for them in the past. Give them time. As the wave moves closer to the shore, their consciousness will unfold. People only limit themselves by clinging to the crystalline form. However, if individuals who cling to crystals were to let go of their concepts and experience the power of the spherical form, they might grow faster than they are ready to grow. So, be compassionate and be patient. Let people have the space and time to grow at their own rates. ◯ Follow me further up into these rocky foothills, and I will lead you to the Guardian of Leopardskin Jasper. We will enter a cave, and somewhere within the mountain you will meet the Guardian. Do not be surprised by the form in which the Guardian appears, for you may simply encounter a vortex of energy. ◯ We will rest before we begin our journey.

19

ATTRACTING BENEFICIAL INFLUENCES

The path was rocky and steep. I was glad we didn't have to walk far before the Guardian of Sodalight pointed out the narrow opening of a cave.

As soon as we squeezed through the entrance, the passage widened and the sunlight disappeared. I wondered what, if anything, would light the path, since we carried no lamp. My answer came when, in the darkness, the deep blue glow surrounding Sodalight's body became more evident. It gave us just enough light to see by if we kept close behind him.

We followed the passageway downward for about fifty yards until we entered a large, bone-dry cavern. Sodalight's voice echoed as he spoke: "We have entered one of the Earth's major deposits of Leopardskin Jasper. Feel its energy. You probably haven't experienced anything like this."

I opened all my senses to Leopardskin Jasper's energy. I can only describe it as grounding and earthy. Then I felt a swirling cloud of this energy collect in an area about three feet in front of me. The cloud was several yards in diameter. I knew that if I walked into this whirl of energy, I would be able to speak the words that flowed from the heart of the Guardian of Leopardskin Jasper.

I stepped into the whirl and entered the most unusual state of consciousness I had ever experienced. I felt like I had become the Earth itself. If I placed my attention on a specific geographic location, I knew everything the Earth knew about that place. I was aware of the Earth's nervous system sending messages to each part of the planet through a network of Leopardskin Jasper. Then I felt the responses to these messages returning to my heart. They carried reports on the energetic changes that had recently occurred in various places.

As I wondered whether this Leopardskin Jasper network spanned the entire planet, the swirling energy began forming words, and I felt compelled to speak.

I am like the planet's nervous system: I collect information from within the planet and from its surface. I learn what the planet needs to maintain global balance, and then I work to fulfill those needs. ◐ When I receive information that some part of the Earth requires a change, I determine what the Earth requires to restore balance in that area. Then I send magnetic impulses to other gemstones or earthstones telling them what must be done. It is their role to initiate and direct whatever changes are required. ◐ I have a direct line of communication with the Guardian of the Earth. I also act as a repository, reservoir, and regulator for the millions of different influences, vibratory rates, and energy flows within the Earth and between the Earth and its atmosphere. ◐ I do not need to cover the Earth completely to know what is happening within every part of it; I only need to be in certain strategic locations. The strategic location on the human being is the neck. When I encircle the neck, I can touch the whole aura and get to know the entire person. This is somewhat similar to the way I get to know the entire Earth, even when I am located in only a few key places. When a strand of Leopardskin Jasper spheres is worn, the energy contained in the spheres flows into the aura, where it captures information; then the energy returns to the spheres. In this way I learn the wearer's needs. ◐ In the Earth, my magnetic impulses draw what is needed to balance certain areas of the planet. When I am worn by a human being, my vibratory rate amplifies my wearer's needs so that whatever is required to achieve greater balance will be drawn to that person. ◐ When I express a planetary need to another earthstone, that earthstone works to define the need more clearly and to determine a possible way to satisfy it. I cannot tell you how this mechanism works in people, because I don't understand all aspects of the human being. However, I have noticed a parallel between a human being and the planet in this respect. I know that for both the Earth and the human being, I move the need and the force that will fulfill it closer and closer together. ☉ When Leopardskin Jasper is cut into spherical form, circular patterns appear on the spheres. My magnetic impulses emanate from these circles. The circles are like control knobs. When they read an aura and identify its needs, they can judge what is a true need and what is an artificial one. An example of an artificial need is a child's "need" to have ice cream for dessert. The child's true need might really be for an apple. Similarly, when a certain imbalance occurs in the planet, the surrounding area might think it needs what I shall call "ten points" of compensation to restore its balance. From a global viewpoint, however, the true need might be only three points of compensation. ☉ The more circles apparent on my spheres, the stronger and more effective the spheres will be in amplifying what is needed by the individual. A greater number of circles also increases my ability to discriminate between true and artificial needs. This is one reason why the more or larger spheres an individual wears, the more powerful are my effects, as long as the spheres contain circles.

REGULATING ENERGIES

One word that characterizes my effects is "regulation." In essence, I am a regulator of energies. I know that to sustain life, all living things must be regulated with extreme precision. I also know that every part of a living organism depends on every other part. If one part suffers an imbalance, other parts will be affected. ☉ Thus, one organ would not be in distress if another part of the body weren't also out of balance. The human body is similar to the Earth in this way. Earthquakes, certain weather patterns, and other natural events occur because something has happened to upset the balance. These events are manifestations of the Earth's striving to reestablish balance. ☉ Part of my mission is to maintain global balance by regulating the planet's energies. For example, if an earthquake creates an imbalance in a certain area, I help to restore balance there through my regulating effects. ☉ When I am worn around a human being's neck, I bring greater balance and regulation to the physical body as a whole. I do this by highlighting the area of greatest need. This highlighting helps the body draw whatever vibratory rate it needs to help restore balance to the area. This vibratory rate and the individual are then magnetically drawn to each together, like the north and south poles of two magnets. ☉ Do not be surprised at what I might help draw to the body. It might be a physician or certain foods or medicines or a book on a new healing method. All these things are just vibratory rates. Yes, a physician with particular knowledge is a vibratory rate, as is a book. Medicines, herbs, fresh mountain air, and a trip to the beach are also distinct vibratory rates. I do not distinguish between vibratory rates and the physical forms they take. ☉ I do not remove disease either from the Earth or from human beings. I just help the body draw to itself whatever is needed to correct the imbalance that is being expressed as a disease. I do not take responsibility for what occurs when an individual becomes more balanced as a result of my influence. My responsibility is simply to bring the physical body and what it needs closer to each other. ☉ Despite their similarities, each Earth human is unique. This is why a human body will sometimes reject an organ transplant from another human being. When a body rejects an organ transplant, it's because the vibratory rate of the organ donor is too different from that of the recipient; or, more specifically, the regulatory mechanism of the recipient is too different from that of the donated organ. When this is the case, the organ will not be able to live in the recipient's body, and the body will reject it. ☉ If a human being wears Leopardskin Jasper spheres long enough, that person's overall regulatory mechanism will become more defined and specific. It will also become strong. As a result, the individual's personal magnetism and individuality will increase. The definition of who that person is will become more specific. Therefore, those who wear Leopardskin Jasper almost continually are not good organ donor candidates. Their organs become less adaptable to the regulatory mechanisms of other people's bodies.

ATTRACTING AND REPELLING

As the person wearing Leopardskin Jasper becomes more self-defined, individuals from this planet or other planets who have dishonorable intentions will be magnetically repelled by the person wearing the Leopardskin. Just as I can attract that which is harmonious, I can also repel that which is disharmonious. The more Leopardskin Jasper worn, the stronger the repelling force will be. Still, it may take many months of continually wearing Leopardskin Jasper before this force becomes strong enough to repel others. ○ Leopardskin Jasper can assist people who constantly attract disharmony into their lives by helping them to attract sources of greater harmony and to repel the negative influences that create disharmony. ○ With or without Leopardskin Jasper, life continually strives to achieve a state of balance. This is reflected, consciously or unconsciously, in every action a person takes. People who continually attract disharmony often tend to overcompensate in their attempts to achieve balance. They swing too far in the opposite direction, thus further upsetting their own balance. ○ Such a tendency is reminiscent of a child who thinks he needs ten cookies when, in reality, two will suffice and ten may give him a stomachache. Leopardskin Jasper can help convince the child or the adult that two cookies are sufficient. It will do this by drawing only those two cookies into his or her life. Also, if people have set up circumstances which continually attract the other eight cookies, Leopardskin can help repel these elements of overcompensation as well as other negative influences. ○ However, if the individual resists the positive influence I initiate and insists on opening the door to negative influences and inviting them in, there is nothing I can do to repel them. This is true even when the resistance is unconscious. One must remember that mental energy is much stronger than physical energy. My work is focused on the physical. Yet—and this is not meant to be confusing or paradoxical—when I touch the aura, I can help attract what is needed and help repel what is not needed by the mind and emotions. However, I do this only as these needs relate to the physical body. ☾ As I get to know people's auras, I get to know people better than they know themselves. I get to know their needs better than they do. I know what influences are most harmful to them. Sometimes people enjoy the influences that harm them and are unwilling to deflect them. In other words, they are not ready or willing to accept the gifts of Leopardskin Jasper. ☾ I work powerfully for the Earth, because the Earth is one hundred percent willing to work with me. Likewise, I can be a powerful tool for human beings when they are one hundred percent willing to make the changes or to accept the influences I help attract. If people wear Leopardskin Jasper, I will bring the vibratory rates they need into their lives. These vibratory rates are like gifts. I cannot tell people to accept them. ☾ My mission for the planet has been and always will be as I have described. People may find other applications as they begin to understand Leopardskin Jasper and the way it affects people when it is fashioned into spheres. That is the nature of human beings: to experiment, to explore, and to expand their awareness. It is for this reason that people have earned the right to become aware of the effects of the spherical form. ☾ You are alive because of two spheres: the sun and the Earth. Doesn't it make sense that if you fashion life-giving substances, such as gemstones, into spheres, that you will gain additional life from them? Isn't that obvious? Perhaps it is not so obvious to everyone—yet. It took many centuries before people all over the planet came to understand that the Earth revolved around the sun. These days people think, "Of course, the Earth revolves around the sun. How obvious." ☾ At the far side of this cavern, you will find a passageway that leads to a different network of caverns. There you will meet the Guardian of the earthstone you call Poppy Jasper. ☾ Before you leave, I want you to know that this discourse was an important part of my work. Now you have the opportunity to understand more clearly the mission and effects of Leopardskin Jasper without having to endure many years of trial and error. Now you have a direction to follow to increase your understanding of the possible effects of Leopardskin Jasper on both human beings and animals. Indeed, animals may experience greater effects than human beings when they wear Leopardskin because their minds won't get in their way. Their minds don't constantly tell them that they need ice cream instead of apples.

"Thank you for sharing this information," said Michael.

It is my duty.

I was suddenly ejected from the swirling energy. It did not surprise me, since it is apparently Leopardskin Jasper's nature to repel that which is no longer needed. To my right I saw the blue glow of the Guardian of Sodalight. He began to move silently toward the other end of the cavern. There he entered another tunnel, and Michael and I followed.

This time the path was relatively level, but the passageway was small and narrow and required some crawling to move through. Luckily, the spirit of adventure squelched any feelings of claustrophobia I might have had. Finally, the tunnel opened into a large cave filled with stalactites and stalagmites. Water dripped uncontrollably from the saturated walls and ceilings, making the air extremely damp. We began to wind our way through the tall stone formations. Somewhere in this cavern, I knew we would meet the Guardian of Poppy Jasper.

POPPY JASPER

20

ENLIVENING THE BODY

Without warning, in the center of the wet cavern, a campfire appeared.
This unusual fire produced no smoke, nor did its light dance on the cavern walls.
It simply radiated a constant glow, allowing us to see the entire cave more clearly.
The Guardian of Sodalight showed no concern about the fire; it merely seemed to
be his cue to request the presence of Poppy Jasper's Guardian.

Again a formless swirl of energy collected a few feet in front of me. I noticed that
its vortex was spinning in the direction opposite to that of Leopardskin Jasper's.
I walked into the swirl and caught my breath. My body felt charged with new
energy. Even more striking was the change in my perception. I no longer saw the
cave walls as rock. Now they were alive—a living part of my own body.

Michael and the Guardian of Sodalight also looked different. I saw only a dim
outline of their forms, for now I perceived their bodies as masses of water and
minerals. Within each of them vibrated a coil of concentrated, brilliant light that
seemed to give life to the collections of water and chemicals. I knew this light
must be Soul.

Then I felt an urge to rest my mind, listen, and serve as a vehicle for the words
of the Guardian of Poppy Jasper.

All earthstones and gemstones are involved in the process of fulfilling the Earth's needs. Our relationship to each other is like the
relationship of the organs in your body: we all work together for
a single purpose. We are all components of the whole picture,
and all of us are required to keep the Earth functioning. ◌
Just as your organs formed as the rest of you was forming, I
formed as the planet was forming. You will find most of the
earthstones are similar in this regard. ◌ I am like a cousin to
Leopardskin Jasper. My work follows his. My mission for the planet
is to provide it with the equivalent of adrenaline. When your
adrenaline flows, you work harder and faster. Often adrenaline
flows because you are excited, and it generates a feeling of joy
that keeps you going. It can also give you the extra energy you
sometimes need to get through challenging situations. This extra
energy is what I give to the Earth. I do this whenever Leopardskin
Jasper determines there is a need for it. ◌ I am not as widely
distributed within the Earth as Leopardskin Jasper, and the
pockets in which I am found are smaller. It is not necessary
for me to be distributed evenly throughout the planet, just as
it is not necessary for you to have a heart in every part of your
body. ◌ The Earth only needs several major deposits of Poppy
Jasper. The planet's circulatory system distributes my vibratory
rate wherever it is needed. This circulatory system consists of
lines of magnetic flow. Communication throughout the planet
is swift along these magnetic pathways. The human body has
a similar communication system; your brain quickly regis-
ters a painful stimulus in any part of your body. The Earth is
as complex as the human body. However, we are not here today to
learn about Earth physiology. ◌ Leopardskin Jasper recognizes
the Earth's needs. It collects the information that something must
be done. Poppy Jasper provides the energy and push to get it done.
When Poppy Jasper receives information from Leopardskin Jasper,

its reaction can be described as that of a positive attitude. A positive attitude is the key to getting work done most efficiently and to everyone's benefit. You have probably experienced this yourself. When you do something with positive energy, more gets done, you feel better for doing it, and others are positively affected by your good humor.

ENERGY VORTICES

You noticed that my vortex swirls in a downward direction. This is because I get my energy from the atmosphere. The vortex of my vibratory rate pulls this atmospheric energy down through the soil to the Poppy Jasper. ☉ When there is a certain job to be done, I spin a "baby" vortex off from the main vortex of the Poppy Jasper deposit. Sometimes the baby vortex is thrown toward the area in need. Other times it is thrown toward the gemstone or earthstone that can affect the area more directly than I can. The baby vortex spins in the direction opposite to that of the main vortex. If it spun in the same direction, the main vortex would not be able to propel it with any degree of force. ☉ As the baby vortex spins in an upward direction, it brings uplifting energy to its target. This uplifting energy is positive, happy, and joyful. It imparts a good attitude and good humor. It acts like adrenaline, inspiring, invigorating, and enlivening the next earthstone or gemstone in line to carry out the mission identified by Leopardskin Jasper. Wouldn't you agree that you react more positively to stimuli that are uplifting and positive? ☉ Sometimes the other earthstone becomes aware of its task as soon as my energy enlivens it, and sometimes others help to define its task. I have a similar effect when I am worn on the human body. I can enliven and wake up areas that appear to be sleeping.

"What do you mean when you say you 'wake up' areas?" asked Michael.

When your stomach is empty, you might say that it is asleep, because it is not secreting any digestive juices. When you eat food, the stomach "wakes up." It becomes enlivened and starts to secrete its juices. I am like that food. ◌ My energy also helps to break up crusty patterns, physical impediments, and blockages that prevent energy from entering certain areas of the physical body. Now, blockages do not always manifest in pockets or specific places in the body. Cells throughout the body often have a blocked or tight quality. Energy cannot flow through blocked cells the way it should. When Poppy Jasper is worn, I cause these blockages to be released. Sometimes these releases manifest as spontaneous muscle twitches and stretches. Some call these stretches "unwinding" movements. ◌ When your physical body becomes freer of these impediments, it is able to accept more energy. This enables your body to do things it was previously unable to do. More energy also makes you feel good. When you're given a little more adrenaline, your outlook is brightened and becomes more cheerful. You feel joyful and happy to be alive. By wearing Poppy Jasper, you may also attain a deeper recognition of your connection with the life of the Earth, and this too will invigorate you. The more you wear Poppy Jasper, the more you will experience all these effects.

GREATER HARMONY

Recently, a change occurred that allowed me and several other earthstones to gain conscious awareness of our own functions and how we work together. Before this change, many earthstones worked by instinct alone and performed their jobs as if in a dream. ◌ With this increase in awareness has come the potential for greater harmony among all parts of the Earth. It also has brought greater responsibility and the potential to work with more difficult situations. If one functions only by instinct or "on automatic," one may not be able to function accurately when unusual circumstances or variables arise. With conscious awareness, I can cooperate more effectively with the other conscious earthstones to resolve these unusual circumstances. ○ As the human race is growing, your technology is changing. Yet, as a race of beings, you still are basically unaware of the nature of your planet. As a result, you do things to the planet that hurt it. We earthstones must find creative solutions to balance what you do to the planet. We must find ways to keep the Earth alive and, consequently, to keep you alive. ○ Some unknown force—Spirit, perhaps—has inspired people to fashion earthstones into spheres so that they can be worn. This inspiration is truly a gift to the planet. When people wear earthstones, they become more in tune with their planet. Their understanding of the planet grows, and they become aware that their planet is indeed alive. Because the Earth is such a perfect reflection of the human body, as people begin to wear and know the earthstones, they will also begin to know themselves better. ○ I give people the motivation, inspiration, and energy to act that I give to other earthstones. Therefore, one who sits still should not expect to wear Poppy Jasper and remain still. Perhaps the worst thing you could do with Poppy Jasper would be to give it to someone who lives in prison. The person will want to move, do something, and change. This person might become very frustrated if he or she were physically prevented from doing so. ○ You have caught me within a moment of time. When you leave, I will continue my work. ○ There is much more we could talk about. However, you must first grasp the information I have given you. You must take it a step or two further. You must understand enough to be able to ask focused questions, and then we will have much more to talk about. You will know where to find me when you are ready. ○ I provided the fire only to help you see this cavern more clearly, for I know that darkness often makes human beings uncomfortable and reluctant to move. Actually, it is not really a fire at all; it just looks like one. ☉ Perhaps this light will have a symbolic meaning for you. Perhaps the symbol will help you understand how I work on the human being. But be careful not to take symbols too far.

"Thank you," said Michael.

Even as the vortex moved away from me, my body continued to feel Poppy Jasper's energy. All my muscles took turns stretching as they released stresses and blockages. These releases were not uncomfortable. Indeed, they were as refreshing as a first stretch in the morning.

The

Guardian

of

BLOODSTONE

21

COORDINATING HEALING ENERGIES

We did not have to wait long before another whirlpool of energy emerged from the cavern walls. Its vortex swirled in an upward direction, like that of Leopardskin Jasper's.

"This is the Guardian of Bloodstone," said Sodalight. "As you enter the aura of each earthstone and gemstone, you experience their characteristic energies firsthand. At the same time, the Guardians get to know you. In knowing you, they learn more about all human beings and, therefore, how to work more effectively for those who wear them."

"As you enter this vortex, you may feel like you're stepping into a tornado. Yet the wind you will feel is only Bloodstone's energy moving through the molecules of your body. When you reach the calm center of the whirling vortex, you will feel the greatest 'at-one-ness' with Bloodstone."

I walked into Bloodstone's vortex and felt the tornado exactly as Sodalight had described. When I entered its tranquil center, a line of communication seemed to open, and I felt the urge to speak.

PLANETARY ENERGIES

I have a relationship with the Earth and with all the earthstones. When I see an imbalance or disharmony occurring on the planet, I know exactly what is needed to correct it. Sometimes another earthstone calls my attention to these areas; Leopardskin Jasper is one who often does this, but there are others as well. Then I use my own energies to help resolve the disharmonious situation. ○ I help collect and coordinate the energies of different earthstones and gemstones that the planet needs to rebalance itself. I act like a lighthouse to illuminate the target area and direct the energies of the other earthstones toward it. ○ To correct the imbalance I've identified, I also draw to the area a supra-physical form of the color rays. Color rays in this form are easily recognized and accepted by the Earth. The colors I tend to draw are the predominant colors of Bloodstone itself: red, orange, yellow, and green. Bloodstone contains less blue, indigo, or purple. This is not surprising. Although these colors are necessary for life, the Earth is more nourished by red, orange, yellow, and green.

"You say Bloodstone recognizes imbalances on the Earth. How do earthstones correct the disharmony created, for example, by toxic waste dumps?"

This is a serious situation in which all the components of the Earth must work as a team, as we always do, to keep the Earth alive. We must all work together, just as all the organs of your body work together to keep you alive. ○ One of my roles in the team is to gather information about the disharmonious situation, draw up a plan, and present this plan to the Guardian of the Earth. My proposal includes a description of the problem and its magnitude. I also suggest a priority level the Guardian should assign to the problem and provide a list of the available resources—that is, earthstones and gemstones—closest to the area. Finally, I tell the Guardian how much energy those resources can contribute and how the earthstones plan to solve the problem. ☾ Using your example of a toxic waste dump, I will describe how we earthstones work together to solve such a problem. ☾ A toxic waste dump is top priority. Within days after the toxicity is deposited, we earthstones analyze the situation, and I draw up a proposal. This proposal usually includes a plan to protect the planet by creating a callus-like shield around the toxic deposit. This shield is much like the callus your skin forms around a splinter you haven't removed. ☾ A black earthstone, whose Guardian you have not yet met and whose vibratory rate acts like a shield, is chosen to encase the deposit. This earthstone calculates the rate at which the toxic vibratory rate is penetrating the Earth. Then it determines how swiftly it can get its own energy to the area to begin manifesting itself and start forming a callus. Once these calculations are made, the earthstone decides how far from the toxicity it will need to start concentrating its energy. ☾ I finalize our proposal and submit it to the planet's Guardian. Then, if the situation has, for example, a priority level of thirty, the Guardian might not answer us for weeks. If the situation has a priority level of one, we receive an answer as soon as the Earth has completed a day's cycle. ☾ During that time, the Guardian examines the proposal's possible effects. To do this, the Guardian assumes that the proposal has been put into effect, then waits until the Earth has made a complete rotation and the sun has shone on the entire planet. This allows the Guardian to evaluate the proposal's ramifications on the entire Earth. Then, depending on the problem's priority level— and whether our proposal to balance one part of the planet would imbalance another—the Guardian accepts, rejects, or redefines our plan. ☾ If the Guardian of the Earth accepts our plan for isolating the toxic waste dump, the vibratory rate of the black earthstone begins to collect in the area at the selected distance. At the same time, certain earthstones direct the sun's magnetic energy toward the black earthstone. This gives the earthstone so much extra life and vitality that its molecules begin to form a callus around the toxicity at a much faster rate than normal. ☉ I should point out that earthstones and gemstones grow at a faster rate when there is a special need for their presence. Toxic waste deposits are an example of such a need, since it is crucial that the Earth protect itself from them. ☉ Nevertheless, it would probably take several years before the black earthstone could create a shield one or two molecules thick. And it could be several decades before the shield would be big enough to be obvious. It would continue to grow until it created a callus thick enough to protect the rest of the Earth from the toxic waste. ☉ By the way, the sun affects the earthstones and the planet itself more than you might think. Solar energy does not recognize the limitations of physical matter. It flows right through the planet and is absorbed by the earthstones, even those several miles beneath the surface. This solar energy creates the Earth's magnetism. ☉ This magnetism is part of what enlivens the earthstones and gives us our energy. Communication lines among earthstones are also magnetic, as are the lines of investigation every earthstone uses to scout the planet. The earthstones store this magnetic energy, but only to a degree. Consequently, if the sun were to die, so would we earthstones. Ultimately, the sun's energy keeps us alive.

HUMAN ENERGIES

My work for the human being parallels my work for the Earth. When you wear a strand of Bloodstone spheres around your neck, I sense areas that are particularly out of balance or disharmonious. I see what is needed to correct these imbalances and disharmonies. Then I bring these areas to your attention, just as I bring disharmonious areas to the awareness of the Earth's Guardian. ☉ Then, if you give me permission, I act like a lighthouse and encourage certain healing energies to come to these areas. Instead of the Guardian of the planet, you must give this permission. This permission might simply be your sincere willingness for change in the disharmonious areas I have highlighted. ○ As soon as I receive permission, I direct your body's own energies toward these areas so they may assist in the required changes and rebalancing. The energies I call are both physical, such as white blood cells, and supra-physical. The supra-physical energies I draw are mostly in the form of color rays. ○ If you are not in tune with the messages I am giving, you may feel increased pain, soreness, or redness in the area. I do not cause this discomfort. These effects simply occur if you are resisting, not paying attention to, or not accepting the awareness I am trying to bring. ○ When you wear Bloodstone spheres around the neck, I focus on the area of greatest disharmony first. When placed over a specific area chosen by you, the physical and supra-physical forces I call are brought to that area, even if it's not the area of greatest disharmony. In both cases, physical changes will result. ○ All I do is draw energies to the area. This does not mean they will automatically cause the area to heal. It simply means that you will now have additional resources to help a positive change occur in the area. In other words, I take no responsibility for healing, and I take no responsibility for altering the cause of a situation. Therefore, once you acknowledge the disharmony and are willing to accept a change, you will be wise to take further action, just as the Earth does. ○ When the Earth acknowledges a situation and gives me permission to collect energy at a certain place, it initiates a change somewhere within itself. An obvious example is a volcanic eruption. One interpretation of such an event is that the Earth erupts the medicine it needs to heal or rebalance a particular area. ○ Similarly, you can take action by going to a physician, taking the proper medicine, accepting a particular therapy, or performing some other action to take total responsibility for the area in question. ☾ My primary mission is for the Earth. Yet, the way I function for the Earth almost perfectly parallels the way I function for human beings when I am worn in spherical form. ☾ Bloodstone is a symbol of the Earth and of nature. The supra-physical colors I express are in harmony with nature. They feed the trees and plants, the minerals and rocks, and the planet itself. Consequently, by wearing Bloodstone, human beings can forge a stronger connection with the Earth and be nourished by the very same energies that nourish the planet.

"Can you explain the difference between the way earthstones and gemstones work?"

Earthstones and gemstones work on different levels of vibratory rate. In general, the earthstones focus their work on physical and supra-physical energies. Gemstones work in a broader arena; their work also includes energies with a much higher vibratory rate than the physical. Because of the earthstones' focus, if the physical body's doors are closed to healing energies from the inner levels, earthstones can help open these doors. ☾ My work is simple, basic, and straightforward. I think you now have a good idea of who I am. For this interview, I have given you enough information.

"Thank you for sharing this information," said Michael.

Thank you for the opportunity.

As Bloodstone's vortex and I separated, I felt an unmistakable flow of gratitude and a mutual understanding develop between us. I was most thankful to realize that this new understanding seemed to be forming not just between Bloodstone and me, but between Bloodstone and the human race as a whole.

22

ANCHORING POSITIVE CHANGE

"Now we will stretch your concepts of reality even further," said the Guardian of Sodalight. "Keep the focus of your mission pure and your attention on the core of your being. Then walk with me."

Together, Sodalight, Michael, and I walked right through the wall of the cavern. My mind complained that this was impossible, so I did what I could to keep my mind separated from the rest of my body. I let it look at the situation with all its doubts and objections until I began to laugh, not believing what I was seeing. Indeed, we were inside the rock. Somehow the molecules of my body were occupying the spaces between the rock's molecules.

"You will not find Ivorite in large deposits but in veins such as these," explained the Guardian of Sodalight. "Position yourself inside one of these veins as best you can." It was easy to distinguish exactly which rock was Ivorite. Since it was time to meet the Guardian of Ivorite, its vibratory rate stood out from the energies of all the surrounding rocks.

Once I had entered the Ivorite vein, I realized that my body was positioned horizontally. Within the rock I had no sense of up or down, and the law of gravity seemed to be suspended. Then I sensed the familiar feeling that the Guardian wished to speak. I allowed the Guardian's words to flow through me.

I am Ivorite. My importance is often overlooked by human beings, but it is not underestimated by my fellow earthstones. The earthstones respect one another greatly, for we know that each one of us has been formed on the planet for a purpose. There is not one of us the Earth could do without. We are all important pieces of the puzzle. ⊙ So far, you have learned that many earthstones play a role in detecting imbalances and focusing their energies to correct them. This is done on both a local and global scale. ⊙ My purpose is to make sure that the sum of these energies is kept in balance. I provide an anchor. I ensure that the changes initiated by the other earthstones do not occur so rapidly that the balance of the whole planet is upset. My function is to hold the reins and prevent changes from occurring too swiftly. I remind the Earth that its changes must occur slowly. Slow changes are best for the Earth's overall balance and benefit, and especially for the life that lives on its surface. ⊙ Ivorite is found in capillaries all over the planet, with only a few deposits large enough to be mined for the purpose of being worn by human beings.

PUTTING CHANGE IN PERSPECTIVE

When my spheres are worn around the neck, I provide an anchor for the human being's changes, just as I provide an anchor for planetary changes. As a result of my work, people can put their changes in perspective more easily. ⊙ Of course, a human being consists of so many levels that I could not possibly anchor every change on every level. However, people's changes usually have focal points, and this is where I do my work. My focus is on the area of life that is experiencing the most change, activity, and growth. This area is usually reflected as the most highly charged area in the aura. ⊙ The earthstones behave similarly when working for the Earth; they place most of their attention on the areas undergoing the greatest number of changes. As an earthstone, I too am naturally drawn to these areas because that is where my energy is needed most. When I am worn by a human being, my vibratory rate fills the aura; then I find the area that is most charged, regardless of what level of the aura it has manifested in. I throw an anchor on this area. ☉ When people experience rapid changes, they often lose perspective. They lose sight of where they have come from and where they are going. Ivorite helps people regain perspective and gives them the chance to readjust their lives accordingly. ☉ As soon as I am removed from the aura, the anchor is also removed, and people are able to resume their changes at their previous rate. Hopefully, however, they will have made some adjustments and can continue in a more balanced way. ☉ Often, when you place a great deal of attention on one area of your life, you neglect other areas. Attention is life. If your attention is withdrawn from every area except the one that is changing the most, all your other aspects will suffer from a lack of life force. ☉ When you wear Ivorite, the area you have given the most attention is put "on hold." This will allow you to nourish and give attention to the other, neglected areas. If these areas need to release something, they will be able to release it; if they need to change, they will be able to change; if they need to relax, they will be able to relax; or, if in the name of overall balance, they simply need more attention, they will receive it. With these needs taken care of, when the Ivorite is removed, you will be in a better position to handle your changes. ☉ When you have experienced a healing, a beneficial change, or some degree of progress, my presence helps stabilize that progress. I help establish a new state of balance that includes this change. Then, when you remove the Ivorite, you will be more inclined to take the next step forward than to slip back to your previous state. ☉ Therefore, Ivorite can be an important part of any therapy, whether that therapy is for specific parts of the physical body or for the body as a whole. Ivorite can also be an effective addition to emotional, mental, and spiritual therapies. It is especially beneficial in cases where the physician finds that the patient tends to slip back after receiving a treatment. When Ivorite is used as an adjunct to other therapies, it should be worn for a maximum of several hours and only after the other treatment is completed. ◯ Have you ever attended a rewarding seminar, been blessed with a spiritual experience, or read an uplifting book, and wished you could hold on longer to their uplifting effects? Wearing Ivorite for several hours after such an experience will help stabilize your uplifted state, thereby helping you to integrate it more profoundly into your being. ◯ If I am used with another earthstone or gemstone, my effects will be canceled out. This will happen if other stones are included with me in the same necklace, or if you wear a necklace of another earthstone or gemstone while I am being worn. ◯ The Earth is different in this regard. It knows how and when to place its attention on me in order to experience my effects. To work for a human being, my vibratory rate must be singled out, and I must be worn alone.

"Among all the gemstones and earthstones we have met so far, this property seems to be unique to Ivorite."

Correct. ◯ Because changes are a barometer of growth, people often perceive them as good things. Indeed, many people look forward to changes. They feel that the more changes they are experiencing in their lives, the faster they are growing. Since life constantly strives for balance and upliftment, the greatest changes occur in the areas where an individual is most immature and inexperienced. ◯ Yet sometimes people do not feel completely ready for certain changes, or they feel overwhelmed by them. When changes seem overwhelming to you, it is probably because they are happening too rapidly and your other aspects are trying to tell you they also need attention and nourishment. This is the time it is wise to wear Ivorite. Then the focus of change will be put "on hold," and your other aspects will be nourished and given what they need. Once the Ivorite is taken off, the original focus of your changes will again have all your attention. This is why it is best not to wear Ivorite continuously for more than one week at a time. Then, when you remove the Ivorite, your body will not be shocked by the effects of change returning to your life.

"Thank you for sharing this information," said Michael.

As you would say, may the blessings be.

"May the blessings be," Michael replied.

I stepped out of the Ivorite vein. Then the Guardian of Sodalight led us up through the rock to the Earth's surface as though we were on an elevator. There we rested under a cloudy sky in a field of waist-high wild grasses. Sodalight encouraged us to relax completely in preparation for our meeting with the Guardian of Opalight.

OPALIGHT

23

RESOLVING KARMA

After we had rested awhile, the Guardian of Sodalight led us into another group of foothills. There we entered a cave through which a cold wind blew. We walked against this wind deeper and deeper into the darkness, with only the faint glow of Sodalight's aura to light our way.

The wind stopped when we reached the entrance to a tunnel. Through the opening I could see that the tunnel was actually a long, wide cavern, brightly illumined by white light. Peering further inside, I saw it was made entirely of Opalight and that the source of the light was the earthstone itself.

Sodalight said that he and Michael were to wait at the entrance and I was to enter the cavern alone. I stepped inside. The light emanating from the cavern began to bounce back and forth between my aura and the cave walls. This process continued until the Opalight seemed to know all it needed to know about me.

I soon noticed that the light was growing dimmer over certain parts of my body. With this observation came the knowledge that the darkest of these areas were associated with situations from my most distant past; lighter areas were related to events of the more recent past. Every part of my body now reflected a different degree of light or shade. Thus, I realized that every part of me had been formed as a result of past conditions. It struck me that, with these variations of light and darkness covering me, I probably looked much like Opalight itself.

Then I heard Michael begin to ask a question, and I felt the answers forming in my heart.

"How does your appearance affect your mission and effects?" Michael inquired.

The light I reflect is the light of Soul. This light shines constantly on the physical body and, as you see, becomes gradated from dark to light in my presence. When I am worn in spherical form, the light of Soul bounces back and forth between the wearer's aura and the Opalight spheres. In the process, I highlight certain areas of the aura and darken others to let Soul know the physical body's condition.

"Why wouldn't Soul already be aware of the physical body's condition?"

As long as Soul wears a physical body, it has the responsibility to care for it. Yet Soul also has a mind. The mind often clouds the truth, because it is one of the mind's duties to challenge Soul's communication with the physical body—and thus ultimately to strengthen that communication.

IDENTIFYING KARMIC CONDITIONS

Every cell in your body and every condition you have has been dictated by the past, by your karma. Consequently, what you do in the present has the power to change the way your conditions and your cells will be in the future. ◌ I can be used as a tool to pinpoint and make you aware of areas of the body with conditions whose causes are most deeply rooted in the past. These conditions are often the most difficult to resolve and are usually the most serious. When you are wearing Opalight, these areas manifest as the darkest areas in your aura. Not all the dark areas I highlight in the aura reflect physical ailments. Some reflect mental or emotional conditions that are or will be affecting the physical body. ◌ I bring your attention to the areas of greatest need. Attention holds the hand of light, and light holds the hand of love. Therefore, when attention is placed on these deeply rooted conditions, light enters the area. Light is the healing force. And when light enters, so does love. Love is like a liquid catalyst that helps changes occur. It is the magic element that allows miracles to happen. ◐ I also highlight the positive qualities and conditions that have grown out of the past. I bring people into the present by helping them release past situations that are holding them back. In this way, I help people feel that things are not as bad as they seem, and this is comforting and encouraging.

FALSE CONCEPTS

When part of the mind has false concepts about the physical body, it inhibits the body from healing and making other positive changes. Consequently, the mind's attitudes about a certain condition could impede Opalight's work. ◐ If false concepts are present, Opalight will quiet the part of the mind that harbors these concepts and prevent them from affecting the physical body. For example, the Opalight might learn from your aura that you have a hip ailment because of a certain situation in the past. Your mind might think there is a different reason for this hip ailment. The Opalight will quiet the part of the mind that harbors the incorrect concept and will work on bringing the truth to your awareness. ◐ The mind is vast, and most people have not yet even imagined its true potential. Therefore, even when I block part of the mind, a vast amount of it remains available. When Opalight blocks the part of the mind inhibiting the body's positive changes, it is hoped that the individual will start to use other, clearer parts of the mind—those that are not limited by false concepts and are more receptive to the truth. Indeed, individuals who wear Opalight and begin to feel their mental energies becoming dulled should try to place more attention on using another part of the mind. Meditation, contemplation, and certain spiritual exercises can help one do this.

RESOLVING KARMA DURING SLEEP

When I am worn in a necklace of spheres, my vibratory rate touches as much of the aura as possible. When my energy has filled the aura, I act like a filter to diffuse, calm, and soothe any harsh or rough vibratory rates contained there. This effect can often help people become calmer and even help them to sleep. Sleep benefits the body and it benefits my work. ☾ In order to make significant changes, people must often resolve past entanglements. This is one of the reasons I help people sleep: much of this resolution is best accomplished in the dream state. When the body is asleep, it is much easier to focus light, and thus love, on the darkest areas of the aura. ☾ As the days pass, one may start to wake up with an almost uncanny knowingness that something has been resolved during the night or that it's time to take a particular action. ☾ For example, you may realize that you need to see a doctor for a certain condition, or you may wake up knowing that a particular condition is related to a past situation. This knowledge will feel so natural that you may not be consciously aware that something from the past has been resolved or that something new has been learned. This knowledge will simply be a part of you. Therefore, one should at least wear Opalight to sleep. ☾ Because of my ability to help people sleep, I can be an effective aid for insomnia. Be aware, however, that if the insomnia is caused by an external substance—such as drugs, caffeine, certain foods, or chemicals—I can do little to assist. Artificial stimulants supersede the calming and soothing qualities I offer. I can be very helpful, on the other hand, if you cannot sleep because of natural causes. Then my calming effect will often be just powerful enough to allow your own natural sleep abilities to take over. ☾ I bring light, love, and attention to areas of need. Yet that is where I stop. If you insist on not seeing what I have illuminated, I cannot convince you to look. Nevertheless, as long as Opalight is worn, I will continue to shine my light on and thus draw attention to those areas. ☉ Although my vibratory rate is still an essential piece of the Earth's living puzzle, my mission and effects are focused primarily on people. One might think that I could do much good for the Earth by allowing it to realize its own limitations and helping it overcome them, but this work is done more effectively by other gemstones. Many of these gemstones are not yet available to human beings. I am, and I can do this work for people. ☉ Do not underestimate the power of the earthstones, though you may think of us as rocks and not true crystals. We are particularly powerful when fashioned into spheres and worn by human beings. We become enlivened by people's auras. ☉ My work is simple and basic. I work for everyone in the same way, because my mission is the same for everyone. Yet, although my mission never changes, different individuals may experience different effects when they wear me. This is true of any gemstone, earthstone, or oceanstone. Our missions and purposes reflect who we are. How we are perceived may be as varied as the individuals who perceive us. It is the same with you: you are who you are, but everyone you meet has a different perception of who you are and what you do. ☉ You shall meet the Guardian of Riverstone next. Good night, and farewell.

Opalight withdrew from my aura, and I ambled out of the cavern feeling as though I had just awakened from a good night's sleep. Then I joined Michael and the Guardian of Sodalight in the adjacent passageway.

RIVERSTONE

24

ACCELERATING CHANGE

"Are you ready to meet the Guardian of Riverstone?" asked Sodalight.

"Yes," replied Michael and I, both eager for another adventure. We were not disappointed, for moments later the cave floor lost its solidity, and we began to sink into the Earth. I don't know how deep we sank, but miles of rock seemed to pass by us. I noticed that the pressure increased and the space between the Earth's atoms seemed to decrease as we moved. We stopped when our feet reached a layer of rock saturated with flowing water.

"We will meet the Guardian of Riverstone within this watery rock," said Sodalight. Again we started to sink, this time into the wet stone. As we entered it, I sensed a quickening throughout my body as the energy flows in every one of my cells sped up. At the same time, my cells became highly impressionable. Then I put aside all thoughts and opened my heart for the words of Riverstone's Guardian.

I can only be with you for a short time. As the Guardian of Riverstone, it is my responsibility to keep my attention on the wild energy and the force of change I bring. I must constantly keep up with the changes I initiate. ◌ My purpose is for the Earth, and it is for the Earth that I have my life. It is only when my rock is shaped into spheres and worn by man or woman that I can affect the human being in a way similar to that in which I affect the Earth. ◌ I exist deep beneath the surface, although the movement and upheavals experienced by the Earth also allow some Riverstone to come to the surface. I do my greatest work for the planet at various depths beneath the surface. Although I am scattered throughout the planet, I am not as abundant as I might seem. It is not necessary that I be plentiful, because I am powerful. When I am taken out of the Earth, I no longer work with the planet.

THE POWER OF MOVING WATER

A charge runs through Riverstone, attracting energy and then causing it to flow and move. Like wild, unbridled horses, the energy of Riverstone races in every direction. ◌ I do not generate energy within myself. Instead, I absorb a type of energy released by moving water. Within Riverstone, this energy moves from one molecule to the next. As it does, it is transformed, increasing in velocity, strength, and power. ◌ My energy fuels change. When another rock, crystal, or element needs my energy to initiate a change, it creates a magnetic attraction. I respond by transmitting energy to it. This enlivens the rock or crystal and enables it to carry out its mission. ◌ The movement of my energy is like that of an airplane, which gains speed and momentum on the runway and then takes off into the air. My energy gains momentum as it flows from one molecule of Riverstone to the next until it is launched into the planet. The longer the runway is, the more speed an airplane can gather before it takes off. For a similar reason, you will find that Riverstone exists in long veins. My energy is released either at the end of a vein or somewhere along the vein where it is needed. ○ You know that change is necessary for growth, and growth is necessary for life. The life energy of a planet could easily become stagnant and unchanging. I prevent this from happening. Among other things, my energy assists in the movement of the plates of the Earth's crust. Surely you know that the energy that causes the continents to move against each other must come from somewhere. It comes from the living rock that lies beneath the planet's surface.

ACCELERATING CHANGE

I can be particularly powerful for the human being, because human beings are made mostly of water. In the human being, I have a vast source of potential energy to tap into and transform. ○ Since the body is surrounded by an aura rather than rock, it is to the aura that I give my energy. When you wear a strand of Riverstone spheres around your neck, my energy focuses on exciting your entire aura. ○ When I energize the aura, the result is that everything—including what you call karma—is sped up. Whatever mode of activity the body is experiencing is accelerated. If the body is in a cleansing mode, the cleansing is sped up; if the body is in a specific, focused healing mode, the healing is accelerated. You must be careful, however, when using Riverstone, because I can also speed up the vibratory rate of a disease. Therefore, the focus of the healing mode must be clear and specific. ○ When I am worn, the vibratory rate of every cell in your body speeds up. This does not change the direction of the body's vortices of energy, nor does it increase your metabolic rate. It simply leads to a rise in your overall vibratory rate, and this causes overall changes in the body.

Michael needed clarification. "Are you saying that one's movement in a certain direction will speed up, so that the need for a change in direction will occur sooner? Do you also mean that one will resolve a situation or move through an experience more quickly?"

Yes, I mean both those things. How quickly these effects are produced depends on how long the Riverstone is worn. It also depends on how disciplined you are in focusing on the change you desire. The results of wearing Riverstone with a focus are different from those of wearing it without one.

FOCUSING CHANGE

When I say wearing Riverstone "without a focus," I mean wearing it with no direction, goal, or dream for your life in mind. It could also mean wearing it with no other influence of the Earth—that is, no other metal, gemstone, or earthstone. No focus to your changes means that your life is continuing as usual. You wake up in the morning, go to work during the day, come home in the evening, and fall asleep at night. ◐ If you wear Riverstone without a focus, undirected changes will occur and confusion will result. These undirected changes might be in your outlook, attitudes, feelings, physical circumstances, or in the way you react to certain stimuli. Wearing Riverstone this way might be helpful, however, if you need a tool to help you get out of a rut or out of a situation that is preventing you from achieving a goal. Actually, this intention itself would provide a focus. ◐ I do not know how deeply into the aura Riverstone's energy goes, nor do I know whether it stops at the emotional or mental level. As soon as the Riverstone is removed, the force behind the changes stops. ◐ When Riverstone is worn with a particular focus, it can be an especially helpful tool. This might involve wearing it with another element, earthstone, or gemstone somewhere on your body. I'll use gold as an example. If you wore Riverstone at the same time you wore a gold ring, I would stir up your gold consciousness. Gold's effects on your body might become more acute and therefore more obvious to you. In this way, I would help you move through the experiences offered by the vibratory rate of gold. ◐ This effect also occurs when you wear me with any other gemstone. I can help you move more swiftly through the experiences or changes characteristic of that particular gem. For example, if the gemstone has a specific healing effect, this effect is accelerated. If the gemstone has a balancing effect, I hasten the movement toward balance. ◐ Be aware, however, that as your life speeds up, it might seem to go further out of balance. This may appear to contradict what I have described as my effects, but it really doesn't. Actually, you will be letting go of the things creating the imbalance at a much faster rate. ◐ If you enjoy meditation or spiritual contemplation, you can wear Riverstone around your neck either during your quiet time or just beforehand. During spiritual practice, you focus on the spirituality within you, and this is indeed a strong focus. ◐ When I am used as an adjunct to meditation or contemplation, your whole being becomes energized. Then, I help you make the changes that will lead to greater spiritual experiences. Often it is physical blockages that prevent people from placing their attention more fully on their inner goals—yes, physical blockages. My action, plus your inward focus of attention, will help break up, change, and resolve anything obstructing your focus. This in turn will help you focus more completely. ◐ The use of Riverstone in spherical form is just an example of human beings' ingenuity and resourcefulness. It is wise to look to the Earth, which gives you life, for the tools to master life or take greater control of it. You and your fellow human beings are intelligent. I am sure you will discover many ways to use a tool like Riverstone. You are limited only by your degree of resourcefulness. ◐ You now know my basic nature and you have been given some examples of how I work. Use me for the tool I am. I am very powerful when I am in spherical form and awakened by a human being's or an animal's aura. ☉ Now that you know me, use me with respect and responsibility. That is all.

"Thank you," said Michael.

We were lifted out of the watery rock and slowly rose to the surface. Then the Guardian of Sodalight suggested we rest in the bright sunshine. We felt revitalized and refreshed by the sun's warm, life-giving rays. Yet we did not relax altogether, for we were aware that our mission was not complete. Our attention had turned to Rhodonite and the knowledge we would gain from its Guardian.

RHODONITE

25

STABILIZING THE EMOTIONS

After we had rested and refreshed ourselves, we walked to the base of a low cliff. There Sodalight pointed out the veins of a pink and black rock within the cliff walls. He called this rock Rhodonite. As we studied the veins, wondering how they had been formed, I sensed that someone was approaching.

Greetings, said the Guardian of Rhodonite.

The individual before us was small, no more than five feet tall. Because of the great amount of energy surrounding the Guardian, I could not clearly see any features or determine whether this individual was male or female. The Guardian faced me and sat down on the ground. I sensed that I should sit nearby, so I moved closer. A moment later, I found myself sitting in the Guardian of Rhodonite's aura.

Shall we begin?

"Yes. Will you tell us of your mission for the Earth and for the human being?"

UPLIFTING THE PHYSICAL

My mission for the Earth is to draw the pink ray to the rock of the planet. The pink ray is the color ray that comes from the emotional plane. This color represents and draws to itself higher vibratory rates than those of the physical level. As this higher vibratory rate is called to the physical, an upliftment occurs. This upliftment is slow, steady, and gradual. ○ All living things are continually growing and evolving. I help the Earth grow by drawing its physical vibratory rate toward the higher vibratory rate represented by the pink color ray. This changes the Earth's patterns into new ones reflecting a higher state of consciousness. ○ When human beings wear Rhodonite in spherical form, my effects on my wearers are similar to my effects on the Earth. I give gradual, steady upliftment to the physical body and emotions. I also give human beings a strong foundation. Because I am of the Earth, I provide a sense of solidity and security, qualities of the planet. The human vibratory rate evolves much more quickly toward higher states of consciousness; therefore, I work more rapidly for human beings than I do for the Earth. ○ I quickly draw people away from a strictly physical point of view to a more encompassing one. I do this by raising the individual's vibratory rate to the emotional level. As a result of my work, the individual's emotions are rearranged: any emotions that are scattered, out of balance, or undefined are brought into greater order and become more grounded. This happens because unbalanced emotions are not in harmony with Rhodonite; indeed, one cannot wear Rhodonite and continue to have emotional im-balances. As a result of all these changes, the individual gains a more stable foundation. ○ Gemstones are tools. They will produce their effects whether or not the wearer realizes what those effects are. However, if the wearer recognizes a gemstone's abilities and is aware of what it can be used for, it will be able to work with more focus, depth, and energy. My uplifting effect on the physical body, which parallels my effect on the Earth, occurs regardless of whether the individual is aware of it. However, my effect of soothing the emotions in order to create a strong emotional foundation occurs only to the degree that the person is aware of, understands, and is open to this effect. ◌ The speed at which my effect on the emotions occurs depends on how willing the wearer is to allow me to do my work and to accept the changes I bring. You see, I make fundamental changes.

REBUILDING YOUR EMOTIONAL FOUNDATION

Each emotional experience you have is like a brick in your emotional foundation. For each brick, there is an optimal place for it to be laid in the foundation. In this place, it contributes most to the foundation's stability. Emotional imbalances occur when "bricks" are not laid in their proper places. ◌ Therefore, if you have emotional imbalances and you wish to create a more solid emotional foundation, some of your out-of-place bricks will have to be moved. You will also have to fill some holes or make some bricks fit more tightly. And, of course, before you move the bricks to their optimal places, you will have to learn which of them are out of place. This is what I mean when I say that Rhodonite makes fundamental changes. ◌ The rebuilding of an emotional foundation is an ongoing process because people are constantly growing—physically, emotionally, mentally, and spiritually. As long as Rhodonite is worn, the wearer will be able to place any new emotional experiences in the optimal place in his or her emotional foundation. ◌ For those who are emotionally unstable, I work on the scrambled pieces of the emotional puzzle that are causing the emotional imbalance and instability. I read just these pieces so that each one fits better in the emotional puzzle. Once greater emotional stability is attained, the person can take further steps toward emotional well-being by wearing a necklace of Roselle, Ruby, or Rhodocrosite in addition to the Rhodonite necklace. The Rhodonite will help the person maintain stability as he or she experiences the changes these other gems initiate. ◌ It takes several minutes for Rhodonite to become charged by the aura. After that, my effects continue to build for as long as I am worn. Wearing a necklace of 8-mm or 10-mm Rhodonite spheres day and night for a minimum of three weeks will probably allow enough time for some emotional rearranging to occur. It may at least provide you with enough time to get to know your emotions well enough to remain somewhat balanced during an emotional trauma—although, to do so, you must also be wearing Rhodonite during the traumatic experience.

"Are there specific therapies you can offer?" Michael asked.

When worn around the neck, Rhodonite touches the core of your being and is in the best position to access your emotional aura. This is also the best place to wear Rhodonite to fulfill its tendency to call a higher vibratory rate to the physical body. ◌ My mission does not include working on specific parts of the physical body. However, because I have a specific vibratory rate, I am sure Rhodonite will have an effect if placed anywhere on the body. That effect will probably vary from one individual to the next.

"Do you see your mission evolving in the future?"

The Earth moves very slowly in the upliftment of its physical matter. I shall be here a long time, providing the planet's physical matter with a magnetic pull toward a higher state of consciousness. I work on the physical molecules themselves. I teach or remind them that something greater than the physical exists. ◌ The more that

Rhodonite is worn by people, the more that I, as the Guardian of Rhodonite, will understand how I can assist them. My primary mission is for the Earth. It is only when I am fashioned into spheres that I can benefit people. ◯ The next Guardian you shall meet is responsible for an earthstone with properties very different from mine or from those of the other gemstones whose Guardians you have met so far. This is the earthstone you know as Malachite. Spirit itself will lead you to Malachite's Guardian. The Guardian of Sodalight has completed his mission with you.

"Thank you for taking the time to share of yourself. You honor us with your presence," said Michael.

The honor is mine.

Then the Guardian of Rhodonite simply vanished. One moment I was inside the Guardian's aura, and the next I was alone with Michael, the Guardian of Sodalight, and the rock with the Rhodonite veins.

Michael and I each embraced the Guardian of Sodalight. Then we thanked him for guiding us into the Earth and for introducing us to many of the Earthstone Guardians. Now we would again look to Spirit as our only guide. My intuition told me that even more profound information about our planet was about to be shared.

MALACHITE

26

HARMONIZING THE BODY

As I turned my attention inward, I became caught up in a wave-like, rhythmic motion that flowed first down and then up my body. After several repetitions of this movement, the upward wave did not stop at the top of my head but kept going. I rode with it farther and farther upward until I found myself hovering in space and looking down upon the Earth.

There I met Michael and the formless Guardian of Malachite. The Guardian had manifested as a vortex of energy. It was easy for me simply to move into this vortex.

You have met me high above the Earth, *the Guardian began,* so that we may have a greater view of the planet and of my function for the Earth. When a greater picture of the whole is seen, a more complete understanding can be gained.

A LIVING LIBRARY

Briefly, my purpose is to keep records of information about the Earth. ○ I was not brought to Earth, nor did I form as the planet formed. A certain race of beings—and I believe you have heard about them from other Gemstone Guardians—took materials already existing on the planet to form Malachite. ○ Remember that one of the main duties of these beings is to keep records about the planets. These records include information about a planet's evolution and the life which inhabits the planet, be it mineral, plant, animal, or human. These beings record how these life forms interact both with each other and with the planet. Some of these records are kept on the planet, some are taken with these beings, and some are both kept on the planet and taken away. ○ Malachite was formed to be the storehouse of information about the Earth. In addition to information about the Earth's life forms, Malachite stores data about the mechanical workings of the planet itself, as well as the planet's relationship to its solar system, moon, sun, and to a lesser extent, the galaxy to which it belongs. ○ Not just any rock can be planted on a planet and expected to keep information specific to that planet. For the information to be accurate, the substance that contains it must be formed specifically from the elements of the planet. Therefore, Malachite is not found in any other place except the Earth. Each living planet has its own particular rock for containing information about that planet. ○ Information can also be stored in Quartz. However, how I store information and the kind of information I store is different from that stored by Quartz. Almost anything you can imagine can be stored in Quartz, including dreams, ideas, formulas, and even illnesses. I have been programmed to gather information about the Earth. I can only accept and store information I have gathered from the planet or that is given to me by the race of people who created Malachite.

MALACHITE'S WAVES

The wave-like motions you experienced just before meeting me are the key to the way I gather information. The black or dark green bands characteristic of my appearance initiate these waves. To explain the mechanics of how my wave motions collect information about the planet, I will speak simply and in illustrative terms. ◌ Each wave motion, or frequency, that I send into the Earth is tagged with a certain date but is otherwise free of information. As it travels through the Earth, it gathers information. When it returns to the Malachite, the information is deposited and cataloged. ◌ My waves travel in a relatively straight line and perpendicular to the black Malachite bands that send them. They bounce back into the Earth whenever they reach the Earth's surface. For example, waves that originated from Malachite in the ground under Arizona might bounce off the underside of the Earth's surface in China and flow back into the Earth. Then they might bounce off the surface some where in Antarctica, and later off the surface in Germany, before returning to a Malachite deposit somewhere else on the planet. ◌ Eventually the waves will reach some Malachite somewhere, because there is an attraction between Malachite and the wave frequencies it emanates. It doesn't matter whether the wave frequencies return to the Malachite from which they originated—in this example, to Arizona—or to some other piece of Malachite. ◌ There may be as many as ten million pieces of Malachite scattered throughout the planet; yet each of these pieces is part of the one body of Malachite, which in a way is me, the Guardian of Malachite. In this way, Malachite is different from people, animals, or plants: in order for them to maintain life, all of their cells must be attached to each other. Malachite need only be somewhere in the Earth to be part of the one living being that is Malachite.

"If a wave motion originates in Arizona and reaches Malachite in Canada, would the Arizona Malachite know the information deposited in the Canadian Malachite?"

When a wave frequency is received, the date and whatever information it has collected is logged in. This information is in the form of vibratory rate patterns. The Malachite in Arizona is told, "Your wave emanation has returned. You no longer need to attract that frequency. It came home in Canada, and we have received its information." ◌ By the way, you have been using the words "vibratory rate," "frequency," and "energy" synonymously, when in fact they are different—at least as far as I am concerned. ◌ Remember that the Malachite in Arizona is a part of the whole body of Malachite. On the physical level, it does not necessarily contain the information deposited in Canada. Yet, one can access from any single piece of Malachite all the information contained by Malachite everywhere. This can be compared to the way each cell of the human body contains genetic information about the entire body. Of course, this is an analogy, intended only to help you understand how the whole of something can be reflected in just one part of it.

"Can you tell us how Malachite works with people?" Michael asked.

In order for Malachite to work for human beings, it must be cut into spherical form. When a human being holds an uncut rock of Malachite, it will do practically nothing for the person. ◌ Now, if one were to place that Malachite rock in a potted plant, it would begin to send wave emanations through the soil contained within the pot. And, if one buried the Malachite rock outdoors in the Earth, it would work for the planet as though it had never been harvested. ◌ When Malachite spheres are worn and not bound by metal, something magical happens between the Malachite and the human being. Of course, something magical happens when any therapeutic earthstone or gemstone in spherical form is worn. I don't know whether you will ever understand all the mechanics of why the spherical form can touch a human being so deeply and in a way no other shape can. I am somewhat surprised that your people are ready for knowledge of the power of the sphere. Spirit, which orchestrates all life, including that of gemstones, must have a reason for deeming your people ready and bringing them knowledge of the spherical form. ◌ Malachite's spheres start to produce effects when they are awakened by the wearer's aura. Then Malachite's waves move down and up, down and up the body in a soothing, rhythmic flow. Each time they pass the Malachite spheres being worn, the waves deposit information.

THE BODY'S MUSIC

To better understand how Malachite works with human beings, you must understand more about harmony and disharmony. Looking at these concepts in musical terms may help. ◌ The C-major chord is a simple, harmonious chord which consists of three notes: C, E, and G. When these three notes are played, the resulting chord is one that is pleasing to the ear because it is in harmony. Disharmony occurs when notes that do not belong in the same chord are played at the same time. If, for example, instead of a C note, an F note is played with the E and G notes, disharmony results. ◌ Now, it is interesting to speculate about what would happen if the notes themselves could hear each other play. If the notes were aware of each other, and the F, E, and G notes were played, the notes might recognize that they weren't in harmony with each other. Then, rather than the F note, perhaps the C note would be played, and the harmonious C-major chord would be produced. ◌ Physical disharmony occurs when parts of the body do not know what other parts of the body are doing. It's as though parts of the body cannot hear which "notes" other parts are playing. Therefore, the body has no awareness that disharmony exists. ☉ For example, if your ankles are playing a C note, your knees are playing an E note, and your hips are playing a G note, you will be able to walk smoothly because your legs are working in harmony. However, if your ankle starts to play an F note instead of a C note, disharmony will result. Then, if you tried to walk, you might feel discomfort or pain. ☉ What I want to illustrate is that, if each part of your body doesn't work well with some or all of the others, or if each part doesn't know what the other parts are doing, it is easy for disharmonies to develop. When a certain part of your body plays a note that is out of harmony with the rest of the body, your body may be unaware of the resulting disharmony—and therefore make no effort to prevent or correct it. If this disharmonious note continues to be played, the disharmony will develop into pain or disease.

HARMONIZING THE BODY

When a strand of Malachite spheres is worn, the Malachite "hears" the disharmonious notes in the body that your body doesn't hear. The first result of the Malachite wave frequencies moving down and up the body is that, in effect, the "volume" is turned up. This allows your body to hear the disharmonious chords. Its reaction may then be: "Oh, that sounds awful! Ankle, stop playing the F note! You should be playing a C note instead." ☉ When you have been wearing Malachite long enough, you may begin to hear the body's harmonious music. Although it will be less pleasing, you may also hear the body's disharmonious music. Depending on how many disharmonies the body has, it may take several weeks or months for the ability to hear this music to unfold. Yet, even if you don't hear music, you may come to a great knowingness and understanding of your physical condition. You may even come to realize that there is potential for healing in areas where you thought health was no longer possible. All this will result from all parts of the body becoming aware of all other parts. ○ Malachite helps every cell of the body know every other cell, just as every little piece of Malachite on this planet knows every other piece. I find it interesting that, unlike human cells, my "cells" are not all touching each other, and yet I know myself better than most human beings know themselves. I can teach your cells how to know every other cell in your body, just as eons ago when Malachite was first formed, Malachite was taught how each of its cells could communicate with all the others. ○ When one part of the body knows what is happening in another part, it is much easier for the body to call all its forces together to combat a disease. Let's say, for example, that your liver has a tumor tucked away in it. Even if this tumor becomes malignant, the rest of your body may have no idea it is there. (I am not sure exactly why physical bodies often tuck harmful things away. Perhaps as the owner of your liver, your tumor, and the conditions which gave you the tumor, you don't want to know that certain actions of yours have resulted in such a disease.) Since your mind is not aware of it, the majority of your physical body will be unaware of it too. If you don't want to face the truth, neither will your physical body. ○ In this situation, I can help your physical body discover the tumor in your liver. I will let every cell of the body know what is happening in every other cell. Then, if the cells find a tumor hidden in your liver, your body's natural survival mechanism will call on your immune system, eliminative organs, and whatever other systems the body needs in order to start to work on that tumor. ○ This whole process will be greatly facilitated if you are willing to take responsibility for the circumstances that created the tumor. If you say, "Well, I didn't create the tumor. I was exposed to some chemical at work, so it wasn't my fault. It was my employer's fault," you may still have issues to resolve and take responsibility for. Have you let go of your anger toward your employer? Have you forgiven your employer? Are you willing to accept the lessons this experience is giving you, and are you now willing to take the steps to resolve it? Answering each of these questions positively and with honesty is one way of taking responsibility. ○ Individuals who don't want to know that there may be tumors lurking in their livers and those who don't want to be in harmony within themselves will not want to wear Malachite. ○ Everyone who wears Malachite experiences different effects. This is because the side effects of my wave-like motion are felt in so many different ways. In some people, Malachite breaks up stagnant fluids and releases congestion; in some it increases circulation; and in others it opens chakras. Some people say it opens the third eye, and they give credit to Malachite for the spiritual experiences that result. Malachite's wave-like motion simply stirs and breaks up anything in the way of establishing and increasing harmony throughout the body. ○ Indeed, Malachite's goal is to have every cell in the body playing the note of a harmonious chord. The music emanating from one who has worn Malachite spheres for a long time is beautiful. This music is the vibratory rate of harmony expressing itself in sound. When all the cells are in harmony, no note cancels out or dampens the sound of any other note. The individual rings with music. ○ If you possessed a microphone that amplifies the sounds of your body, after wearing Malachite for one month, you would hear some parts of the body playing harmonious chords and others playing disharmonious ones; this is because some parts of the body harmonize more swiftly than others when Malachite is worn. There might also be some parts of the body from which you would hear no music at all. In these areas, the notes would be canceling each other out. ○ To hear discordant music is better than to hear no music at all. Once the body is aware of discordant music, it does everything it can to make that discordant music harmonious. The parts of the body where no music is heard are the ones you should worry about, because the body is still unaware that disharmony exists there. ☾ I have mentioned the microphone and a potential application of it to hint at what is to come. This microphone is a fundamental diagnostic tool that already exists, though perhaps not yet on this planet. With this microphone, you can hear the music emanating from various parts of the body. For example, it lets you hear the change in the stomach's music after you have eaten something that caused disharmony there. ☾ Once you hear the disharmonious music your body is singing, you may not want to eat the food that caused the disharmony. And once you hear how beautiful the body can sound when it is working in harmony with itself, you will be inspired.

ACCESSING PLANETARY INFORMATION

"Can you tell us how human beings can learn about our planet from Malachite?"

So, you wish to know how to access the information stored in Malachite. As masters of your planet—that is, if you assume mastery of your planet—you have the right to this information. At this time, you Earth people are still slaves to your planet and slaves to your limited concepts about your relationships with other planets in the solar system and galaxy. ☾ For some reason, many people in power on Earth feel that the general public cannot handle certain truths that are already known. These truths concern your planet, your moon, Mars, and the other planets in your solar system, as well as visitors from other planets. Knowledge is power—and, in this case, power is knowledge kept from the masses. As we hover here between the moon and the Earth with the sun behind us, I will tell you that the public is being told only a watered-down fraction of what is already known. ☾ People pray for this information, and they are ready for it. Many are asking individuals from beyond the Earth for this information. Hence, much information about the planets, the moon, and the solar system is being given through individuals who "channel" beings from other places and other times. Unfortunately, much of this information is inaccurate. If the people in power would realize that the masses are ready for this information, and if they would share it, your people would not be running the risk of receiving incorrect information. ○ The individual from Planet X who communicates through one of your people might have the best intentions and, in fact, might give you accurate information about Planet X. However, the laws of Planet X are not necessarily the laws that govern planet Earth. Therefore, if you utilize some of this technological information, you may waste a good deal of money, time, and perhaps even lives. ○ People on your planet seem to enjoy authority, especially when it comes from a distant source. For Earth humans, the farther away an individual comes from, the more authority that individual has. It doesn't matter whether this person comes from another country, planet, or far away in time. ○ The Earth is not what it was during the Age of Atlantis— not by any means. The world has changed considerably. Since Atlantis, crystals and minerals have been planted, vibratory rates have changed, people's consciousness has risen, weather patterns and elements in the atmosphere have changed, and the Earth's polarities, magnetic lines, and power points have shifted. The Earth is in many ways a different planet from what it was during the Age of Atlantis. ○ If you want to know about the workings of your planet, do not communicate with an individual from Planet X who may have only visited the Earth once or twice. Do not communicate with someone from ancient Atlantis if you want to know about the planet today. If you want information about the Earth, you need not look beyond your planet to find a wealth of information beyond your wildest dreams. The information is here. It is within the planet. It is within Malachite.

"When you spoke of people in power withholding information, were you referring to scientists or to people in government?"

Your scientists, your military, and your government have collected more information about things such as the moon and extraterrestrials than you might think. However, since they are reluctant to share this information with the rest of the people on the planet, there are other ways to obtain it. It can be obtained from Malachite. ◯ The longer people wear Malachite, and the more its waves move down and up the body, the more prepared people will be to accept the information contained within the Malachite. By using Malachite in a specific way, people can tap this information.*

EXTRATERRESTRIALS AND MALACHITE

"I have heard that extraterrestrials have a special interest in Malachite. Is this true and, if so, can you tell us why?" inquired Michael.

Every living planet has a certain rock which stores information about it, like Malachite does for the Earth. Malachite is special, because it is like a treasure chest with no lock. One has only to open the lid. I do not know why this is so. The technique for accessing my information is simple and remarkably easy, and you need no special technology to practice it. Those who meditate or perform spiritual exercises have already developed the part of the brain that accesses this information most accurately; therefore, they will have the most success. Yet anyone can develop this ability. ◯ Although each planet in the physical universe has its idiosyncrasies, each also has much in common with other planets, especially those with similar mineral contents. Quartz-based planets and their people

---

* See MICHAEL KATZ, *Gemisphere Luminary Therapy Guide*
FOR A TECHNIQUE TO ACCESS PLANETARY INFORMATION FROM MALACHITE.

have an affinity with the Earth like no others. It is only natural that the people from these Quartz-based planets would want an easy way to access information about another Quartz-based planet. ◌ Extraterrestrials particularly desire freshly mined Malachite. This is because I can be contaminated after I am mined. The patterns of information I store can be disrupted by nuclear radiation in the atmosphere. My ability to absorb radiation does have some benefit, in that Malachite spheres will absorb harmful radiation from a wearer's aura. Unfortunately, when the radiation is absorbed, the information contained in the Malachite is altered.

"Is information lost when spheres are cut from the Malachite rock?"

No, because the information is contained within my crystalline matrix. Remember, you can extract all of Malachite's information from any of its pieces, just as you can find genetic information about the entire body in each of its cells.

"Why do you think we are receiving this information now?" Michael asked.

Are carpenters considered master carpenters before they have learned how to use all the tools of carpentry? No. People are now ready to learn to use some of the tools that will help them attain greater mastery of their lives on Earth. I think this is one of the reasons you are interviewing the Gemstone Guardians. ◌ The gemstones and earthstones are perhaps the most powerful tools you have on this planet. We are not simple tools—we are complex. We are not just the hammers and the screwdrivers—we are sophisticated power tools. To use us to our maximum potential, our users must possess intelligence, knowledge, resourcefulness, and creativity. ◌ Before we close, I would like to clarify why Malachite exists at all. Why does the Earth need a rock containing so much information about itself, its history, how it works, and how it interacts with life and the solar system? It is a spiritual law that every living planet that supports life must have a method for keeping records about itself. It is a rule of the game. ◌ Libraries have always been treasured. I am like a library. Therefore, I am a treasure of your planet in a way that no other gemstone is a treasure. Now that you know more about me, you can open the treasure chest and partake of what is inside. Those who do so are indeed honored and blessed, for they will have taken the steps to accept what is available and what, in fact, has already been given to them. I say they are blessed, because not everyone will have the strength to accept the information Malachite has to offer. ◌ It is an honor to be interviewed and to have the opportunity to share information about Malachite. Apparently, it is time that some truths about Malachite be known and that instructions for receiving greater truths be given. ◌ That is all.

"May the blessings be," said Michael.

May the blessings be.

The wave-like emanations flowing within my body stopped, and I found myself looking down through my own eyes at the planet Earth. The freedom of being in space without a spaceship and without even a space suit was exhilarating. I felt like flying around the moon to learn for myself the secrets that Malachite said are being kept from the people. Alas, that adventure will have to wait for the telling of another story.

I prepared to meet the Guardian of Lapis Lazuli and once again found myself
hovering in space and looking down on the Earth. Michael, as usual, was
at my side.

As we watched the Earth below, the light illuminating the planet began to bend. It
was as though the Earth's image was printed on transparent paper, and some giant
unseen hand was folding the paper over and over again. Paradoxically, no matter
how many times it was folded, the Earth's image remained the same size. Then it
came to me that I was watching the planet move backward in time.

Suddenly I was back on the Earth. In front of me loomed a massive gold throne.
On it sat a middle-aged man wearing a gold crown and blue and gold robes.
His eyes were as royal blue as his garments.

I am the Guardian of Lapis Lazuli. I brought you to this time in history so you could see it was my power that gave all the kings of this era their power. I was a gemstone like no other. ☉ We will remain in this time in history until I have answered your questions about the past. When we are done, we shall unfold time and return to the point from which we started. Then we will speak of the present and of the future. ☉ I do not have a specific purpose or mission, either for the Earth or for its people. This is because I was not brought here to have a particular effect. ☉ I was given to your planet in exchange for a large quantity of something that was taken from the Earth. I do not know what I was exchanged for. I do know that the people living on the Earth at that time had nothing to do with the exchange. Furthermore, those who made this exchange had no idea that what they were giving to the Earth would become so powerful. They did not know that when the Lapis Lazuli was planted in the Earth, the planet's vibratory rate would make the Lapis very potent. ☉ Those who left the Lapis have never returned to your planet. If they had, they might have been surprised at the way Lapis reacted to the Earth's atmosphere and at the powerful effects it had on the people who wore it. ☉ Lapis Lazuli is not plentiful in the physical universe. However, it is abundant on a few planets, including the one from which I come. Interestingly, Lapis reacts quite differently to each planet, whether it is brought there or grows there naturally. ☉ You may wonder why so many crystals have been planted on the Earth. Yet it's not surprising when you consider how many races of people are comfortable with and adept at interplanetary travel. Trade creates a diversity among planets, just as it does among the nations of the Earth. For example, because of such trade, the Japanese eat hamburgers and wear blue jeans, and Americans eat sushi and drive Japanese cars.

"Do you know when Lapis was brought here?" Michael asked.

It was during the Age of Atlantis. However, my greatest strength was realized during the Egyptian era. Although Earth people today associate Lapis with Egypt, I was used in many places on the planet.

THE EGYPTIAN ERA

"What effects did you have on the Earth and its people during the Egyptian era?"

My vibratory rate acts like a stimulant for the Earth. I send waves of stimulation through the channels of the Earth to the various power points, charging them in the process. ○ I do the same thing for the physical bodies of human beings: I stimulate their channels and power points. You call the body's channels "energy meridians," and you call its power points "acupuncture points" and "chakras." ○ During my prime, this stimulation of the meridians and chakras was strong and its effects were profound. The fact that my energy flooded every chakra appeared to defy the laws of nature, and my energy gave those who wore me the awareness of how they could further bend those laws. ○ Particularly profound was the effect I had when my energy opened the higher chakras. The individuals of that time were not accustomed to having their higher chakras opened and stimulated. These people were more physically oriented. Their attention was rooted in the Earth, and they drew most of their energy from their lower chakras. The powers they experienced when their higher chakras were opened were great. Indeed, it gave them tremendous power over the minds of those who did not possess Lapis Lazuli and over many natural forces such as gravity.

"Did Lapis have anything to do with the building of the pyramids of Egypt?"

Although Lapis was not directly involved, many of the architectural feats accomplished during the Egyptian era could not have been done without my presence. Remember, I gave those who wore Lapis Lazuli physical, emotional, mental, and spiritual powers. I was worn by the royalty. The powers I granted made the royalty seem like gods to the people who did not wear Lapis. ◌ Lapis gave its wearers the awareness, understanding, and ability to accept the presence of interplanetary visitors. These visitors helped them build the pyramids. Without Lapis, leaders of the time would not have been able to accept what the extraterrestrials wished to build on their land. ◌ The pyramids were built for many reasons, and they had multiple functions. In them were burial chambers and places for initiations and secret classes. There were also rooms where energies converged in such a way that great healings and transformations could occur. These particular rooms also served as terminals where people could be transported to other places, not only in consciousness but physically as well.

"Do you mean that people could be transported to other places on this planet or to other planets?" Michael asked.

Both. This transportation was mostly enjoyed by the royalty, who often made a game of transporting themselves from one pyramid to another. However, it was also practiced for the beneficial effects of the expanded state of awareness gained when they entered one pyramid and exited another.

"I can see how that could change one's concepts."

Exactly, and shatter one's limitations.

"Can this still be done in the Egyptian pyramids?"

The pyramids have been destroyed. They're not what they once were.

"Can any pyramid be used for transportation?" Michael pursued.

Only if the transportation is done on the level of consciousness. It was not just the shape of the Egyptian pyramids and the way the energies flowed around them that allowed physical transportation to occur. Layers of special material were laid beneath the transportation chambers. This material played with the forces of gravity and magnetism. There were other forces involved too, but we are not here to talk about the pyramids. ◌ People enjoy hearing about the past. However, the past cannot be accurately verified. My effects in the present can be verified, either scientifically or through direct personal experience.

"Shall we return to the present?" suggested Michael.

Yes.

Instantly we found ourselves hovering over the Earth again. This time the Earth's image began to open up and unfold. When it was finished, I noticed that some geographical changes had taken place.

HARMONIZING HEART AND MIND

Since the Egyptian era, my energy has waned considerably. Today my stimulating effects on the Earth have become mild. Instead of affecting the entire planet, I can only stimulate the areas within a certain radius of where I am found. My effect on people's meridians and chakras is also a fraction of what it used to be. Now my focus is primarily on the heart, throat, brow, and crown chakras. ◌ Those who are attracted to Lapis are attracted strongly. The energy I radiate can touch people very deeply. It touches them through the heart and the mind. Lapis can help people experience the energy and power they possess within. This power is greatest when one's heart energy combines with one's mental energy—in other words, when the emotional and mental aspects are working in harmony and are not at odds with each other. ☉ I work on creating a greater connection, communication, and understanding between one's emotions and mind. When feelings are brought to the mind, mental processes become richer, more fruitful, and bountiful. When mental processes touch the emotions, the emotions become understood. The establishment of a good connection between the heart and mind opens many possibilities. It expands horizons and increases one's potential. ☉ Often we are our own hardest masters. When our hearts and minds are working in harmony, among other things, we tend to become easier on ourselves. I bring a feeling of relief that can be felt within moments of connecting with Lapis's energy. This feeling may be one of the reasons people are drawn to me. ☉ I can help people break free of past situations that may be causing them problems today. I do this especially for those who have had an association with Lapis in the past or who were incarnated during the time I was in my prime, regardless of where on the planet they lived. I can help these people most, because they have already made a connection with Lapis Lazuli. Of course, I can also benefit those who have not had a connection with Lapis. ☉ I give my wearers courage and the fearless, adventurous spirit needed to realize their dreams. I show them their dreams and help them feel that they can attain them. Once you feel you can attain your dreams, resources will be drawn to you like iron filings to a magnet. If you continue to wear me, I will also help you realize these dreams. ☉ The vibratory rate of my royal blue color affects people deeply. This is because it touches the optic nerve in an unusual way. Your optic nerve picks up impressions of what you see with your physical eyes as well as impressions of what you see in your dreams and inner visions. All these impressions stimulate this nerve, which is connected to the part of the brain that serves as the storehouse for memories. The vibratory rate of my color impresses the optic nerve in a way that reminds the brain of a primordial memory. This memory is from the individual's core. It is a memory of that which links the individual to his or her source.

"What do you mean by source?" Michael asked.

God. And it is not only my color that reminds people of the energy or Spirit that connects them with God. The vibratory rate of Lapis itself also plays a large part in stimulating the optic nerve, and hence the brain, to recall this memory. ◌ For this reason, people are also comforted by my royal blue color, though they may not know why. When people feel comfortable, they feel freer, and with freedom comes confidence. This confidence is what allows people to start remembering all the things they want to be and to connect more deeply with their goals and aspirations and dreams.

SOUL'S JOURNEY

"You have the reputation for being wise, and I sense your wisdom. I have wondered what the overall purpose of gemstones is. Do you know why Spirit has created them?" Michael asked.

From one point of view, Soul is on a journey home. Before Soul can reach its goal and return to its own infinite source, it must master many lessons and develop many strengths. Along the way much help is provided. On Soul's journey are signposts, guiding lights, and spiritual paths, as well as spiritual masters, guides, healers, and other helpers. Tools, such as books and gemstones, are also provided for

Soul. All of these are available to help individual Souls fulfill their destinies and return to their true home in God, the infinite source of all life. Each of these helpers of Soul is distinct and different. Each is powerful and not to be underestimated.

"So, gemstones are another set of tools available to assist Soul."

Yes. Gemstones are among the many tools provided to assist Soul, whether or not Soul uses them. Those who are wise use the tools that lie at their feet rather than struggle constantly with their bare hands. Yes, God created your hands, but God also created tools.

"Is it common for wearers of gemstones to have dream experiences about the gemstones they are wearing?"

This is truer today than it has ever been. Today awareness is expanding and invisible clouds are being removed from people's consciousness. The Gemstone Guardians themselves are being given a greater awareness of their own capabilities. ☾ In other words, we have been given the awareness of how to work directly with people. We can teach people and work with them in their dreams, meditations, and contemplations as well as in the waking state. Although we always could work with people, and some of us have done so, today we are being asked to work more directly with them. We have also been asked to work more directly with each other.

"Why do you think this is happening at this time?"

Destiny. It was predicted eons ago that there would be a time when, in the semi-darkness, a greater light would start to shine. That time is now. Since the end of the last century, an opening and awakening has been occurring. This is happening everywhere—on every planet in every galaxy, in every universe, and on every plane of existence. ☾ Everywhere there is a rejoicing. Yet with this opening, awakening, and brightening comes a profound responsibility. With it come many lessons, and perhaps many hardships, for it is also an opportunity to grow. Growth means change, and change means letting go of things that are no longer necessary, though we may hold them very dear. We cannot remain attached to who we were and grow at the same time. ☾ This opening began with a crack in the door, and slowly, slowly, the door is opening. By now it has only opened a few inches, but it will continue to open for some time to come. ☾ It is indeed an interesting time you have been born in. ☾ I have spoken only briefly about the effects of Lapis, of what happens when the mind and emotions work together, hand in hand. I cannot overemphasize the importance of connecting these two aspects. In that connection is Lapis's power. It is very simple. Indeed, Lapis works so simply that it can be easily overlooked. ☾ Those who are fortunate enough to own a strand of high-quality Lapis spheres are indeed blessed with a powerful tool. Feel the power I radiate today, and then imagine what I must have been like in my prime when my abilities on this planet were one or two hundred times what they are today. It is awesome, humbling, and perhaps even frightening to realize the power and potential of those who wore me in the ancient days.

"Is there anything else you would like to share?"

The beginning pianist can only play a few notes at one time and make them sound beautiful. But a master pianist can play a seemingly infinite number of notes and make them sound even more beautiful. You are working toward mastery of Spirit and Self. Since Spirit is life, there is no reason that this mastery cannot be reflected in the mastery of everything you do in life. ☾ You have experienced time and again the plight of the beginning pianist struggling to make a composition sound beautiful. You will all have to work on mastering greater and greater pieces of music. Set your sights in that direction, and you will attain it. It takes practice to become a master, yet the potential to do so is available to everyone. Lapis Lazuli can help you attain mastery, perhaps more so than any other gemstone. This may be mastery of bread baking, piano playing, or Spirit itself. ☉ To become a master, first you must see your goal and then you must feel that you have attained it. I can help you have these feelings. I can help you see your goals and dreams and give you the courage to attain them. ☉ Michael, you have experienced Lapis Lazuli before. Let it play music in your heart. Let it strike the chords, for they have been played before. And don't accept your own limitations.

"That is good advice. Thank you very much," Michael replied.

Now I shall leave you. May the blessings be.

"May the blessings be."

The Guardian of Lapis departed, and I sped through a tunnel of light so quickly that the atmosphere around me shook. Several moments later, I found myself back on the Earth, sitting comfortably on the living room sofa.

The

Guardian

of

ONYX

28

BECOMING GROUNDED

I expected to meet the Guardian of Onyx in a dark place, perhaps in a dimly lit cavern deep within the Earth. I was surprised when Spirit led us to a grassy area near a mountain brook. There the Guardian of Onyx sat waiting on a large rock. When he saw Michael and me, he stood, stretched out his hand to shake ours, and greeted us amiably.

The Guardian of Onyx looked as ordinary as any person on Earth. He had jet black hair and dark brown eyes, and he spoke in a quiet, gentle voice. This Guardian seemed to be a rather likable fellow. Judging from the location he chose for his discourse, he dearly loved nature. I felt this love—a kinship with all living things—as I entered his aura.

Although it is considered an earthstone, the material you call Black Onyx has not been made entirely by the planet. Black Onyx is comprised of the Earth's elements, yet has been enhanced by human beings. By this I do not mean that it is man-made. Onyx is surely alive, even though its color has been enhanced to make it appear black. This enhancement only contributes to my mission. Indeed, it makes me what I am. The effects of most other gemstones are dampened by treatment. Without treatment, Black Onyx would not be. ◔ As its Guardian, I have been assigned to watch over Onyx, to guide its vibratory rate, and to care for and work with the people who wear it.

"Does your mission include only the Black Onyx on Earth?" Michael asked.

Yes. My guardianship is for the Earth's Black Onyx only.

THE ROOT CHAKRA

"What is your mission?"

I work exclusively for human beings. My mission is to stabilize, strengthen, and support the root chakra. My vibratory rate, combined with my color, works on stimulating all the chakras except the crown. I give the chakras strength at the deepest level so they may function properly. ◔ Some people have negative attitudes about the root chakra or consider it less important than the other chakras. If the root chakra were not necessary, it would not have been included in the human body. When the root chakra is balanced and functioning properly, you have the strength to develop the higher chakras. Indeed, you need a strong and stable root chakra to help you withstand the changes that will come into your life as you develop those chakras. ◔ It is the nature of my vibratory rate and of my color to absorb the seven color rays and bring them into the body. My energy enters the root chakra. Then it rises up through the body, giving the chakras the message that it is all right for them to open up and accept colors and other beneficial energies as the body needs them. Some of my energy leaves through the sacral chakra, but most of it continues to rise up through the body. As my energy passes each chakra, it deposits the vibratory rate of the colors each chakra is programmed to accept. My energy reinforces the chakras' ability to accept these color rays. It also enlivens their receptivity to all colors. ◯ When my energy reaches the stomach chakra, I let go of the green and yellow vibratory rates, because that chakra has a magnetic attraction for these two rays. The heart chakra has a magnetic attraction for the red and orange rays; this attraction calls the red and orange vibratory rates from my make-up. At the throat chakra I release the blue-ray vibratory rate. And at the brow chakra I let go of the indigo and purple vibratory rates. In some individuals, I deposit the indigo ray with the blue at the throat chakra. My energy does not reach the crown chakra. ◯ All beings react to light, and all beings have chakras, or energy centers, including animals. Perhaps plants do, too—and if one knew how to look for them, their energy centers might be found. Therefore, I believe that all living beings will react to Onyx in a similar way. ◯ Although it may seem paradoxical, when all light converges on a single point, there is darkness. When this phenomenon occurs on a spiritual level, the negative pole of creation is formed. Perhaps this is why black is a symbol of the negative and white a symbol of the positive. ◯ The nature, purpose, and importance of the negative force is to temper Soul. Ultimately, it strengthens the individual—the hard way. Yet, please do not consider Black Onyx a negative stone. When Onyx is worn during a negative situation, its vibratory rate allows light to shine on the situation and reveal its positive side.

RELEASING BAD HABITS

Onyx can help people break certain patterns or habits. These habits may be physical, emotional, or mental. ◐ I can help the body become strong enough to accept an optimal amount of color rays on its own. When the body does this, the individual's vibratory rate rises. When one's vibratory rate rises, one often recognizes patterns and habits in one's life. This is because a habit is a form of disharmony, and where all colors of the rainbow exist in balance there can be no disharmony. ◐ With this rise in vibratory rate, you might also see that a certain habit is not all bad, because through that habit certain lessons are being learned. Nevertheless, you might also come to realize that you no longer need the habit. Then it will just be a matter of further raising your vibratory rate to completely dissolve your ties with the habit. In most cases, habit resolution also involves dissolving karmic ties with the entity associated with the habit—tobacco, for example, in the case of a smoking habit. ◐ To change a habit, you must first recognize it; otherwise, a complete change cannot occur. When you see the reason for certain habits and understand why patterns keep recurring, you will have taken the first step required to change those habits or at least to change their underlying causes. ◐ My effect on patterns and habits is a side effect of my primary mission. However, it is a noticeable one and common to everyone who wears Onyx. The side effects of most gemstones are not experienced by everyone who wears them. In this way Onyx is different from most gemstones. Still, the details of each person's experience with Onyx will be unique.

"Would you explain the mechanics of how you help people let go of habits?"
asked Michael.

First, I allow you to become aware of the habit. I do this by intensifying your attachment to it. Yet I do this only to the point where you recognize that the attachment exists. In this way, I help you see that what is destructive is not so much the habitual behavior itself, but your attachment to it. ☾ How many people do you know who smoke or drink but don't think they have a smoking or drinking problem? When Onyx is worn, an individual who has, for example, a smoking habit will find that the attachment to smoking intensifies. This doesn't mean that the person will smoke more cigarettes or that the habit will get worse. Instead, this intensification will encourage the person to recognize that the attachment exists. With this will come the realization that "I'm out of control! My habit is controlling my life!" ☾ As the attachment to the habit intensifies, I also give strength. I do this by making sure that each chakra is receptive to the color rays and that the color rays entering the body are being distributed properly. ☾ This is important, because it will prevent the person from losing balance when the realization dawns that he or she is out of control. Instead, the person will have the strength to let go of the attachment and say, "This habit once controlled me, but no more. It is no longer a part of me." Perhaps the person will even continue to smoke, but the attachment to the habit will have been released; the individual will have mastered the habit. ☾ If you continue to wear Onyx, you will also have the strength to break the karmic ties with the habit controlling you. Onyx will protect your aura whenever the habit tries to return. ☾ One can use one's knowledge of how Onyx works to focus my effects. If my wearers understand my effects, they can decide to put attention on the habit that concerns them most. Those who are unaware of my effects will simply realize that certain habits are controlling their lives.

"If someone wearing Onyx has, for example, twenty habits, would the habits be addressed one at a time or all at once?"

The attachment to the most destructive habit will be addressed first, unless the individual chooses a different habit to focus on. If one chooses a habit which is actually a manifestation of a deeper attachment, I will work on the underlying attachment first. For example, if someone chooses to release a habit concerning food, when the underlying attachment really concerns the person's concept of giving and receiving love, my attention will focus on the person's underlying attachment. ◐ Breaking and letting go of habits causes a change in one's overall balance. This can be uncomfortable, but it is not my intention to initiate more changes than people can handle or to create an imbalance. Because I help the chakras learn to accept the proper balance of color rays, wearing Onyx will improve one's overall balance. Consequently, my wearer will not be overwhelmed by the changes that come with the breaking of habits. Indeed, he or she will have the strength to make those changes.

BECOMING GROUNDED

To gain a better perspective on their inner lives, many people need to become more secure and grounded in the physical body. Onyx will give them that secure and grounded feeling. It will allow them to experience the mind and emotions from a more solid base and thereby gain a greater, more holistic understanding of themselves. ◐ Thus, people who tend to feel "spaced out," disoriented, or detached will benefit from Onyx. So will those who have difficulty concentrating on important tasks or who tend to live almost exclusively on the emotional level. Often such people struggle to maintain adequate awareness of what is occurring around them on the physical level. Onyx can be a helpful tool for these individuals, especially when they must drive, use potentially dangerous power equipment, or perform some other task requiring intense concentration for safety reasons. ◐ At such times, these individuals should place Onyx on whatever part of the body is most comfortable for them. The Onyx could be worn around the neck, placed in a pocket, or laid in the lap.

"Do you anticipate that your effects on human beings will change in the future?"

Although human beings may think they change slowly, you really change quite quickly, especially compared to the rate at which gemstones evolve and change. As long as human beings continue to make Gray Onyx black in the same way you do now, my effects will remain the same.

MEDICINE FROM THE EARTH

"Since you are the last of the Earthstone Guardians to be interviewed for this book, would you care to summarize the work of the earthstones?"

The earthstones are not greater than the gemstones and vice versa. They are just different. Earthstones are crucial for the planet, just as crystals are. ○ Now that you understand how I work and what I do, feel free to experiment with other therapeutic applications. Be creative! I believe this would be the message from all the Earthstone Guardians. When you learn the true nature, purpose, and mission of a stone—whether you call it an earthstone, oceanstone, or gemstone—you will have gained the opportunity to combine this basic knowledge with your creativity and your own knowledge of the human body. In other words, you can experiment. ○ There is not just one way to use a tool. With creativity, you can use most tools in a variety of ways. For every gemstone, there are at least a hundred and one applications of it, especially when you have a more complete picture of the world of gems. ○ Do not underestimate your intuition when working with gemstones therapeutically. Some say intuition is God, Spirit, your higher Self, or your Guardian Angel speaking to you. If you feel insecure about using your intuition, substitute the phrase "inner knowingness" for intuition. Always use your inner knowingness to guide you when using any gemstone. ○ Some people will always need to prove their intuitive insights with mental equations. These people either have not adequately developed the intuition or do not trust it enough. Of course, there are instances when the use of such equations is essential, especially in complex situations. ○ People have already accepted medicinal plants as gifts from the Earth. We Guardians believe that people are now ready to accept medicinal gemstones as gifts from the planet. Both plants and gemstones can be medicinal. Nevertheless, they are very different. Both plants and gemstones are alive. However, the amount of life and healing force contained in the molecular structure of plants is minuscule compared to that contained in the crystalline structure of a gemstone. ○ The life force of a plant starts to diminish once it is plucked from its roots. The life force of gemstones does not change when they are removed from the planet. In fact, the harvesting of gemstones is the first step in preparing them to directly assist human beings. If one tears off a piece of leaf, that piece will immediately start to die. If one breaks off a piece of a gemstone, it will stay as alive as the stone from which it was broken. ○ Plants lose their vibratory rate once they are ingested by the body. The body soon forgets the plant's gift and needs another dose. If you wear a gemstone for one minute and take it off, your body will soon forget the gemstone's vibratory rate. However, it is much easier to wear a gemstone continuously than it is to eat a plant continuously. ○ My comparison between plants and gemstones could continue. I respect plants. I love them, just as I love all the gifts of the Earth, and I am deeply grateful for them. Plants and gemstones can work well together, and you can certainly receive gemstone and herbal therapy at the same time. As long as the therapies are beneficial, they will not conflict with each other. ◐ The more you know about gemstones, the more freedom you will have to choose from a wider variety of the planet's gifts. These gifts will help you through your changes and support you in your growth.

"We will be interviewing some of the Oceanstone Guardians next. Would you like to introduce the first Guardian?" asked Michael.

The oceanstones are out of my realm. Although we exist on the same planet, we are of different worlds.

"Thank you for sharing your wisdom with us."

That you have recognized wisdom in my words tells me there is wisdom in you as well—otherwise, how could you have recognized it? ◐ I expect we will meet again, perhaps even in the physical world.

"I look forward to it," Michael replied.

I looked at the Guardian of Onyx, who smiled. He had a twinkle in his dark brown eyes. I reached out my hand to shake his, and we said our good-byes. He spoke privately with Michael for several minutes while I waited, enjoying the scenery. They seemed to be enjoying each other's company and forming a friendship.

When their conversation ended, the Guardian stretched his arms toward the clear blue sky and inhaled the refreshing mountain air. Then he turned to watch the water as it tumbled over rocks in the stream next to us. It was indeed a glorious day.

MOTHER OF PEARL

29

STIRRING PRIMORDIAL MEMORY

I closed my eyes and was greeted by the sound of waves and the cries of seagulls. Soon the waves I heard began to move through my body, sending a stirring, rhythmic motion through every cell. It was as though my cells were particles of sand on a beach, and waves of life force were surging through them, then receding and surging again. Then I let my attention go deeper, and I heard the sound of the water molecules themselves: they sang.

When I opened my eyes, I was not surprised to find Michael and myself by the sea. A small white cloud was moving toward us over the waves. When it arrived on the beach, I saw it was actually the transparent and shimmering form of a woman. Her face was wrinkled, yet her perfect posture and the love radiating from her aura gave her an ageless beauty.

She sat between Michael and me on the sand. She seemed to know Michael well, and they greeted each other warmly.

Turning to me, she said, There is no need for you to enter my aura. Just close your eyes, relax your mind, and connect with me on a deeper level.

Mother of Pearl is part of a seashell, the house of a sea animal. Every species has its own Guardian, including human beings. I am not the Guardian of the sea creatures in whose shells Mother of Pearl grows. I am the Guardian for the Mother of Pearl that has been harvested and fashioned in some way to be worn by human beings. ◐ If you wish to know the history of Mother of Pearl, study the evolution of the sea creatures that bear shells: the mollusks.

STIRRING THE DEPTHS OF YOUR BEING

My purpose is not for the planet. It is for the human beings who wear me. My mission is to stir. I stir the life force in the cells of the physical body. I stir emotions in the emotional body, and I stir thoughts and memories in the mind. This stirring helps remind my wearers of their true origin. Every cell in your physical body and every aspect of your emotional and mental bodies has a primordial memory. I stir the forces that have kept this memory hidden, so that it may be remembered. It is the memory of the time you were part of the sea. ◐ Now, if you have a scientific background, you may say, "Ah yes, human beings evolved from the sea. All creatures originated as single-celled organisms in the ocean." If you have a spiritual orientation, you may say, "Yes, human beings originated in the ocean, the ocean of love—that unbounded spiritual ocean where all Souls dwell." ◐ There are many side effects, or results, of my stirring. On a mental level, I stir memories, especially recent ones. When memories are stirred, they are remembered. Specifically, I stir the memories of dreams, including daydreams; this makes their symbols clearer and more easily understood. I also stir the mind to look within and beyond itself. ◐ When I stir the emotions, they become more balanced and harmonious. I stir positive and negative emotions in different ways, because they are two entirely different entities. The sharpness of negative emotions, such as sharp tempers and the sharp pangs of fear, is smoothed and calmed. This alone allows the individual to experience greater emotional balance. Those who have difficulty expressing their positive feelings, such as love, will find these feelings becoming stronger, more defined, and thus easier to express. I also give the strength and support needed for this expression to take place. ◯ When I stir the life energy of the physical body's cells, there is an overall calming effect. My stirring is relaxing, rhythmical, and steady, like the rhythm of waves lapping the shore. It is also like the motion of breathing, and it increases the flexibility of the cells. The more flexible the cells are, the more oxygen and life force they can accept. ◯ My stirring also helps calm any mechanism in the body that is overactive. This effect may not be strong enough to help one sleep. Insomnia is often related to strong mental activity. I do not suppress mental activity; when I stir the thoughts, they tend to turn inward. I am calming, sedating, and relaxing, but I am not a sleeping aid. ◯ I have another effect that is a specific result of my vibratory rate: I scatter or absorb certain negative wavelengths thrown at the individuals who wear me. These include the wavelengths of thoughts, emotions, and electromagnetic forces, as well as the emissions of televisions, radios, and microwave transmitters. These can all produce dishar-monious effects on human beings. ◯ These wavelengths are not homogenous; they contain different parts. Some parts I absorb, and some I can only scatter. I am able to do this because of the way my vibratory rate charges the aura. This action can be considered a side effect of my mission. Nevertheless, it is a profound effect of my vibratory rate, and it occurs when the wearer's aura is saturated with my energy. ◯ When the Mother of Pearl vibratory rate has saturated an aura, it affects the wavelengths that enter it, as I have just described. It also affects certain other wavelengths that are already contained in the aura. These wavelengths are the individual's unfulfilled needs and desires.

UNFULFILLED NEEDS

Inside each of you are needs, desires, feelings, and hurts. All of these are reflected from within you out into your aura. When Mother of Pearl has saturated your aura, it recognizes the needs and desires that are unfulfilled. It sees them for what they are—holes in the fabric of your being. ○ I shall explain. Human beings have a natural, innate need to be nurtured, to be cared for, and to be loved. These needs are first felt in the womb and are most apparent in infants and young children. Mothers and fathers are surely aware of all the love, attention, and nurturing a baby needs. ○ Yet people do not stop having these needs as they get older. They are with you for life. I am not talking about the need to own the latest invention on the market. The needs I speak of are part of your fabric. As an infant, you needed to be loved and nurtured in order to survive. Now that you are an adult, these needs are not as critical for your physical survival, but they are absolutely essential for your emotional survival. ○ No mother is perfect. I have been a mother myself for thousands and thousands of years. Not only have I had children of my own, but, as the Mother of Pearl, I have performed a motherly role for Pearl for a long, long time. Even with all this experience, I am still not perfect. Although we do our best, no mother can fulfill all the needs of her children. As children grow into adulthood, they find that Mother is no longer there to fulfill their needs for love and nurturing and that often life does not fulfill them either. ○ Your unfulfilled needs become holes in the fabric of your being. I am speaking of every unfulfilled need—every one. These holes may include the lack of attention you received as a child; an inability to receive the education you wanted; a lack of food, shelter and clothing; or the lack of a relationship that fulfills your need for love. For example, you may have had a relationship that went awry, or you may have loved someone who did not return love in the way you needed it to be returned. No doubt this created a vacuum, an unfulfilled need. It created a hole in the fabric of your being. ◌ Mother of Pearl detects these holes. Then my vibratory rate sings the song of love, of motherly love, and I fill and repair these holes. The more you wear Mother of Pearl, the more effective I will be.

IN THE ARMS OF A LOVING MOTHER

Often, it is not just my vibratory rate that is needed to repair the holes. One must often acknowledge these holes and cry many tears before they can be mended. I can help you with this part of your healing. Yet know that these holes can be mended, for my vibratory rate sings of the source of infinite love, and it stirs within every part of you the memory of this source. I am speaking of that primordial ocean out of which we all grow. It is an ocean of love. As your memory opens to this ocean of love, the love will flow into you and help repair the holes created by unfulfilled needs. ◌ I give the feeling that one is resting in the arms of a loving mother. Therefore, I will help those who need some motherly love, whether or not they are aware of that need. When I am shaped into a sphere and worn by a human being, the person I belong to becomes my child. ◌ Hence, Mother of Pearl is an ideal gift for young children. I will protect the child's inner nature from harmful wavelengths— namely, negative thoughts, emotions, or other influences, such as the radiation from television sets. Be aware, however, that if I am exposed to too much television radiation, I will become saturated in a very short period of time, and then my other effects will be weakened or nullified. ◌ My protection will deflect the brutal thoughts and emotions that accompany abuse. I do not protect a child from the emotions that are important for a child to experience. For example, a parent's anger may be needed to teach a lesson or prove a point. However, if a parent or anyone oversteps the boundaries of teaching anger into destructive anger, I will take it upon myself to deflect this anger away from the child. Although the child may cry and appear shaken, the inner core of the child's being will be protected. It is important for a child's inner nature to be protected and allowed to grow unharmed and undamaged. A child's inner being is delicate and most precious, for it is the foundation upon which the child will build the rest of his or her life. ◯ When the child reaches a certain age, my work will be done. The necklace size you choose for a child will one day be outgrown, and he or she will put me aside or pass me to a younger sibling. Then the child I have cared for will take the inner strength I have helped to protect, and he or she will build upon it. What the child builds on this inner foundation is his or her choice. As a mother, I let go. ◯ As children change and grow into teenagers, a few will continue to enjoy me, just as a few teenagers enjoy their relationships with their parents. Adults are once again drawn to me, less for my protective qualities than for my stirring effects and the rocking, cradle-like feeling I give.

"What is the effect of your iridescence?"

The shimmering, reflective quality of Mother of Pearl helps my vibratory rate enter the aura. It is one of the reasons I saturate the aura so quickly. The more opalescence I possess, the more deeply I can work—be it physically, emotionally, or mentally—and the more clearly the individual will receive my effects. ◯ One of my responsibilities is to assist the Guardian of Pearl. She needs assistance because of how Pearl has been used and worn by people in recent times. The Guardian of Pearl has withdrawn. She has been battered and beaten by the vibratory rate of cultured Pearls. Their vibratory rate dilutes and breaks down the power of the true Pearl. It also places strain and stress on her. ◯ You will have one opportunity—and only one—to speak with the Guardian of Pearl. It is vital that her attention be kept on maintaining her strength. After her discourse, I will answer any additional questions you may have about Pearl.

The energy shifted, and the Guardian turned her attention away from Michael and me. She seemed to be calling to a force that lay hidden deep within the sea.

The

Guardian

of

PEARL

30

REFLECTING INNER BEAUTY

The air grew humid and became gently charged with electricity. I felt certain we were in the presence of the Guardian of Pearl. The Guardian of Mother of Pearl reminded us to listen to Pearl's words with our hearts.

Then the Guardian of Pearl spoke . . . .

You wish to know Pearl. I am as ancient and timeless as the ocean from which I come. ⟳ Prior to the Age of Atlantis I was young, strong, and vibrant. I was a gift from the seas of the Earth to human beings. I reminded them of the source of life. I was also like a mirror in which one could see the reflection of one's true inner self, as well as visions of the future. I was much more powerful than the crystal balls used by mystics today. ⟳ I was a living treasure of the Earth, naturally formed into a perfectly round shape with luster beyond your wildest dreams. Pearls were much larger then than they are today, with an average diameter of approximately one inch. The largest Pearls, which were about three inches in diameter, were rare and treasured by royalty. ⟳ During the Age of Atlantis, my size was halved, as was my ability to reflect wisdom and to offer visions. Yet I was still used, worn, and loved. Often I was given as a gift to a loved one as a symbol of love and of life. Even today, the Pearls given in this manner and worn around the neck shine with the love with which they were given. I absorb the feelings of the giver and reflect them upon the wearer. ⟳ Today I am still treasured as a gift from the sea, but only a faint memory of my youth and strength lingers. I am very, very tired. Yet I am willing to share with you what information I can. You see, I am old, and my power has been diluted by the vibratory rate of cultured Pearls. ⟳ Once I was able to reflect both the positive and negative aspects of people's natures. By gazing into me, people could see their faults and shortcomings and then work to correct them. Now, with the little strength I have left, I choose to reflect only the pure and positive qualities in an individual. This is less draining for me, and it is uplifting for my wearer. ⟳ This effect is the result of the vibratory rate of my luster. When worn around the neck, on a finger, or as earrings, I reflect the beauty contained within the wearer's aura. Be aware, however, that the life span of each Pearl is short. Pearls age as their wearers age and, in the process, their luster diminishes. ⟳ To some, my life cycle symbolizes reincarnation or rebirth. First, I have a life beneath the sea. The opening of the shell is like the transition from the watery womb into the world of human beings. Then I begin life anew. Pearls allowed to live beneath the sea to a ripe old age are the most powerful of all. ⦿ My natural and most powerful shape, the sphere, is also the shape of the Earth and the sun. It represents the source of life for human beings. The naturally formed Pearl sphere can reflect the inner bodies. The rounder my form is, the more encompassing is my work. Those which you call cultured Pearls, whose seed has been planted by human beings, only reflect the human physical body. ⦿ My color is a reflection of the purest light that shines within the aura. Those who are attracted to rose-colored Pearl are drawn to it because they have beautiful shades of red and pink in their auras. The white-colored Pearl reflects the greatest overall beauty. The gold variety reflects the highest connotation of the color gold: the pure light of Soul. Not everyone can wear such golden pearls, simply because not everyone can handle the reflection of this high vibratory rate. ⦿ The people who benefit most from wearing Pearl are those who could use a reminder of their positive qualities. They are also those who would benefit from being reminded of the source of life, since my spherical shape represents that source. ⦿ I have little or no therapeutic value, but as a gift of love I am most dear. When given by a lover, my wearers benefit from being reminded of the love that surrounds them. ⦿ My nature is patient, understanding, calm, and tranquil. Those who want these qualities in their lives may also be attracted to me. So will the individuals who wish to express beauty and purity. ⦿ Now it is time for me to go. In a way, I am sad to leave you, for my mission is a lonely one. I wish that one day you might be taken in your dreams to a time when I was in my prime. Then you might experience for yourself the youthful beauty, power, and energy I once expressed.

The electric charge in the atmosphere intensified for a brief moment. It seemed to be Pearl's way of thanking us and of saying good-bye. Then the Guardian of Pearl was gone.

The Guardian of Mother of Pearl spoke again:

I would like to clarify a few things Pearl said and offer my point of view at the same time. ☾ Pearl was once extremely powerful. Thousands of years ago, this gift of the sea gave people of the land the power to understand themselves. Pearl reflected the individual accurately and clearly. ☾ When people see themselves in a mirror, they may closely inspect their physical bodies. Pearl gave people the chance to closely inspect their inner selves. She let her wearer examine the way his or her inner self was being reflected outwardly. Pearl's mission was to allow people to see themselves as they truly were. ☾ Pearl has let go of the burden of showing people the whole truth about themselves. Truth is often a burden to show as well as to accept. Today Pearl only reflects the highest beauty within each of us. ☾ Every one of us contains beauty beyond description. Pearl continually reminds you of the beauty within yourself. The beauty I speak of is beyond vanity. It is the part of you that is pure Spirit, pure light and sound, Soul itself. This part of you contains no negativity and no distortions. That is why it appears so beautiful.

CULTURED AND IMITATION PEARLS

"Why do cultured Pearls drain and weaken the Guardian of Pearl?" asked Michael.

As the Guardian of Pearl, she is responsible for all Pearls, including cultured Pearls. When worn, cultured Pearls do not behave in the same way natural Pearls behave. Cultured Pearls begin as seeds planted in seashells by human beings. The Pearl is then allowed to grow around the seed. Therefore, the very core of a cultured Pearl is devoid of life, making it incapable of affecting its wearer's inner core. ○ For a long time, the Guardian of Pearl used her own energy and love to compensate for the deficiency in cultured Pearls. This allowed cultured Pearls to behave like real Pearls. However, it was a tremendous drain on the Guardian of Pearl and consequently diluted her energy. Today there are so many cultured Pearls that the Guardian of Pearl does not have enough love and energy in her heart to go around. ○ Imitation Pearls—those made from plastic and designed to deceive people into believing they are true Pearls— simply insult the Guardian of Pearl. They drain her in the same way you would feel drained if you were bombarded with insults all day. The mental aberrations which cause people to create imitation Pearls are certainly not her responsibility. Still, it hurts her that such things are made. ○ Imitation Pearls are completely empty of life. Cultured Pearls, on the other hand, are only half-alive and will drain energy from anyone who wears them. Therefore, cultured Pearls should not be worn by those already in a weakened state. ○ The true Pearl benefits its wearers by reflecting the beauty within them. Yet, because of Pearl's depletion, she can no longer reflect this beauty herself, but must draw upon the life force within the wearer to help her. Therefore, it is not advisable to wear a solid necklace of true Pearls unless you naturally possess plenty of strength and energy. It is also unwise for those who are very weakened to wear this much Pearl, because they need all the life force available to them to sustain or heal themselves. Such people may be able to wear Pearl in combination with other gemstones, for then it will draw energy from the other gemstones instead of from the wearer. Because Pearl draws on the wearer's life force, it can also help balance overabundant energy. ○ If I had only so much money to spend and wanted to buy a Pearl, I would invest in one very special Pearl. If I decided to wear it, I would mount it in a ring with as little metal covering it as possible. Wearing it in a ring would make it easy for me to gaze at its beauty. It would also make it easier to see my reflection and therefore to gain some level of self-awareness. ◉ I am not referring to spiritual self-awareness. I mean self-awareness in a practical, day-to-day sense. In other words, I would start to take notice and ask myself, "How are my thoughts and emotions being expressed? How am I presenting myself? Is this the way I want to present myself?" Often we are not aware of the silly things we do and that we may later regret. Pearl helps us to be more aware and refined, more like the person we would like to be. It helps us move closer to our ideal self-image. ◉ If I wore the Pearl around my neck, other people would tend to see the Pearl more than I would. Therefore, others would see more clearly the kind of person I am. As a result of their feedback, I would become more aware—consciously or unconsciously—of the image I was projecting. I could use this feedback to start smoothing the rough edges of my personality. ◉ I wish to make it clear that I am not the Guardian of Pearl. I have only given you my point of view, and I do not know all there is to know about Pearl.

"Thank you for sharing your wisdom," said Michael.

You are welcome.

The Guardian's form became more and more transparent until it was only a faint shimmer of sparkling light. These sparkles rested in the air between Michael and me until the next gentle breeze scattered them. Then the Guardian of Mother of Pearl was gone.

31

STRENGTHENING YOUR POWERHOUSE

I readied myself to seek out the Guardian of Coral, but before I could begin my search, three beings entered Michael's living room. Faceless and formless vortices of swirling color, they hovered in the air above us. One was red, another was pink, and the third was white.

We have decided to meet you in the atmosphere of your living room, *said a voice emanating from the red vortex.* For the sake of simplicity, call us Red, Pink, and White Coral.

Over the millennia, Coral's shape and color have changed along with the chemical nature of the oceans. The places Coral is found have also changed. Those who live by the sea have always enjoyed Coral. Yet only those who wear Coral in spherical form can fully experience its therapeutic qualities and benefits. ○ The mission of spherical Coral is to provide the human wearer with the opportunity to build strength. When Coral is in the sea, its purpose for the planet is simply to house other ocean life. ○ Once Coral is removed from the ocean, it goes to sleep until it is re-enlivened in a human being's aura. It takes several hours for this enlivenment to occur, because the Coral must adjust: it must learn to respond to the human aura rather than to water. ○ We, the Guardians of Coral, care for the Coral that lies under the sea as well as the Coral worn by people. ○ In general, people are not drawn to Coral as they are drawn to other gemstones. The decision to wear Coral will probably be based on knowledge of what Coral can do. Therefore, we are much like any other tool chosen for a specific purpose. ○ We do not saturate the aura the way other gemstones do. We work on a layer of energy that lies closer to the physical body. This layer, also known as the supra-physical aura, is comprised of the vibrations, or life essence, emitted by your body's cells. ○ Electrical currents run up and down your body. These nonphysical currents give an accurate picture of what is going on in your physical body. Coral senses and reads them. When you wear a strand of Coral, its vibratory rate touches virtually every one of these currents. That is why it is best to wear Coral spheres around the neck. The currents flow both inside and outside of the body; Coral accesses the currents that run inside the body through those that run on the outside.

THE BODY'S POWERHOUSE

There is another aspect of the body which is essential to Coral's work. Like the electrical currents, this aspect would not be found if one were to dissect the body. It is a vortex of energy which swirls within your torso. It is somewhat, but not entirely, associated with the chakras. It is known as your "powerhouse." ◌ Your powerhouse is one of your most important sources of energy, the energy you use for life, growth, and evolution. It is made up of electrical currents and of the life force itself. In a sense, the electrical currents form a structure which contains and stores the vortex of life force within you. Therefore, when we refer to the powerhouse, we mean both this life force and the structure of energy which contains it. ◌ The Coral in the ocean builds a structure for the animals living inside it. When worn by a human being, Coral can strengthen, rebuild, and cleanse the structure that houses the vortex of life force contained within the wearer. Red, Pink, and White Coral each affect this powerhouse in a different way. Before we get into specifics, do you understand what the powerhouse is?

"Perhaps if you elaborate, it would help us understand it better," replied Michael.

The powerhouse is located inside the body in front of the spine and behind the chakras. Think of it as a building, and imagine a roofless, cylindrical structure. ◌ At its top in your crown chakra, it is quite narrow. It remains narrow behind your brow chakra and begins to widen just below your throat chakra. From there it continues to widen until it reaches its greatest circumference in the area between your stomach and sacral chakras. Then it quickly tapers again and ends at the root chakra. ◌ You eat food for energy and you breathe air for life. Your chakras take in yet a different kind of life-sustaining energy. The powerhouse acts as a storehouse for this energy. It feeds the cells of your body through electrical charges that act as little packages or jolts of energy. ◌ People who are overweight do not have bigger powerhouses than people who are thin. It is not the kind of energy reserve that fat is. It is a life-energy reserve. People who are ill or weak often have depleted powerhouses. Healthy people have fuller powerhouses. ◌ Yet, no matter how healthy or vital you are, you can always become stronger. It is the nature of the world in which you live that your powerhouse is constantly being battered by harmful influences, both internal and external. Internal influences include thoughts and emotions. External influences encompass such things as the food and drink you consume and the air you breathe. Any negative influence whittles away your powerhouse. ◌ When you are very, very tired and need a boost, you call upon the reserves in your powerhouse. When you want to eat something that you know you are allergic to and you eat it anyway, you call on the reserves in your powerhouse. When you go somewhere that is polluted, you call on the reserves in your powerhouse to protect you from the pollution. ◌ The life force contained within your powerhouse feeds your enthusiasm for life and your joy for living. It nourishes your desire to grow, evolve, and learn. These activities take a great deal of energy. Consequently, people whose powerhouses are depleted are usually less interested in learning new things or in growing or changing. ◌ You can strengthen, rebuild, and cleanse your powerhouse with things that are constructive, strengthening, or "good for you"—for example, clean air, good food, harmonious thoughts, a positive attitude, or any form of spiritual nourishment. However, Coral can do more to benefit your powerhouse than practically anything else on this planet. ◌ Now, I, the Guardian of Red Coral, will speak to you about Red Coral and its effects on the powerhouse.

REBUILDING THE POWERHOUSE FOUNDATION

The blueprints of your powerhouse were given to you as you were forming in your mother's womb. There the foundation of your powerhouse was also formed. ◊ One of the most beneficial things a pregnant woman can do is wear Red Coral. It will provide the same benefit for the growing fetus that it will for the mother: it will evaluate the entire individual and determine what improvements need to be made in the powerhouse foundation. ◊ I, as Red Coral, compare the vibratory rate of the powerhouse with that of the individual; I evaluate and analyze the difference. Then I pinpoint and attract the specific ingredients that should be added to the vibratory rate of the powerhouse to improve it. This improvement in the powerhouse raises the individual's vibratory rate. This process continues for as long as I am worn. Thus, the longer I am worn, the stronger the powerhouse and its owner become. ◊ I know how to make the strongest possible powerhouse foundation. The deeper and darker the natural red color of the Coral, the stronger are my effects. ◊ Red Coral will always find ways to improve the foundation of your powerhouse, no matter how healthy you are. Your powerhouse foundation is alive. It will change as you change. For example, if you deny yourself certain minerals, the lack of these minerals will soon be reflected in your powerhouse. ◊ I rely on what the body knows about itself. The body knows what it needs and what it lacks; it knows which ingredients it needs to make its powerhouse stronger. The individual, on the other hand, often has no conscious awareness of what these needs are. Hence, I do not work on a conscious level. ◊ I give the body the ability and strength to draw to itself the things that it needs. I do this by magnetically charging key areas of the body. Let's say, for example, that the foundation of your powerhouse lacks a mineral, such as calcium. Your body will recognize this need. I will then "magnetize" the body in such a way that it attracts more calcium to itself. The way each body does this will vary. For example, the body may begin to crave foods containing calcium, or it may become more efficient at extracting calcium from food. ☾ I work with more than minerals. All sorts of things may be missing from your powerhouse foundation—for example, a color ray or some kind of emotional nourishment. Most often, however, the powerhouse foundation lacks oxygen or a nutrient that can be obtained from food. No matter what these things are, I work in the same way to draw them to the body. ☾ When Red Coral is worn alone, the strand should be choker-length: sixteen, eighteen, or twenty inches long, depending on the size of the individual's neck. Now, I must caution you that a solid Red Coral necklace will change the whole structure on which an individual is built. Therefore, its effects will be handled best by those who are brave, determined, and truly aware of what will happen when they wear it. It is difficult to alter one's basic nature, and such changes can be upsetting. Afterward, things will not be done the way they used to be done and energy will not be stored the way it used to be stored. Even one's diet may change. ☾ A solid Red Coral necklace is often more appropriate for men than for women because of the nature of the male physical body. Consequently, a woman may not be able to handle the physical changes resulting from a solid Red Coral necklace as well as a man can. Besides, when women build physical strength, they must simultaneously build emotional strength in order to maintain balance. Combining some Pink Coral with the Red Coral will support the emotional aspect, strengthening its foundation at the same time the physical foundation is being strengthened. ☾ Red Coral attracts the red ray. It does not carry the red ray, nor can it open the body to accept it; it simply attracts the red ray to the wearer.

The red vortex of energy receded into the background, and the pink vortex moved forward and began to speak.

RENOVATING THE POWERHOUSE

Your powerhouse is not just a blueprint or a foundation. It has substance. In this way it is similar to a building. A building is not just its foundation; it also has walls made of blocks or bricks. During childhood and adolescence more and more "bricks" are laid, one on top of the other, on the foundation of your powerhouse. This process continues until your physical body stops growing at adulthood. ◌ Now, no one lives in such a perfect environment that they are always provided with the nutrients they need exactly when they need them. By nutrients, I mean both physical and emotional nutrients. When needs are not met at the moment they are needed, holes form in the powerhouse. These holes are also created when great stresses are placed on the body. Such stresses tax the powerhouse and result in damaged or improperly laid bricks or the placement of insufficient "mortar" between them. ◌ By the time you reach adulthood, all the bricks of your powerhouse have been laid. At that point, if you don't have the energy you would expect to have, it's probably because there is some mortar missing, or some bricks have been put in the wrong place, or some bricks are absent altogether. ◌ Your powerhouse can also be compared to a well. Instead of water, the powerhouse stores life force, which can be called upon whenever it is needed. If there is a hole in your well, water will drain out of it. The farther down in your well the hole is, the more water will drain out. I work to fill the holes in your powerhouse by rearranging its "bricks." In other words, I rebuild the powerhouse. ◌ This is why Pink Coral is such a wonderful gift for children. The younger the child, the deeper within the powerhouse I can work. It is easier to rearrange bricks in a well that is only two feet high than in one that has grown to five feet high. Pink Coral will rearrange the bricks so that they fit in the optimal places in the child's powerhouse. It will do this regardless of what stresses the child may experience or what nutrients the child may lack. ◌ These bricks are simply "sections" of vibratory rate and, therefore, are moved easily under my influence. Of course, I will also readjust and shuffle the vibratory rate of an adult's powerhouse in order to make its bricks fit properly. ◌ If your powerhouse has many holes, energy will seep out of it in all directions. Since your powerhouse is located near your organs, the energy seeping out of it may cause hyperactivity in these organs, especially in the intestinal tract. The abnormally high intestinal activity will cause food to pass through too quickly. This can result in a decrease in the intestines' ability to absorb nutrients. ◌ In some situations, the powerhouse has not been built completely. This occurs for many reasons. In these cases, because the powerhouse has only gotten halfway off the ground, it will not be able to store much energy. People who wake up feeling just as tired as they did when they went to bed often have incomplete powerhouses. During the night the powerhouse is most effective at gathering and storing its energy for the following day's activities. If the powerhouse is only half-built, it can store little or no energy. ◌ Pink Coral will attract whatever is needed to build on the foundation of the powerhouse. To do this, I emulate the natural process which directs the flow and expression of energy in the body. In this way, I increase the individual's overall strength and vitality.

"Are there any specific therapies involving Pink Coral?"

The best way to wear Pink Coral is around the neck in a necklace which reaches the heart. Your powerhouse affects your entire being. The only way I can affect your entire being is when I am worn around your neck. Being worn over the heart gives me better access to your powerhouse. ◌ Pink Coral strengthens and builds on the foundation that the body has already manifested, whether that foundation is good or bad. Therefore, if someone starts wearing Pink Coral and then begins to feel even weaker and more tired, it may mean the Pink Coral is building on an improperly laid foundation. This situation can be prevented by wearing Red Coral before or along with the Pink Coral. The Red Coral will correct deficiencies in the powerhouse foundation before the Pink Coral starts to build on it. I will build on the new and better foundation established by the Red Coral. ⚬ There is another situation in which I work particularly well with Red Coral. This is when the individual's building blocks have been weakened by certain disorders or dysfunctions, especially those of the bones and, to a lesser extent, of the blood and lymph systems. After healing rays have been introduced, and the affected area is cleansed and ready for rebuilding, Red Coral can prepare the foundation. I will then build on the new foundation created by the Red Coral. ⚬ Now let's speak of White Coral.

This time the pink vortex of energy receded, and the vortex of pure white energy intensified and moved toward us.

PROTECTING THE POWERHOUSE

I protect the powerhouse and keep it pure. That is one of the reasons I am so important and wonderful for children. Children often yearn to explore and experience the world around them, but their explorations don't always lead to positive experiences. ⚬ Like Pink Coral, I am much more effective on children than adults, because children's powerhouses have not yet solidified. Nothing about them has solidified, since they are still growing and changing. Therefore, it is easier to protect them and to keep their powerhouses free from impurities. ⚬ I have a particular love for people, perhaps more than Pink and Red Coral do. My feelings for human beings may have much to do with how I affect them. I am like the mother who wishes to protect her children from all that is unpleasant. Of course, you would need to wear a large amount of White Coral to do this completely. ◌ I work well with Pink Coral. When Pink Coral rearranges the powerhouse structure, making it strong and resilient, changes occur in the wearer's life. During these changes, an individual is often more susceptible to outside influences, particularly negative ones. These negative influences can include anything that is not nourishing, whether it be thoughts, emotions, or foods. ◌ I have a reflecting or repelling action. I am like a mirror. This mirror does not surround you but is more or less inside of you. Therefore, everything I reflect passes your consciousness. This allows you to see what is not good for you. You will see everything that I reflect.

"I'm not sure that I understand," said Michael.

Imagine being surrounded by a spherical mirror. If a negative thought comes your way and is deflected by the mirror, you may never even know that it came. On the other hand, if the mirror is placed so that it's somewhat inside of you, the negative thought will come in, but it will be reflected back to the sender before it can affect you. ◌ This is what I do. I will not let the negative thought affect you. More accurately, I will not let it affect your powerhouse; I will not let it affect the core of your being. However, you will still experience it. It is hoped that you will also learn from it, so that in the future you will avoid similar, potentially harmful experiences. ◌ Is that clear?

"Yes," replied Michael.

Although the other Corals may not be completely aware of it, you also have a powerhouse in each of your inner bodies. Red Coral's work focuses on the physical. Pink Coral focuses on the physical and the emotional. I, too, work physically, but I also protect your emotions and your mind. That is why I can protect the core of your being, not only from your own negative thoughts and emotions, but also from those of others. I also protect your core from any disharmonious influence that enters your physical body. ☾ Any kind of negative influence can act like a battering ram on the building blocks of your powerhouse. If the influence continues, blocks can loosen and fall out, creating a hole in your powerhouse. I protect the powerhouse from anything harmful, including harmful chemicals or other physical irritants. You should know, however, that if you continually introduce damaging elements to your body, I will not have the strength to maintain my protective influence.

"Are there specific ways to use White Coral therapeutically?"

I affect the whole being. When worn around the neck, I can touch every part of you. ☾ All Corals work best and do great work with those individuals who understand our purpose. We are most effective with those who are willing to let go of the things that inhibit their vitality, energy, and basic strength. Those who have self-defeating or destructive attitudes, who are confirmed pessimists, or who have little hope that they can change or grow will not benefit from Coral as much as those who have at least a glimmer of trust, acceptance, or hope. ☾ Even if the individual is unaware of Coral's effects, Coral will work—as long as the person has an optimistic nature or is at least willing to accept change or acknowledge that it can occur. Most people are willing to be healed. They just may not know what they are in for when they ask to be healed.

"How do you see Coral being used in the future?"

As long as we exist, we can be used as tools. We will work for the benefit and strength of any individual of any age. You will see changes occur more swiftly in children. Children are easier to change, because they are already changing so much. ☉ Children should wear a combination of Pink and White Coral. The Coral should be worn continually for several days until it becomes attuned to the child. Then the child should wear the Coral for at least twelve hours every day. It can also be worn at night. ☉ If you follow this protocol, you will find that the child's resistance to infection will be strengthened. The child will not get sick as easily and will be less susceptible to negative influences. Children who wear Pink and White Coral will experience an increase in self-confidence, because they will be better able to recognize what is good for them and what is bad for them. This heightened discrimination will be the result of the White Coral. Few children will need Red Coral; it is usually too strong for them. ☉ You may also notice that children who wear Coral want to move beyond their previous limitations. Because they feel stronger, they may try physical activities that they would have never tried before—for example, they might do things on the monkey bars they've never attempted before. They will have a greater sense and awareness of their bodies, and their growth will be more stable. My purpose is to protect the core of your being. Remember that when I am worn, whatever influences come toward you will still touch you. I only deflect them from your powerhouse. Is that understood? I am not like Rubellite, which will shield your aura. I only shield your powerhouse. Do you see the difference?

"Yes, thank you. Would you please summarize the functions of the three Corals and the differences between them?" Michael requested.

Certainly. Red Coral rebuilds the powerhouse foundation; Pink Coral rebuilds the powerhouse itself; and White Coral protects the powerhouse and keeps it pure. ☉ Red Coral improves the powerhouse foundation by drawing to the body the basic nutrients it needs. It entrusts the actual building and maintenance of the powerhouse to Pink and White Coral. ◌ Pink Coral builds, or rebuilds, the powerhouse itself. It rearranges its building blocks, or sections of vibratory rate, so that they are all in their optimal places. It builds the powerhouse on the existing foundation, be it good or bad. This is why it is often important to wear Red Coral with the Pink. Of course, the effects of Pink Coral are also enhanced by White Coral. There are also cases in which all three work best when worn together. ◌ White Coral, by keeping the powerhouse clean and pure and deflecting all negative and harmful influences, maintains the powerhouse's strength and vitality.

IN UNION WITH ALL LIfE

We, the Gemstone Guardians, each have our own missions, and we work in our individual ways. Yet, on another level, we are united. I do not mean just among ourselves. I mean we are united with all life. ◌ We are united with the life of the Earth, with all animals and plants, and with all human beings who wish to be united with us. The difference between human beings, plants, and animals is that human beings can consciously choose the tools and influences they wish to work with. ◌ We are united for the singular purpose of spiritual unfoldment. No matter what our effects are and no matter how we can benefit and assist, it is all in the name of greater spiritual unfoldment. ◌ Gemstones not only help human beings; human beings help gemstones. Within you flows a force that emanates from the highest place—the source of life itself. By wearing gemstones, you enliven them with your aura. In this way, gemstones are touched by the flow of this life force and their evolution is fueled by it. ◌ We, the Gemstone Guardians, have done our best to give you an overview of who we are, what we do, and what our potential is. We have done this because if human beings and gemstones band together and share with each other, we can help each other evolve and grow spiritually. ☾ Never forget that all gemstones contain intense concentrations of the light and sound of the life force. As long as you have a physical body, the gemstones, earthstones, and oceanstones will continue to be some of the greatest tools available to help you grow beyond your current limitations. Those who are blessed with wisdom will consciously take steps to use the tools available to them.

"We thank you and all the Gemstone Guardians for sharing this wealth of information with us," said Michael.

On behalf of all the Gemstone Guardians, may I say that you are welcome. May the blessings be . . . .

The swirling vortices of Coral energies faded until they seemed to disappear. Yet their effects remained. I felt as though their presence had strengthened the foundation of the house and solidified the walls of the living room. Even the air seemed purified. The interviews we had agreed to do were now over.

Returning to the consciousness of my physical body, I became fully aware that I was sitting comfortably on the sofa. I smiled into Michael's happy eyes. We felt truly blessed and honored for having had these inner-world experiences and for the opportunity to accept the gifts of the Gemstone Guardians.

32

THE NEXT STEP AND BEYOND

THE INNER COUNCIL

Nine years ago, I, Michael Katz, had the honor of interviewing the Gemstone Guardians for this book. During that exciting time, I also met regularly with several other inner-world beings. These included the Guardian of the Mineral Kingdom, an inner-world physician, a master teacher at a spiritual learning center, and others. We had many discussions about how best to present the Guardians' teachings. ◌ I learned that these beings are part of a council whose mission is to aid humanity by helping people recognize the healing power of gemstone spheres. The Guardian of the Mineral Kingdom elaborated on the council's mission during one of our meetings: "The changes occurring on your planet are great in both depth and magnitude. We are here to help your people make these changes, particularly the transition from metal to gem consciousness described by the Guardian of Amethyst. As individuals begin to wear and work with gemstone spheres, their consciousness will grow and unfold. As more and more individuals are uplifted, so will humanity as a whole be uplifted." ◌ Over the course of numerous meetings, a plan evolved. It was decided that to accomplish the council's mission we would work together to create a three-fold organization: a publishing house devoted exclusively to the work of the Guardians and the council; an educational division to train both lay people and practitioners; and a gemstone pharmacy to provide people with a reliable source of medicinal gemstones.

BUILDING A PHARMACY

For the next several years, we were busy putting our plan into action. Our first task was to build the pharmacy. "To begin," the Guardian of the Mineral Kingdom explained to me one evening, "you and I will design a collection of therapeutic gemstone necklaces. These will include both solid strands, which contain only one kind of gemstone, and necklaces which incorporate different kinds of gemstones." ◯ "To create the solid strands," she continued, "we will confer with each Gemstone Guardian about the optimal necklace lengths and sphere sizes to be used for his or her gemstone. To create the combination necklaces, I will teach you the art and science of combining gemstones. Together, we will design combination necklaces that maximize the healing benefits each gemstone has to offer." ◯ In the months that followed, thirty new combination necklaces came into being. As they did, I learned that gemstone combinations have a life to them that no single gemstone can express and a value that no single gemstone can match. When gemstones are harmoniously combined in the same necklace, they fulfill purposes and produce effects they could not offer if they were worn by themselves in separate necklaces. ◯ The council members repeatedly emphasized that our pharmacy's gemstones must be suitable for therapeutic use and therefore of only the highest quality. To this end, each Gemstone Guardian met with me at length, teaching me how to recognize the physical characteristics that his or her gemstone must display to be therapeutic. ◯ As we worked to manifest our three-fold plan, it became clear that the Guardians' first thirty discourses had been only the beginning— a glimpse of the vast knowledge they wished to share. New layers of knowledge were revealed when the Gemstone Guardians granted me a new series of lengthy, in-depth interviews. These advanced teachings substantially expanded the information they had shared in their first thirty discourses. ◯ I felt a great urgency to publish these first waves of knowledge from the Guardians, and after some hasty editing, I did so. With these publications, the establishment of our gemstone pharmacy, and the presentation of our first workshops, the first phase of our mission seemed complete.

A NEW FOUNDATION

Although the council and I were pleased to have accomplished so much so quickly, as time passed we began to see that, in order to move forward, a firmer footing was needed. I had become a publisher and pharmacy director rather suddenly, learning my new trades along the way. ◯ With this in mind, the council suggested that I reassess everything I had done so far. The inner-world physician addressed me: "Countless meetings with the council and your ever-deepening experience with the gemstones have given you a broader vision of this new form of medicine. It is time for you to reevaluate your achievements and to recreate them at a new level. This is needed to build a strong foundation—one which will endure the coming transitions. It is upon this foundation that the knowledge and practice of gemstone sphere therapy will be built in the coming centuries." ◯ Experience had taught me that the Gemstone Guardians' teachings comprise a unique new art and science, unlike any other. Therefore, we agreed that an essential element of this new foundation must be a unique name for this new healing modality. Thus, we adopted the name "Gemisphere" and the term "Gemisphere energy medicine" to distinguish the knowledge of the Gemstone Guardians and the council from that of any other source. ◯ To lay the strong foundation the council described, I have been guided to find others who could assist me in this enormous task. This creative team has devoted itself to making the Guardians' teachings more accessible. In reconsidering how to present the Guardians' information, we have formalized and expanded our training programs and restructured our publications. ◯ The Gemstone Guardians' original thirty discourses are now organized into two books: the book you are holding, the *Gemisphere Luminary*, and the *Gemisphere Luminary Therapy Guide*. The *Luminary* introduces the Guardians and their approach to energy medicine.

It is meant to be read first to develop an overall understanding of what gemstones are and how they work when worn as necklaces. The *Therapy Guide* describes over fifty gemstone therapies and techniques in an easy-reference format. It also includes excerpts from the Guardians' discourses on therapeutic quality, as well as instructions for cleansing gemstones of unwanted energies.

ACCESS TO TOOLS

Our new catalog, the *Gemisphere Source*, is a visual journey through our pharmacy. It presents photographs of our entire collection of gemstone-sphere necklaces along with concise descriptions of their missions and effects. Included are solid strands of the gemstones discussed in the *Luminary*, the combination necklaces described earlier, and other gemstone therapy tools. All the gemstones used to create these necklaces and tools are carefully evaluated and hand-selected by our staff to meet or exceed the Guardians' stringent criteria for therapeutic quality.

ADVANCED STUDY

The Gemstone Guardians' advanced discourses are being collected in a series of books called *Gemisphere Energy Medicine*. These discourses expand on the framework laid in the *Luminary* and *Therapy Guide* and provide a much deeper understanding of the actions of gemstones spheres. They also fill in details about the subtle bodies that are only touched upon in the *Luminary*. The therapies in this series are more complex and presented with step-by-step instructions and illustrations.

WORKSHOPS AND TRAINING

For Gemisphere energy medicine to be firmly established on Earth, practitioners and lay people alike must be trained in the many therapeutic techniques that comprise this unique new healing modality. To accomplish this, Dr. Pauline Alison, a key member of our creative team, and I have been developing a hands-on training program. This training draws on all the discourses given by the Gemstone Guardians so far, as well as on other information shared by the council. From this wealth of knowledge we have created introductory workshops and begun a series of week-long, in-residence training courses. At publication time, workshops and the first in-residence course are being presented in the United States and Europe. ◌ The council certainly has more plans for the future. These are to be revealed as time goes on. My colleagues and I look forward to helping in whatever way we can to bring these plans to fruition. In the meantime, my deepest gratitude goes to all the Gemstone Guardians, whose love and wisdom have graced these pages, and to the inner council for their continued love and guidance.

April 1997

PLEASE DIRECT INQUIRIES ABOUT
GEMSTONES, BOOKS, AND WORKSHOPS TO:

GEMISPHERE

P.O. BOX 10026
PORTLAND, OR 97296-0026
503.241.3642   FAX 503.241.9673
www.gemisphere.com